Complete Chess Strategy:
First Principles of the Middle Game

COMPLETE CHESS STRATEGY

Volume 1
First Principles of the Middle Game

Ludek Pachman
International Grandmaster

Cornerstone Library   **New York**

Published by Cornerstone Library
A Simon & Schuster Subsidiary of
Gulf & Western Corporation
Simon & Schuster Building
1230 Avenue of the Americas
New York, New York 10020

This new Cornerstone Library edition is published by arrangement
with Doubleday & Co. and is a complete and unabridged reprint of
the original hardcover edition

The trademark of Cornerstone Library, Inc. consists of the words
"Cornerstone Library" and the portrayal of a cube and is registered in
the United States Patent Office

Manufactured in the United States of America

ISBN 346-12321-6

Contents

Preface

Is it possible to learn how to play the middle-game correctly, or must we rely on our own imagination, combinative powers and experience when tackling this complex phase of the game?

There is no doubt that the theory of the middle-game is vastly different from that of the opening. The latter has been studied in detail, with theoreticians attempting to supply us with the 'best' moves. We must of course try to grasp the strategic and tactical ideas behind each opening, but there is no escaping the need for a wide knowledge of many concrete variations.

When studying the middle-game we cannot learn specific variations off by heart, but are concerned with basic principles and typical positions or manoeuvres. It becomes vitally important to recognize the characteristic features of a position and plan our play accordingly, but how can this be done? My purpose in the present volume is to give the ordinary club player an answer to this question. I am not seeking a new approach to chess strategy, but offering practical guide-lines for the study of the middle-game.

It is well known that the evaluation of many positions and many strategic problems depends on individual style. For this reason no author of a work on chess strategy can escape the criticism that he is bringing in his personal opinion and approach to the game. The objectivity of such a book can only be guaranteed if it is based upon material from master and grandmaster games, and if the advice given represents the views of various outstanding players.

This book is based on games from practical play. Only in a few cases have I restricted myself to quoting a position. Usually the whole game is presented, for the reader must learn above all to view a game as an entity and to recognize the transition stages between one part of the game and another. This has naturally compelled me to limit the number of examples used to illustrate the various strategic ideas.

The material is a mixture of old and new, with examples from modern tournament practice alongside games from the past which have permanent value and are often easier to understand than the complicated struggles from the present chess scene. The reader will also find a relatively large number of my own games. These have not been included because I am so immodest as to think they represent the best examples of correct play, but because every chess-player knows his own games best and can therefore explain his thought processes more effectively.

The present volume is the first of three which aim to give the reader an insight into the whole field of chess strategy. We first have a brief look at the development of chess strategy over the years, then consider basic principles, and in several chapters the reader will learn the special characteristics of individual pieces. The structure of the book remains the same as in previous editions, but the contents have in part been revised and brought up to date.

Ludek Pachman
Solingen, 1973

1 The Development of Modern Chess

1 The Development of Modern Chess

It is no chance occurrence that the development of the modern game began between the fifteenth and sixteenth centuries. Human intelligence, awakening from its hundred years sleep of the Middle Ages, demanded creative games to match the artistic achievements of the Renaissance. Such activity should not only be serious and entertaining, but should also require the fullest concentration, being used as a measure of man's new-found mental faculties which had lain dormant for centuries, their full potential unrecognized. It was to chess that man turned, a game which could boast of a thousand years' history.

Modern chess can be said to have begun in the period between the end of the fifteenth and the end of the seventeenth centuries, mainly in Italy and Spain. At the end of the fifteenth century, Lucena in Spain and a little later the Portuguese Damiano in Italy published chess books which already contained the new rules of the game. In contrast to the game of the Middle Ages, the new movements of the queen and the bishop were introduced. The former was transformed from the weakest to the strongest piece on the board, and the range of the latter was significantly increased. These changes injected new life into the game. The Spanish master Ruy Lopez who battled with the leading Italian players achieving early successes, was later pushed into the background by the ever-increasing fame of the Italian school. In 1574 he was beaten in a match by Leonardo di Calabria. Cesare Polerio began a systematic analysis of individual openings, and this work was continued in the seventeenth century, mainly by Salvio and Greco. The new rules were gradually consolidated until finally, towards the middle of the century, after the introduction of castling in its present form, they became the definitive rules we now know.

At the same time chess theory also began to develop. Outstanding masters of the time wrote works in which the various opening systems were examined, published annotated games and enunciated the first basic chess principles. We can thus look upon this era as the *Beginning of Chess Strategy*.

Hitherto the restricted movement of the pieces had made chess a decidedly slow and uninteresting game. It was rare that a game between equal players ended in mate. Usually the players strove to win material to reach a favourable ending. The new rules suddenly created a wealth of fresh possibilities, with the mobility of the pieces enabling sharp attacks to be launched.

As a result, this was the era of the simple and at that time very effective plan of rapid piece development with a view to attacking the enemy king. These attacks were all the more successful because correct principles of defence were as yet unknown. Players used the most primitive of defensive techniques: direct threats had to be parried and then pieces captured which the opponent had happened to leave unprotected in the heat of battle. Ruy Lopez was aware of the importance of the centre, as is shown by his penchant for the opening move P–QB3, but only as a means of driving away enemy pieces and deploying his own pieces for the attack.

The following game, played around 1580, shows us the chess style prevalent at that time:

1 Polerio–Domenico

Two Knights Defence

1 P–K4 P–K4 2 N–KB3 N–QB3 3 B–B4 N–B3 4 N–N5 P–Q4 5 P×P N×P 6 N×BP K×N 7 Q–B3+ K–K3 8 N–B3 N3–K2 9 P–Q4 P–B3 10 B–KN5 P–KR3 11 B5×N B×B 12 0–0–0 R–B1 13 Q–K4 R×P? 14 P×P B–N4+ 15 K–N1 R–Q7 16 P–KR4 R×R+ 17 R×R B×P 18 N×N P×N 19 R×P Q–N4 20 R–Q6+ K–K2 21 R–KN6 1–0

The above mentioned principles formed the basis of the Italian school in the eighteenth century, whose leading spokesmen and theoreticians were del Rio, Lolli and Ponziani. However, France produced a great rival to this school in the person of F. A. Danican, known to us as Philidor. In 1749 his famous work *Analyze du Jeu des échecs* appeared for the first time, containing ideas which placed him more than a century ahead of his time. Philidor wrote: 'The pawns are the soul of chess, creating conditions for both attack and defence; the win or the loss of a game depends on the good or bad position of the pawns.' This was a completely new concept understood neither by Philidor's contemporaries nor by his immediate successors.

Philidor taught that great care must be taken in handling pawns; they should not be weakened by advancing in isolation but should move forward in close support of each other. He considered a successful pawn advance so important that he gave it priority over the development of the pieces. For example, after 1 P–K4 P–K4 he even rejected 2 N–KB3 as hindering a later P–KB4, or the move 2 N–QB3 as preventing

P–QB3 to prepare P–Q4. He preferred 2 B–B4. As Black he recommended 2 ... P–Q3 after 1 P–K4 P–K4 2 N–KB3, with a view to a subsequent ... P–KB4. It is clear that Philidor was single-minded in his approach, but greatly underestimated the possibilities of piece play.

Unlike most of his predecessors he did not restrict himself solely to the analysis of the opening. His work discussed the relationship between the opening and the rest of the game, and he tried to formulate principles which were valid for all stages of the game. He even dealt with the end-game, his analysis of rook and knight versus rook being unsurpassed to this day for its depth and precision. Unfortunately he did not meet the leading Italian masters over the board, so that his conflicting ideas were never put to the practical test. He had no contemporary chess rivals in France, England and Holland, so usually played only odds or simultaneous games. He was generally considered the strongest player of his time.

The following game, which is characteristic of Philidor's strategic viewpoint, was played by him 'without sight of the board':

2 Brühl–Philidor

London 1783, Bishop's Opening

1 P–K4 P–K4 2 B–B4 P–QB3 3 Q–K2 P–Q3 4 P–QB3 P–KB4 5 P–Q3 N–B3 6 P×P B×P 7 P–Q4 P–K5 8 B–KN5 P–Q4 9 B–N3 B–Q3 10 N–Q2 QN–Q2 11 P–KR3 P–KR3 12 B–K3 Q–K2 13 P–KB4 P–KR4 14 P–B4 P–R3 15 P×P P×P 16 Q–B2 0–0 17 N–K2 P–QN4 18 0–0 N–N3 19 N–N3

P–N3 20 QR–B1 N–B5 21 N×B P×N 22 Q–N3+ Q–KN2 23 Q×Q+ K×Q 24 B×N NP×B 25 P–KN3 QR–N1 26 P–N3 B–R6 27 R–QB2 P×P 28 P×P R.N1–B1 29 R×R R R×R 30 R–R1 B–N5 31 R×P R–B6 32 K–B2 R–Q6 33 R–R2 B×N 34 R×B R×NP 35 R–B2 P–R5 36 R–B7+ K–N3 37 P×P N–R4 38 R–Q7 N×P 39 B×N R–KB6+ 40 K–N2 R×B 41 R×P R–B6 42 R–Q8 R–Q6 43 P–Q5 P–B5 44 P–Q6 R–Q7+ 45 K–B1 K–B2 46 P–R5 P–K6 47 P–R6 P–B6 0–1

Despite the fame and general recognition he enjoyed throughout his life, and despite numerous reprints of his book (the last in 1852), Philidor's ideas were not adopted by any of his successors. In fact, almost the whole of nineteenth century chess was dominated by the ideas of the Italian school, albeit with continuous improvement. Its exponents were La Bourdonnais (1795–1840), Anderssen (1818–1879), Morphy (1837–1884) and Chigorin (1850–1908). Each of them brought something new to the game. *L. C. M. de La Bourdonnais* greatly extended the openings repertoire of the time. Alongside the accepted systems of the Gioco Piano and Evans Gambit, he had a penchant as White for the Queen's Gambit and as Black for the French and Sicilian Defence. In his games La Bourdonnais exploited the principle of central superiority more completely than any of his predecessors, and he was the first to use systematically the central breakthrough as a basis for an attack on the enemy position. His combinations already contained a logic and precision which were sadly lacking in the romantic improvisation of the Italian masters.

3 MacDonell–La Bourdonnais

London 1834, Sicilian Defence

1 P–K4 P–QB4 2 N–KB3 N–QB3 3 P–Q4 P×P 4 N×P P–K4 5 N×N NP×N 6 B–QB4 N–B3 7 B–KN5 B–K2 8 Q–K2 P–Q4 9 B×N B×B 10 B–N3 0–0 11 0–0 P–QR4 12 P×P P×P 13 R–Q1 P–Q5 14 P–QB4 Q–N3 15 B–B2 B–N2 16 N–Q2 QR–K1 17 N–K4 B–Q1 18 P–B5 Q–QB3 19 P–B3 B–K2 20 QR–B1 P–B4! 21 Q–B4+ K–R1 22 B–R4 Q–KR3 23 B×R P×N 24 P–B6 P×P 25 R–B2 Q–K6+ 26 K–R1 B–B1 27 B–Q7 P–B7 28 R–KB1 P–Q6 29 R–B3 B×B 30 P×B P–K5 31 Q–B8 B–Q1 32 Q–B4 Q–K8 33 R–B1 P–Q7 34 Q–B5 R–N1 35 R–Q1 P–K6 36 Q–B3 Q×R.Q8 37 R×Q P–K7 0–1

Adolf Anderssen preferred gambits such as the Evans Gambit and the King's Gambit which he made eminently respectable. These are openings in which White offers material to gain time and space. Even pawn sacrifices to help the co-ordination of pieces were much more soundly based in Anderssen's games than was the case with his predecessors, and his combinations had greater depth and perfection. He planned them beautifully, revealing a thorough grasp of basic tactical elements such as the pin, discovered check, double attack, piece diversion etc.

4 Anderssen–Dufresne

Berlin 1852, Evans Gambit

1 P–K4 P–K4 2 N–KB3 N–QB3 3 B–B4 B–B4 4 P–QN4 B×NP 5 P–B3 B–R4 6 P–Q4 P×P 7 0–0 P–Q6 8 Q–N3 Q–B3 9 P–K5 Q–N3 10 R–K1 KN–K2 11 B–R3

P–N4 12 Q×P R–QN1 13 Q–R4 B–N3 14 QN–Q2 B–N2 15 N–K4 Q–B4? 16 B×QP Q–R4 17 N–B6+! P×N 18 P×P R–N1 19 QR–Q1!? it was later discovered that **19 B–K4** is objectively stronger, as now **19 ... R–N5** could have saved Black; there are many complex variations e.g. **20 B–B4! Q–KB4 21 R×P!** etc. This in no way detracts from the classical beauty of Anderssen's conception. **19 ... Q×N** (*1*)

1
W

20 R×N+! N×R 20 ... K–Q1 21 R×QP+! K–B1 22 R–Q8+! N×R 23 Q–Q7+!! 21 Q×QP+!! K×Q 22 B–KB5+ K–K1 23 B–Q7+ K–B1 24 B×N mate

Paul Morphy understood perfectly the strategic principles of the open game, especially those of the gambit openings. He would achieve maximum effectiveness for his pieces by opening up files and diagonals, and had a splendid feeling for combinations. However, when necessary he could also be satisfied with winning a pawn and converting his advantage in the end-game. For this reason his contemporaries criticized his dryness of style, an accusation which seems incredible to us today. He instinctively knew how to exploit every inexactitude on his opponent's part, such as loss of time or unfavourable placing of pieces, and would then produce the decisive tactical blow.

5 Lichtenhein–Morphy

New York 1857, Scotch Game

1 P–K4 P–K4 2 N–KB3 N–QB3 3 P–Q4 P×P 4 B–QB4 N–B3 5 P–K5 P–Q4 6 B–QN5 N–K5 7 N×P B–Q2 8 N×N? P×N 9 B–Q3 B–QB4 10 B×N Q–R5! 11 Q–K2 P×B 12 B–K3? 12 0–0! **12 ... B–KN5! 13 Q–B4 B×B 14 P–KN3** 14 Q×QBP+ B–Q2 15 Q×R+ K–K2 16 P–KN3 B×P+ 17 K×B P–K6+ 18 K–K1 Q–QN5+ 19 P–B3 Q×NP 20 Q×R B–N5 etc. **14 ... Q–Q1 15 P×B Q–Q8+ 16 K–B2 Q–B6+ 17 K–N1 B–R6 18 Q×QBP+ K–B1 19 Q×R+ K–K2 0–1**

Mikhail Ivanovich Chigorin brought the open game to its highest point of perfection, and the proof lies above all in his games. An indication of his approach is the fact that throughout his chess career he played nothing but open games as White, avoiding the Ruy Lopez which can easily take on a semi-blocked nature. On principle he never played a Queen's Gambit, even though this opening was one of the most popular towards the end of his career. Chigorin contributed a great deal to the theory of certain gambits (Evans Gambit and King's Gambit), because he used these with logic and with success at a time when the technique of defensive play had considerably improved. Also as Black, Chigorin strove for an active game. His ideas were particularly noteworthy in the defence to the Queen's Gambit where he tried to open up the game by the move ... P–K4. A similar idea is behind the system named after him: 1 P–Q4 P–Q4 2 P–QB4 N–QB3; also in the Semi-Slav opening which we often see nowadays: 1 P–Q4 P–Q4 2 P–QB4 P–K3 3 N–QB3 P–QB3 where the eventual thrust ... P–K4 is a key motif; and even more so in the system which was revolutionary at the time: 1 P–Q4 N–KB3 and 2 ... P–Q3, a forerunner of one of the most popular openings in present-day chess, the King's Indian. He discovered new ideas for Black's defence to the Ruy Lopez and these form the basis of a number of well-known defensive systems. Like his predecessors Chigorin was always aiming for active play and creating attacking chances which he exploited with logic and energy. In defence he avoided passive set-ups and placed the emphasis on counterplay. However, his creative approach was seen at its best in his constant search for new unexplored paths along which he ventured despite the great risks involved, thereby providing us with many artistic moments. Despite the successful advent of the hyper-moderns, Chigorin's creative chess ideas influenced many of his contemporaries and representatives of the younger generation. We need only mention the Hungarian master R. Charousek and grandmaster O. Duras, the most important figure in the history of chess in Czechoslovakia.

The Italian school was not the sole approach to chess thought up to the middle of the nineteenth century. We have already mentioned the completely contrasting views of Philidor, but in England chess took another direction, with *Howard Staunton* as the leading exponent of the English style. Staunton's main concern was to obtain a sound position, and he was content with a slight advantage which he could, if necessary, press home by fairly accurate end-game play. He avoided risky combinations, sacrificing material only if the consequences were clear-cut. The following game is a good example of the advantages of such play, and Staunton carries out his plan in a way that a modern master would be happy to endorse.

6 Cochrane–Staunton

London 1842, Queen's Gambit

1 P–Q4 P–Q4 2 P–QB4 P–K3 3 P–K3 P–QB4 4 QP×P B×P 5 P×P P×P 6 N–KB3 N–KB3 7 B–K2 N–B3 8 N–B3 B–K3 9 0–0 0–0 10 P–KR3 Q–K2 11 P–R3 P–QR3 12 P–QN4 B–Q3 13 P–N5 N–K4 14 N–Q4 KR–B1 15 B–N2 N–B5 16 B×N R×B 17 P×P P×P 18 N3–K2 R1–QB1 19 Q–Q3 N–K5 20 N×B P×N 21 QR–B1 Q–R5 22 R×R R×R 23 N–Q4 N–N4! 24 P–K4 24 N×P? N×P+! 25 P×N R–KN5+! 24 ... Q–B5 25 P–N3 N×RP+ 26 K–N2 Q–N5 27 N×P!? Q×N 28 P–K5 B–B4 29 R–KR1 N–N4 30 P–B4 N–K5 31 P–B5 Q×BP 32 Q×P+ Q–B2 33 Q–Q8+ Q–B1 34 Q–Q5+ K–R1! 0–1

It was in the London tournament of 1851 that the English style first came into contact with the Continental style which was closely identified with the Italian school. This tournament, which took the form of a series of matches, ended in a convincing win by Anderssen who beat his chief rival Staunton 4–1 in the penultimate round. Although such a score hardly represented the relative strengths of both players, Anderssen was nevertheless clearly superior. The chess public viewed the result as a victory for the Italian over the English school.

The development of modern chess strategy begins with the work of *Wilhelm Steinitz* (1836–1900). For thirty years he was considered the strongest player in the world and for ten of these years he defended for the first time in chess history the newly introduced title of World Chess Champion. However, the greatest significance of his personality lies in the fact that his work began an era in which chess became a scientific game. During the first part of his career (1862–1873) he was still wholly under the influence of the Italian school, but later he started to search for new paths. In his chess column in *The Field*, and later in the *International Chess Magazine* and in his unfinished *Modern Chess Instructor*, Steinitz harshly criticized games which had hitherto been regarded as the summit of chess art. His final judgment was truly heretical at the time: effective attacks had almost always been the result of bad defence, and the approach to chess consisted mainly in aimless manoeuvring without any soundly conceived plan based on strategic principles.

Along with this criticism he devoted a great deal of energy to the task of formulating new principles of correct play. Lasker later summarized as follows Steinitz' new concepts in the field of chess strategy:–

1. There is an 'equilibrium of position'.
2. Sharp attacks can only be attempted when this equilibrium is disturbed, never before.
3. It is fundamental that attacks must only be aimed at the 'weak points' in the enemy position.
4. The defence must be conducted with the utmost economy of means and must not tie down pieces unnecessarily.

These basic principles do not of course exhaust everything that Steinitz brought to the development of chess strategy. He was the first to recognize the importance of small positional advantages. He pointed out the significance of 'weak points', isolated and doubled pawns, and explained the value of the Q-side pawn majority and the superiority of the bishop pair in open positions, showing at the same time how to exploit these advantages. He demonstrated that pawns, especially those protecting the castled king, are at their strongest on their original square. He championed the idea that the king is a strong piece which in certain circumstances can even be used effectively in the middlegame. He was the first to show that a correctly conducted defence can be just as valid a strategic plan as is an attack, and he stressed the need for a blocked centre when attacking on the wing. Finally, Steinitz was the first to understand the strategy of closed positions which his predecessors had simply avoided when possible.

Opening theory was enriched by many of his ideas. Even today the Steinitz Defence and the Steinitz Attack are played in the Ruy Lopez, as is his variation in the French Defence, and he was the first to play the Queen's Gambit in its present form.

His main weaknesses lay in the fact that he often exaggerated the importance of the basic elements, especially in the opening (weaknesses in the enemy camp, his own pawn position and possible win of material). On the other hand, he undervalued dynamic elements, such as the possibility of an effective attack arising from rapid development. In many of his games he deliberately provoked his opponent into attacking and thus suffered several unnecessary defeats. However, these weaknesses in no way detract from the vast contribution Steinitz made as the founder of modern chess strategy.

There is often talk about the Steinitz school and about individual advocates of his methods, but in my opinion it is completely illogical to view Steinitz as the creator of a certain style in the history of chess strategy. His basic principles were the foundation for the development of modern chess, and as such can be compared to the rules of formal logic in science. Perhaps this is why his successors interpreted his ideas in various ways. In addition, certain parts of his output of a more disjointed nature, such as articles, annotations and lectures, were open to misleading interpretations.

Among his successors was *Dr Siegbert Tarrasch* (1862–1934) one of the strongest masters of his time and even more important as a chess teacher. He set about the task of drawing up a series of chess principles based on the teachings of Steinitz and offering a practical method of correct play. He expounded these 'rules' in his books *Die Moderne Schachpartie* (Modern Chess) and *Dreihundert Schachpartien* (300 Games of Chess) which played a tremendous part in propagating basic chess theory among the broad mass of chess-players.

Later (e.g. in the works of Aron Nimzowitsch), Tarrasch was strongly criticized for his alleged dogmatism. It is true that he tried to formulate principles which were generally applicable and as a result sometimes overlooked the individual characteristics of certain positions. However, many of his disputed ideas have been rehabilitated in recent times. For instance, his defence to the Queen's Gambit forms part of the chess armoury of such leading players as Keres and Spassky.

At approximately the same time, another master began to develop the teachings of Steinitz, although in a completely different direction. This was probably the most profound chess thinker of all time, the outstanding second World Champion, *Emanuel Lasker* (1868–1941). Lasker extended the principles of Steinitz, and lent many of them a greater precision. In contrast to Steinitz and Tarrasch, Lasker was not concerned with finding the absolutely correct move, for his basic premise was that chess represents a struggle between two individuals, each with his own specific characteristics, good and bad. The game cannot be viewed as an exact science, since its inherent complexity and time-consuming problems inevitably produce errors, even from the strongest of players. Lasker was the greatest and perhaps so far the only chess psychologist. We shall devote more time to his ideas in our chapter 'Systems of Chess Thinking'.

By far the greatest number of people, and chess players are no exception, are of a practical disposition and therefore all too readily inclined to achieve results with the minimum expenditure of effort. For this reason, it is easy to understand why Lasker's deeply conceived ideas found no advocates, whereas Tarrasch's precepts influenced many masters whose careers began at the turn of the century.

Tarrasch's fundamental ideas about 'economy' in chess thinking, and simplification of all problems which occur in a game, were brought to the highest peak of perfection by the third World Champion, *José Raul Capablanca* (1888–1942). A great deal of praise was bestowed upon Capablanca and he was generally considered a chess phenomenon. His play was distinguished by truly amazing accuracy. He rarely committed serious errors, possessed a fine positional instinct and in particular displayed a mastery of the end-game and of simple middle-game positions which he could bring to a successful conclusion by exploiting even the slightest advantages. Capablanca's games represent the culmination of chess technique, his constant aims being simplification, avoidance of unclear situations and refusal to take any risks. After his successful World Championship match against Lasker in 1921, he went through many tournaments, including New York 1927 (in which the six leading grandmasters had to play four-game matches against each other), without suffering a single defeat. It almost seemed as if chess had reached the absolute zenith of its development. Capablanca himself stated that chess held no more secrets for him, and he talked about the death of the game once the leading masters had acquired the necessary technique to draw against one another. Nevertheless, at the very moment of his greatest triumph Capablanca was nearing his fall.

Before we turn to the conqueror of Capablanca, we must say a few words about the very important 'Neo-Romantic' movement, so named by its leading exponents *Richard Réti* (1889–1929), *Aron Nim-*

zowitsch (1886–1935) and *Saviely Tartakower* (1887–1956). These hypermoderns took as their starting point the teachings of Steinitz which they supplemented by several important strategic principles and above all by a new concept of the struggle for the centre. They demonstrated that a pawn centre (e.g. pawns on K4 and Q4) is not always necessarily advantageous and may even present a serious weakness if immobile and exposed to flank attacks. The practical application of these ideas resulted in a veritable revolution in opening theory. The new defences to 1 P–Q4 seemed at first so bizarre that they were designated, initially as a joke but later seriously, 'Indian Defences'. The move 1 N–KB3 which had been known for a long time, suddenly took on a new meaning in association with the idea of a flank attack directed at the enemy centre, and was called by Réti 'Opening of the Future'. This new concept of the centre was the most important contribution of the Neo-Romantic school, and we shall examine it in more detail in the final chapter of Volume 2.

In his book *My System*, Nimzowitsch expounded further strategic ideas concerned with the blockade, the pawn chain and the manoeuvre. We shall also be examining these. The hypermoderns gave a new lease of life to the development of the game. In particular, Nimzowitsch strongly attacked the simplifying principles of Tarrasch and the concept of a body of generally applicable rules. However, the hypermoderns also were to a certain extent dogmatic in their rejection of dogma. In order to prove that even the correct principles of Tarrasch could not be applied universally, they tried to find exceptions at any price. This led them into adopting many bizarre, unnatural and disadvantageous set-ups, resulting in unpleasant defeats. It also explains why the hypermoderns could achieve successes against Tarrasch and the older masters but could not prevail against Capablanca's precise, simple and efficient play.

Chess history can thank one man for the fact that the Capablanca legend was not of even greater duration and did not lead to the feared demise of chess. This man was the brilliant *Dr Alexander Alekhine* (1892–1946), a chess genius of the highest order. He had made a deep and thorough study of the teachings of Steinitz and revealed an accomplished playing technique along with an outstanding positional insight. He had learnt from Lasker to take into account the personality of his opponent and was the first to grasp the former's difficult concepts. However, all these good points would not have been enough to guarantee him victory in the match for the World Championship. Alekhine possessed extraordinary powers of imagination and an incredibly rich flair for combinative play. He sought not only victory but beauty. He was not afraid to take risks, and he revelled in complex positions which made demands upon his intuition as well as his tactical skill. He managed to discover aspects of play which bordered on the metaphysical, which lay beyond the limits of acquired principles and which almost defied human understanding. Knowledge and experience were not enough; what was required was a fund of creative power.

Alekhine was a true chess artist,

in the Chigorin tradition. In 1927 he beat Capablanca in an historic struggle for the World Championship. It was a triumph of the artist over the technician, of intuition over method.

Alekhine's victory was significant, because it pointed to the inexhaustible possibilities of chess whilst refuting arguments about the stagnation of the game. Alekhine's work heralded a new creative approach to chess theory and practice.

The reader should know enough of the development of chess to be able to understand present trends. We have necessarily limited ourselves to one or more of the leading representatives of each era when discussing the growth of chess ideas, but this in no way means that they were the only players involved. Each era threw up many masters and theoreticians who contributed something to the game. We have given character sketches of the towering personalities of chess history who managed to convey in both theory and practice the essential ideas of their time.

It would also be feasible to look for parallels between the growth of chess ideas and the general development of thought in human society, for despite its individual characteristics chess cannot be divorced from other aspects of culture. Our game mirrors the intellectual level and cultural trends of the times. However, such a theme would require a separate, comprehensive treatment of its own, beyond the scope of this work.

Let us consider the present chess scene. In the post-war years the Soviet masters attained an extraordinarily convincing predominance in World chess, which led to the

term 'Soviet school' being applied to them. Various authors, in particular Alexander Kotov, used the phrase dogmatically with nationalistic and political overtones, whereas in reality no such school exists. Among the leading Soviet players there are some whose style reminds us of Alekhine e.g. Bronstein, Tal, Geller. On the other hand, the style of Smyslov, Petrosian and Taimanov is akin to the polished technique and precision of Capablanca. As for Botvinnik, Keres and Spassky, they present a versatility of style. Sometimes they prefer quiet positional play, accumulating and exploiting small strategic advantages, and at other times they opt for ultra-sharp positions offering complex tactical problems.

Nevertheless, Soviet chess-players have made a great contribution to the development of modern chess. For the first time in the history of chess, a truly scientific research programme was carried out in an attempt to solve theoretical problems. A student could offer chess research for his thesis, and work on chess theory was organized, with thousands of players participating. This gave a great impetus to the development of chess, and not only in the Soviet Union. Foreign players were outclassed for many years by the Russian players, until they too finally adopted the same methods of deep systematic preparation and collective analytical research.

And now a new chess phenomenon has appeared on the scene, in the shape of the present World Champion Robert Fischer. A close study of his games gives us an insight into the chess trends of today and the near future. Fischer resembles Capablanca in his mastery of chess technique and his rapid sight of the board. However, he is willing to accept double-edged positions which the Cuban automatically avoided. Fischer, like Lasker, relies upon errors from his opponent, often risking a great deal because he knows that nowadays this is the only way to win games. In contrast to Capablanca's time, playing technique among masters and grandmasters has improved considerably! We could thus describe Fischer's style as a synthesis of Capablanca's and Lasker's. At the same time, Fischer shows us, in the field of chess, what can be achieved by a narrowly specialized human mind.

Fischer began his basic chess study by examining and revaluing the games of his predecessors. This is how it should be. Every chessplayer who wishes to become a top-class master must acquire comprehensive theoretical knowledge, become acquainted with the works of entire generations and at the same time be able to make his own contribution to the development of modern chess.

2 The Fundamentals of Chess Strategy

It is often asked how many moves ahead a master or grandmaster can visualize, and there is a commonly held opinion that the difference between a top-class player and a beginner lies in his ability to calculate. Admittedly, exact calculation is indispensable if a player is to make progress, but it is not the only skill required and is by no means the most important difference between the master and the average player. There are many players who can produce good, accurate combinations but who nevertheless fail to achieve master strength. This is mainly because of their inability to draw up in advance *a logical plan arising from the nature of the position*. It is only possible and indeed desirable to calculate specific variations when we are dealing with certain clearly defined positions. In most positions it is the correct plan which leads us to the required moves. Two examples should make this point clear.

The above position (*2*) occurred in Duras–Barasz from the 1912 Breslau tournament. Grandmaster Duras now sacrificed the exchange in order to begin a mating attack on the king: **35 R×N! R×R 36 R–B8+ K–R2 37 Q–R8 Q–B3** forced, as 37 ... Q–R4 or 37 ... Q–N5 allow 38 N–R4 which would now fail to 38 ... P–KN4 **38 R–R8+ K–N3 39 Q–KN8!** Up to this move, Duras would have had to work out everything by *exact calculation*, but he could now use his *judgement* to evaluate the position as clearly won for him, in view of the exposed black king.

Of course, such an outstanding tactical player as Duras could have tried to go even further in his calculations, but even if he had managed this, it would have been an unnecessary waste of energy. Any experienced player well knows that the advantage of the exchange is of no help to the defence in such positions, and that a winning combination must be at hand. So it proved in the game continuation: **39 ... R–Q6** the threat was 40 P–R3 **40 N–R4+ K–N4 41 N–B5 R–K3 42 P–KR4+ K–N5** if 42 ... K–N3? 43 R×P is mate; or 42 ... K–R4 43 N×NP+ wins **43 N×RP+ K–R4** 43 ... Q×N 44 R×Q R×R 45 Q×NP+ R–N3 46 Q×BP wins **44 N×P+ K–N5 45 N–R6+ K–R4 46 N–B5+ K–N5 47 R–R7! R–K2 48 N–R6+ K–R4 49 N–B7+ 1–0.**

We can thus sum up White's thought processes from move 35 as follows:

1. Exact calculation of the sequence of moves up to move 39, more or less forced for both sides.
2. Evaluation of the resulting position as won for White, in view of the exposed black king.

In some cases such a forced series of moves leads either to mate or decisive material advantage, making an evaluation of the final position either unnecessary or quite easy. In general, however, it is more difficult to weigh up the prospects for both sides after a given series of moves, than it is to calculate these moves themselves. Or consider the first move of this combination, 35 R×N! which is at first sight surprising. Ideas such as this are again more difficult than the calculation of a forced sequence of moves.

In this particular instance, Duras had already carried out the idea of occupying the QB-file with his major pieces. As we shall see later, one possible way of exploiting an open file is to penetrate to the eighth rank. The surprising 35 R×N! was therefore the logical consequence of a proper understanding of the given position. Such an understanding of the nature of a position, including the weaknesses in the enemy camp and a knowledge of how one's pieces work together effectively, is a prerequisite for discovering similar combinations.

A further requisite is undoubtedly the ability to visualize and combine. This can to a great extent be acquired by practice, but in part demands natural gifts, such as imagination, without which (we must not be afraid to admit it) one cannot reach the heights in chess.

To arrive at the correct move in our next position, we need totally different thought processes.

This comes from Nimzowitsch–Rubinstein, Dresden 1926 (*3*). Both sides are not at grips, so to speak, so there is no question here of direct threats which force a specific reply. What is important is to find the *correct plan* and only then to select moves which best fit in with this plan. Careful examination of the position reveals that White has two small advantages:

1. One of his rooks already occupies the open K-file and the second rook is ready to double up if required.
2. White's KB on QB4 is the most

active of all four bishops, limiting in particular the movement of Black's king.

None of these advantages, however, can be immediately exploited. After ... B–Q2 Black is covering all the squares on the K-file, and White's bishop needs support from the other pieces before we can talk of danger to the black king. White's knight is particularly badly posted, as KR5 will not be available after ... P–KN3.

White's correct plan is therefore as follows:

1. His knight must head for the strong KN5 square.
2. Direct threats against the black king must be combined with pressure down the K-file.
3. He must avoid a premature exchange of both rooks on the open file.

What has Black in the way of a counter-plan? As White's position offers no weaknesses to attack, Black must aim to ward off direct threats and simplify the game through exchanges.

With these points in mind, the reader should have no difficulty in following the game which continued: **18 N–R1!** heading for KN5 **18 ... B–Q2 19 N–B2 QR–K1 20 R1–K1 R×R 21 R×R N–Q1** 21 ... R–K1 would fail to 22 Q–Q5! which shows us that Black's king position, threatened by the powerful white KB, stops him carrying out his policy of exchanging pieces **22 N–R3 B–B3** again 22 ... R–K1 cannot be played, because of the pretty continuation 23 Q–R5! R×R 24 N–N5! P–R3 25 Q–N6 P×N 26 Q–R5 mate **23 Q–R5 P–KN3 24 Q–R4 K–N2 25 Q–B2!** there is no direct attack after 25 N–N5 P–R3, so White prevents the harmonious

co-operation of the black pieces by attacking the weak QP **25 ... B–B4** if 25 ... Q–N3 26 P–QN4! is possible e.g. 26 ... R–K1? 27 R×R B×R 28 B–B3! N–B3 29 B–Q5 etc. **26 P–QN4 B–N3 27 Q–R4** simpler and more logical would have been 27 Q–K1! when Black has no defence to the threats on the K-file e.g. 27 ... B–K5 28 N–B2! winning a pawn **27 ... R–K1 28 R–K5! N–B2** if 28 ... P–R3 Nimzowitsch gives 29 P–N4! with a decisive attack e.g. 29 ... P×P 30 P–B5! Q×R 31 P–B6+! Q×BP 32 Q–R6 mate; or 29 ... P–N4 30 BP×P! threatening 31 Q–R6 mate **29 B×N Q×B 30 N–N5 Q–N1 31 R×R B×R 32 Q–K1!** once again the K-file proves its importance. Despite the great reduction in material, Black's pieces are so badly placed that they cannot prevent the White attack without a decisive loss in material. For example, if now 32 ... K–B1 White wins by 33 Q–K5! B–Q1 34 N–K6+ K–K2 35 Q–B5+! K–Q2 36 N–B8+! etc. **32 ... B–B3 33 Q–K7+ K–R1** or 33 ... K–R3 34 N–K6 **34 P–N5!** winning at once, for if 34 ... P×P 35 N–K6 P–R4 36 Q–B6+ K–R2 37 N–N5+ K–R3 38 B–N4! wins **34 ... Q–N2 35 Q×Q+ K×Q 36 P×B 1–0.**

A plan such as we saw here, beginning with move 18, is called a *strategic plan*. When we are drawing up such a plan by considering the given elements of a position, we are using *strategy*. (This and other terms such as 'strategic aim' and 'tactics' have the same meaning in other fields such as war and political science). With every plan it is clearly important to know what we are trying to achieve, our 'strategic aim'. In the last example White's aim was to utilize his active pieces and control of the K-file in order to destroy the co-ordination of Black's pieces and institute a successful mating attack.

It might appear that the main strategic aim of all games is to mate the enemy king. However, such a superficial conception of strategy was only applicable in the early days of chess, when an attack on the king was the only available plan known to players. We have already pointed out in our introductory chapter how greatly chess ideas have changed since that time, along with an improvement in technique and a deeper understanding of the game. In modern games between top-class players, even the capture of a weak pawn may no longer be the strategic aim. Instead we often see a bitter struggle for small positional advantages such as the control of an open file, the weakening of enemy pawns, the creation of a passed pawn etc.

However, it is clear that the best of plans comes to nothing, if it cannot be carried out properly, in chess as in life. *Tactics* is the name we give to the methods used in executing our own plans or countering those of our opponent. The *manoeuvre* and the *combination* are two major examples of tactics.

Let us have a further look at the Nimzowitsch–Rubinstein position, and in particular at moves 23 to 25. These three queen moves first brought about a weakening of Black's pawn position with . . . P–KN3, then led to the misplacing of his KB with . . . B–B4. Such a sequence of moves, with the aim of either improving one's own position or weakening the opponent's, is called a *manoeuvre*. If this manoeuvre forces certain replies, then we talk

about a *forcing manoeuvre*. In the last position, White's queen moves practically forced Black's moves, but moves 29 to 34 are an even clearer example of this type of manoeuvre.

If we turn back to the Duras–Barasz game, the sequence beginning 35 R×N! has the appearance of a forcing manoeuvre, along with an unusual element: right from the start there is a change in the material balance on the board, to the disadvantage of the side carrying out the manoeuvre. White sacrifices the exchange with the aim of exploiting the exposed position of Black's king. The fact that one side deliberately brings about a position involving a material disadvantage to himself (even if sometimes only temporary) is somewhat of a strategic contradiction, since according to our basic concepts one of our most important goals is to achieve *material superiority*. A forcing manoeuvre which is based on certain strategic contradictions is called a *combination*. This term is very often confused with *sacrifice*, but this is wrong for two reasons.

Firstly, because the strategic contradiction which is the basis of every combination does not necessarily involve the sacrifice of material. The side carrying out a manoeuvre may accept a certain positional disadvantage such as a weak pawn, the exchange of a well-placed piece, an exposed king etc. These and similar freely accepted positional disadvantages are of course just as much strategic contradictions. During the rest of the manoeuvre the active side reaches a position which is more advantageous than the original one, and this again is the hallmark of a combination, although sacrifice does not come into it.

Secondly, there are sacrifices which are in no way connected with a manoeuvre. In our chapter 'The value of the pieces', we shall demonstrate that the value of individual pieces is relative, depending upon the kind of position they are in. We shall then see 'positional' or 'strategic' sacrifices which are not part of a combination but arise from considerations about the effectiveness of certain pieces.

There are other concepts in the field of tactics, such as the double attack, the pin, the discovered check, traps etc. It is not the task of this book to deal with these in detail, but the reader will meet them as he studies our examples.

As the above comments may well appear abstract and difficult to the beginner, we shall close this section with another famous game which will illustrate the basic concepts we have been trying to explain.

7 Botvinnik–Capablanca

AVRO tournament 1938, Nimzo-Indian Defence

1 P–Q4 N–KB3 2 P–QB4 P–K3 3 N–QB3 B–N5 4 P–K3 P–Q4 5 P–QR3 B×N+ 6 P×B P–B4 7 BP×P KP×P 8 B–Q3 0–0 9 N–K2 P–QN3 10 0–0 B–R3 11 B×B N×B 12 B–N2? 12 Q–Q3! **12 ... Q–Q2 13 P–QR4 KR–K1** (*4*) 13 ... P×P 14 BP×P KR–B1 was also possible.

Nowadays this type of position is well known to anyone who has studied the Nimzo-Indian Defence. However, at the time this game was played, the opening had been little analysed, which accounts for Botvinnik's inexact 12th move. It is clear that Black has the advantage

on the queen's wing. He has two strategic plans at his disposal:

1. He can temporarily block the queen's side by ... P–B5 then play his QN to ... QN6 via ... QN1–QB3–QR4, either forcing White's QR to the passive QR2 square or winning the QRP.
2. He can open the QB-file at the correct moment, occupying it with his rooks, then use his ... QB5 square as a post for his knight or rook.

White on the other hand has a central pawn majority. His *strategic plan* is to prepare P–B3 and P–K4 followed by a king's side attack with P–K5 and P–KB4–5.

14 Q–Q3

Already beginning the tactical execution of the above plan. It is worth noting that this move allows Black to carry out his first plan with a gain of tempo. Botvinnik correctly judges that this will give him a free hand in the centre and on the K-side, thus making his task easier.

14 ...   P–B5?

Whereas Capablanca misjudges his prospects and opts for the weaker of his two plans. 14 ... Q–N2! was the best move, retaining the possibility of opening the QB-file at an opportune moment, and at the same time controlling his vital ... K5 square. After this move he would even stand better, as a result of White's inexact 12 B–N2?

| 15 Q–B2 | N–N1 |
| 16 QR–K1 | N–B3 |

Black could have played 16 ... N–R4 to make White's central advance more difficult to carry out. However, White can then institute a king's side attack, as shown in the following variation given by Botvinnik: 17 P–R3 P–B4 18 B–B1 N–QB3 19 P–B3 N–R4 20 P–N4. Moreover, White could have prevented this move by 16 N–N3, if he had so desired

| 17 N–N3 | N–QR4 |

If 17 ... N–K5 White has 18 N–R1! and if Black then tries to intensify his control of ... K5 by 18 ... P–B4 he has to reckon with the possibility of 19 P–B3 N–KB3 20 P–R3 followed by 21 P–N4.

| 18 P–B3 | N–N6 |

During the last 5 moves both sides have executed a manoeuvre in line with their strategic plans. Black now wins the QRP and White carries out his central advance.

19 P–K4	Q×P
20 P–K5	N–Q2
21 Q–B2!	

Avoiding the serious tactical error 21 P–B4? N6–B4! when Black either forces the exchange of queens or plays his knight to ... Q6, with a winning game in both cases.

| 21 ... | P–N3 |

This and the next move are played to forestall P–B4–B5–B6 in conjunction with N–B5, which is how Botvinnik won a later game against Alexander in the 1946 Radio Match USSR v. Great Britain.

| 22 P–B4 | P–B4 |
| 23 P×Pep! | |

White must clearly not allow his pawns to be blockaded by ... N–B1–K3, when Black could carry out his queen's side operations undisturbed.

23 ...	N×BP
24 P–B5	R×R
25 R×R	R–K1

Some analysts were of the opinion that 25 ... R–KB1 would have held the game, but Botvinnik gives the strong continuation 26 Q–B4! with the following possibilities:
1. 26 ... Q–R7 27 P×P! Q×B 28 P–N7 K×P 29 N–B5+ K–R1 30 Q–R6 R–B2 31 Q×N+! etc.
2. 26 ... Q–Q2! 27 R–K6 N–QR4 (*27 ... N–K5 28 Q–K5 N×N 29 R–K7*) 28 B–R3 R–B2 29 Q–N5! etc.

| 26 R–K6! | R×R |

If 26 ... K–N2 27 R×N! K×R 28 P×P+ etc. leads to a quick mate. In all these variations Black's troubles stem from the unfavourable position of his queen which is away from the main scene of action.

| 27 P×R | K–N2 |
| 28 Q–B4 | |

Already threatening 29 N–B5+! P×N 30 Q–N5+ etc.

| 28 ... | Q–K1 |
| 29 Q–K5 | |

Black's KN is now pinned and his other knight out of the game. White has a strong passed KP and is threatening to bring his last piece into the attack by 30 B–R3. It is clear that the position must contain tactical elements which are favourable to White. In other words, Botvinnik has achieved his strategic aim of an irresistible K-side attack.

| 29 ... | Q–K2 (5) |

It is already too late to retreat his QN. If 29 ... N–QR4 (*29 ... N–Q7? 30 B–B1 N7–K5 31 N×N P×N 32 P–Q5*) 30 B–B1! threatening both 31 B–R6+! K×B 32 Q×N, and 31 Q–B7+ followed by 32 B–R6. Black would be forced to play 30 ... Q–K2 allowing the same continuation as in the game.

Black appears to have prevented the threatened 30 B–R3 and now hopes to advance his Q-side pawns. However, Botvinnik decides the game by a splendid *combination* involving the sacrifice of two pieces with the aim of queening his KP.

30 B–R3!!	**Q×B**

Or 30 ... Q–K1 31 Q–B7+ K–N1 32 B–K7! N–N5 33 Q–Q7, a *manoeuvre* to force his pawn home after 33 ... Q–R1 34 B–N5 etc.

31 N–R5+!	**P×N**
32 Q–N5+	**K–B1**
33 Q×N+	**K–N1**
34 P–K7	

All Black's moves were forced and he cannot stop the pawn queening. He must try for perpetual check but Botvinnik has calculated that his king can escape.

34 ...	**Q–B8+**
35 K–B2	**Q–B7+**
36 K–N3	**Q–Q6+**
37 K–R4	**Q–K5+**
38 K×P	**Q–K7+**
39 K–R4	**Q–K5+**
40 P–N4!	

But not 40 K–R3? P–KR4! drawing

40 ...	**Q–K8+**
41 K–R5	**1–0**

An interesting fact emerges from this game: both sides carried out their chosen strategic plan and attained their strategic aim. However, whereas Black only achieved a material advantage by capturing White's QRP, White obtained a decisive K-side attack. Black's error lay in considering only the possibilities in his own position without taking into account the real prospects which his strategic plan gave to his opponent.

THE CHARACTER OF THE POSITION AND CHOICE OF PLAN

The choice of plan in every case depends upon the concrete position on the board, so must correspond to this position. Before we can draw up our strategic plan, it is vital to judge the position correctly and pin-point its individual characteristics. Which factors determine the character of a position and how can they lead us to the correct plan?

We cannot of course answer these questions fully in the space of a chapter, since they are the clue to the whole of chess strategy which is the subject of these volumes. However, we can state that the character of position is determined by the following factors:

1. The material balance.
2. The effectiveness of the individual pieces.
3. The value of each pawn.
4. The pawn structure.
5. The position of the kings.
6. The interrelation and co-ordination between pieces and pawns.

Some of these factors are permanent, whilst others are only temporary. The quality and structure of the pawns are important fixed elements, for they cannot be transferred from one wing to the other as can pieces.

The pawn position only changes gradually, whereas it is usually easy to alter the position of pieces. As a result we have the apparent contradiction that in most cases it is the pawns which largely determine the character of a position, despite their comparatively small value. Of course, material superiority and the position of the kings are other important permanent features.

Let us examine a few positions to see how we can assess their essential character and select the corresponding strategic plan.

This position (6) occurs in a little-known variation of the Ruy Lopez after the moves **1 P–K4 P–K4 2 N–KB3 N–QB3 3 B–N5 B–B4 4 P–B3 N–B3 5 P–Q4 P×P 6 P×P!? B–N5+ 7 N–B3 N×KP 8 0–0 B×N 9 P×B 0–0 10 P–Q5! N×QBP 11 Q–Q3 N×B 12 Q×N N–K2 13 P–Q6! P×P 14 B–R3** (6).

There has been insufficient practical testing of this line and experts differ in their evaluation of it. What are the determining factors?

1. Black is two pawns ahead in material, not counting his pawn on ... Q3 which must fall.
2. White's queen, knight and bishop are actively posted and his rooks are ready to occupy any of the open files. Black's pieces, on the

other hand, are passively placed and he is a long way behind in development.

Both these factors determine the nature of the given position, and so form the basis of the respective plans to be adopted by both sides.

1. White must use his active pieces to create tactical threats in a direct attack on Black's position. (e.g. B×P, Q–KR5, R–K1 N–N5 etc.).
2. Black must try to counter the immediate threats, complete his development and exploit his material superiority through simplification.

It would require deep and accurate analysis of the possibilities for both sides, before we could determine which of these plans offered the best prospects. However, this point does not concern us here. What is more important to us is that this position illustrates a *static factor* (material advantage) alongside a *dynamic factor* (lead in development, actively placed pieces), the first permanent, the second temporary. This succinctly explains the position: both of these factors are in conflict and demand quite different plans from both players.

Our next position also comes from the Ruy Lopez after the moves **1 P–K4 P–K4 2 N–KB3 N–QB3 3 B–N5 P–QR3 4 B–R4 N–B3 5 0–0 N×P 6 P–Q4 P–QN4 7 B–N3 P–Q4 8 P×P B–K3 9 P–B3 B–K2 10 B–K3 0–0 11 QN–Q2 N×N 12 Q×N Q–Q2 13 QR–Q1 QR–Q1** (7).

Material is equal here, and both sides have developed the same number of pieces. Which plan should each side select?

The key factor in this position is the asymmetrical position of the pawns. If we divide the board into two halves by drawing a line between

the K-file and Q-file, Black has four pawns to three on the queen's wing, whereas the opposite is the case on the other wing. An additional factor is White's pawn on K5 which is already in his opponent's half of the board and restricts Black's possibilities on the K-side. A black piece cannot go to ... KB3; after ... P–KB3 or ... P–KB4, Black must always reckon with P × Pep, and after ... P–KN3 a hole is created on ... KB3. The respective strategic plans are as follows:

1. White will attack on the K-side by piece-play (e.g. Q–Q3, B–B2 or N–N5 etc.), exploiting the restrictive power of his KP. In addition he can, after careful preparation, advance his KBP to KB5.

2. Black will parry White's K-side threats and prepare in his turn a Q-side pawn advance by ... N–QR4, ... P–QB4 etc.

Our next example comes from a variation of the well known Rauzer system of the Sicilian Defence, after the moves **1 P–K4 P–QB4 2 N–KB3 N–QB3 3 P–Q4 P × P 4 N × P N–B3 5 N–QB3 P–Q3 6 B–KN5 P–K3 7 Q–Q2 B–K2 8 0–0–0 0–0 9 N–N3 9 P–B4! 9 ... Q–N3!** *(8)*

The dominant factor here is the position of the kings on opposite flanks. Both sides must strive to hurl

their pawns and pieces against the enemy king without wasting time. In such positions, it is usually a matter of 'first come, first served'. White will therefore advance his KBP and KNP, and sometimes his KRP, as quickly as possible, whilst Black will utilize his QRP and QNP in the same way.

A less important factor, which must nevertheless be taken into account, is the weakness of Black's QP. As a result Black must look to the protection of this pawn (... R–Q1, ... Q–B2) whilst carrying out his main plan.

The choice of the correct plan must depend upon the specific characteristics of the position rather than general principles only. Consider the following position which arose in the 5th game of the Spassky–Fischer match in Reykjavik, 1972, after the moves **1 P–Q4 N–KB3 2 P–QB4 P–K3 3 N–QB3 B–N5 4 N–B3 P–B4 5 P–K3 N–B3 6 B–Q3 B × N+ 7 P × B P–Q3 8 P–K4 P–K4 9 P–Q5 N–K2 10 N–R4 P–KR3** *(9)*.

The game continued:

11 P–B4 (?)   N–N3

Acceptance of the sacrifice would give White the advantage in all variations after 11 .... P × P? 12 B × P P–KN4 13 P–K5!

12 N × N   P × N

13 P×P?

It was discovered after the game that 13 0–0, followed by an eventual P–B5, would have been stronger, with approximately equal chances.

   13 . . .   **P×P**

White's plan is easy to understand and apparently strong. His pawn advance has made it difficult for Black to utilize his K-side pawn majority because of the doubled pawns, and at the same time White has obtained a protected passed pawn in the centre. He also has two bishops against bishop and knight which is usually a permanent advantage as we shall see in a later chapter.

According to all *general principles* White should now stand better, but in reality the opposite is the case, as the *specific characteristics* of the position reveal. White's bishops have no scope and his pawns are immobile, whereas Black's pieces soon begin to exert strong pressure, as follows:

   14 B–K3

In a later game Kraidman–Pachman (Netanya 1973) Black also obtained the advantage after 14 P–QR4 P–QR4 15 R–R2 Q–Q3 16 QR–KB2 B–Q2 17 B–B2 P–KN4 18 Q–K2 B–N5 19 Q–K3 B–Q2 20 B–Q1 N–N5!

   14 . . .   **P–N3**
   15 0–0   **0–0**

16 P–QR4	**P–QR4!**
17 R–N1	**B–Q2**
18 R–N2	**R–N1**
19 R2–KB2	**Q–K2**
20 B–B2	**P–KN4**
21 B–Q2	**Q–K1!**
22 B–K1	**Q–N3**
23 Q–Q3	**N–R4!**
24 R×R+	**R×R**
25 R×R+	**K×R**
26 B–Q1	

Or 26 B–KN3 N–B5 27 B×N NP×B and the black pawns on the K-side become mobile.

   26 . . .   **N–B5**
   27 Q–B2??

It was essential to play 27 Q–N1 but even then Black can play his queen to . . . QB2 and then strengthen his position by advancing his K-side pawns.

   27 . . .   **B×P!**
   0–1

If 28 Q×B then 28 . . . Q×KP wins.

Often the position of a single pawn may be the dominant strategic factor, as in our next position. Unzicker–Botvinnik (*10*).

White's plan is simple: to direct his attack against Black's weak QP, then choose the correct moment to open up the K-side by P–N4. It did not take long for the German grandmaster to carry out this plan successfully, in his game from the European Team Championship at Oberhausen 1961: **18 B–B3! B–K3** if 18 ... B×P 19 Q–N2 B–B3 then both 20 P–N4 and 20 KR–K1, threatening 21 P–K6, are very strong **19 KR–N1! P–QN3 20 Q–N2 R–QR2 21 R–N5 R–Q2 22 P–N4! N–K2** after 22 ... P×P 23 B×NP B×B 24 Q×B White is threatening both 25 Q×P and 25 P–K6 **23 B×N K×B 24 K–R1** of course 24 P×P B×P 25 B×P was also playable, but White would then have to reckon with the possible counterplay 25 ... P–N4 26 P×P R–N1 **24 ... P–N3 25 R1–QN1 K–B1 26 P×P B×P** if 26 ... P×P 27 R–N1 wins **27 B×P Q–R5 28 B–K4! Q×BP 29 B×B P×B** or 29 ... Q×B 30 R×NP K–N2 31 R–KB6 Q–N4 32 Q–B3 followed by 33 R–KB1 winning **30 R×NP K–K2 31 P–K6 1–0**

The same strategic motif is seen in the following instructive game:

8 Reshevsky–Capablanca

Margate 1935, Queen's Gambit

1 P–Q4 N–KB3 2 P–QB4 P–K3 3 N–QB3 P–Q4 4 B–N5 QN–Q2 5 P×P P P×P 6 P–K3 B–K2 7 B–Q3 0–0 8 Q–B2
8 ...   P–B4?!
Black avoids the position arising after 8 ... P–B3, which we shall discuss in our chapter 'The Minority Attack'. The text move seriously weakens the QP which White now plans to subject to continuous positional pressure.
9 N–B3
White cannot win a pawn immediately by 9 P×P N×P 10 B×N N×B+ 11 Q×N B×B, as 12 Q×QP fails to 12 ... B×N+, and 12 N×P allows 12 ... B×P.

9 ...   P–B5
This prevents the opening of a file onto his QP, but in no way frees Black from worries about this weak pawn, as the rest of the game shows.
10 B–B5   R–K1
11 0–0   P–KN3
The weakness of the QP is already evident in the variation 11 ... N–B1? 12 B×B R×B 13 B×N B×B 14 Q–B5, when the pawn falls.
12 B–R3   N–B1
13 B×B   R×B (11)

Black's position seems impressive at first glance. If he can carry through a Q-side pawn advance with ... P–QR3 and ... P–QN4, he may gain the initiative. However, with his next few moves Reshevsky creates another way of attacking Black's QP.
14 B×N!
A strategically well-based exchange, removing one of the defenders of the QP.
14 ...   B×B
15 P–QN3!
A powerful move. Black dare not exchange pawns, as after 15 ... P×P 16 Q×QNP he loses a pawn at once. White now threatens 16 P×P giving the following lines:
a. 16 ... R×P 17 Q–N3 followed by 18 N–Q2, again with decisive pressure on the QP.

b. 16 ... P×P 17 P–K4! and White's central pawns are more dangerous than Black's Q-side majority.

15 ...   **Q–R4**

Parrying the threat by putting pressure on White's QN, but the placing of Black's queen now allows another advantageous manoeuvre by White.

16 P–QN4!   **Q–Q1**

Forced, as 16 ... Q×NP? fails to 17 QR–N1! Q–Q3 18 R×P threatening 19 R×RP, or 19 R–N5, or 19 R1–N1.

17 Q–R4!

Not only attacking the QRP but also threatening 18 Q–N5 winning that fatal QP around which the whole game hinges.

17 ...   **P–QR3**
18 P–N5!   **R–K3**
19 QR–N1

And now the threat is 20 P×P P×P (20 ... R×RP 21 Q–N5 etc.) 21 R–N7. Note that this cannot be played at once, as White's queen is lost after 19 P×P R×RP 20 Q–N5 R–R4! 21 Q×NP? R–N1 22 Q–B6 R–N3.

19 ...   **R–N1**

Black cannot play 19 ... P–QR4 20 P–N6! R×NP 21 R×R Q×R 22 R–N1 when at least two pawns fall.

20 R–N2   **B–K2**

In order to answer 21 R1–N1? with 21 ... P–QR4! 22 P–N6 B–N5.

21 P×P   **R×RP**
22 Q–B2   **N–K3**
23 R1–N1   **R–R2**
24 P–QR4! *(12)*

Black has managed to contain the immediate threats, but his pieces are tied to the defence of his weak QNP and QP.

24 ...   **N–B2**
25 N–K5   **Q–K1**

26 P–B4?!

A very dubious pawn move. Admittedly White can now switch to a K-side attack by P–B5, when he is ready, but the move seriously weakens his KP and cuts out the possibility of a central pawn advance by P–B3 and P–K4. For this reason, it would have been better on the previous move to play K–R1 and manoeuvre the KN to K2 via KN1, followed by N–N5 exchanging Black's important defensive knight. This manoeuvre is still possible, as time is not such an important factor here.

26 ...   **P–B3**
27 N–N4   **Q–Q2**
28 P–R3   **K–N2**
29 N–B2   **B–R6**
30 R–R2   **B–Q3**
31 N2–Q1!

The next vital stage of his plan, intending N–N5 exchanging Black's knight, when White's remaining knight is ready to occupy QB3.

31 ...   **P–B4**

Black wishes to prevent all chances of P–N4 followed by P–B5.

32 N–N5!   **R–R4**
33 N×N   **B×N**
34 N–B3   **Q–K3**
35 Q–B2   **P–N3**
36 Q–B3   **R–Q1**
37 R2–N2

Threatening 38 R–N5 with more

pressure on the QP. Black parries this by tactical means.

37 ...　　　　　Q–K2!

With the idea: 38 R–N5 R×R 39 R×R Q–R6! 40 N×P P–B6! e.g. 41 N×B P–B7 winning.

38 R–N4　　　　R–Q2
39 K–R1　　　　B–Q1

We now see the drawbacks of White's P–KB4. As White has to defend the KP, this restricts the activity of his pieces and so reduces his pressure on the Q-side. Nevertheless, Reshevsky still finds an advantageous plan, consisting of two phases:

1. His K-side pawns are advanced in order to prevent a possible counter-attack by ... P–KR3 and ... P–KN4.
2. His king is brought to QB2 to sap the strength of a possible ... Q–QR6, and then R–N5 will allow him to attain his strategic aim, the capture of Black's QP.

40 P–N4　　　　P×P

Otherwise 41 P–N5 would completely blockade Black's K-side, and White's king could calmly proceed to QB2.

41 P×P　　　　Q–Q3
42 K–N1　　　　B–B2
43 K–B2　　　　R–B2!

Threatening a dangerous counter-attack by 44 ... P–KN4 45 P–B5 R–B3 and 46 ... R–KR3

44 P–N5　　　　B–Q1
45 K–K2　　　　B×P?

This leads to a rapid loss, as Black's queen will prove useless on ... QR6. He had a much better plan in 45 ... Q–K3! 46 K–Q2 Q–B4 compelling White to defend his Q3 square with 47 Q–K2.

46 R×NP　　　　Q–R6
47 K–Q2!　　　　B–K2
48 R–N7　　　　R×RP

A last fling, as an attempt to guard his QP by 48 ... Q–Q3? fails to 49 R7–N5 R×R 50 P×R! and the passed QNP is decisive. After the text move White cannot of course play 49 N×R? Q–Q6+! 50 K–B1 B–R6+, or here 50 K–K1 B–R5+.

49 Q×P　　　　R–R4
50 Q×P

After lengthy manoeuvring White has finally attained his strategic objective, giving him a winning game. For more than 30 moves, his whole planning has been centred on Black's weak QP.

50 ...　　　　　R–R4
51 K–Q3　　　　Q–R1
52 Q–K6　　　　Q–R6?
53 R–Q7　　　　R4–KB4

Anticipating the threatened 54 R1–N7, but losing to the second threat.

54 R–N3!　　　　Q–R8
55 R×B　　　　Q–KB8+
56 K–Q2　　　　1–0

In our next game, we quickly reach a position in which neither side has any real points of attack. Let us see how to evaluate such positions and form a strategic plan.

9 Capablanca–Ilyin-Zhenevsky

Moscow 1925, Sicilian Defence

1 P–K4 P–QB4 2 N–QB3 N–QB3 3 P–KN3 P–KN3 4 B–N2 B–N2 5 KN–K2 5 P–Q3! 5 ... P–Q3 6 P–Q3 N–B3 7 0–0 0–0 8 P–KR3 P–QR3 8 ... R–N1! 9 B–K3 B–Q2 (*13*)

Already the position possesses certain distinctive characteristics. Both sides are equal in development. with the pieces roughly balancing each other out. The pawns offer no weaknesses to be attacked, so what will be the basis of the respective plans?

10 Q–Q2	**R–K1!**

A well-known strategem in such positions, in order to answer 11 B–R6 with 11 . . . B–R1, preserving his strong bishop.

11 N–Q1

Sooner or later this move will be forced, so White prepares to counter the pressure of Black's KB on his QNP by playing P–QB3.

11 . . .	**R–QB1?**

Again an inexactitude, as it does not fit in with the correct strategic plan. 11 . . . P–QN4 should be played at once, so that the rook can later go to QN1 without loss of time.

12 P–QB3	**Q–R4**
13 P–KN4	**R.K1–Q1**
14 P–KB4(?)	

More precise was the immediate 14 P–N5 N–K1 15 P–KB4, as the text move allows Black to set up a better defensive position with his bishop on K1 and knight on Q2.

14 . . .	**B–K1!**
15 P–N5	**N–Q2**
16 P–B5	**P–N4**
17 N–B4	**P–N5**
18 P–B6!	**B–B1!**

And not 18 . . . KP × P? 19 N–Q5 with a bad position for Black

19 N–B2 (?)

Capablanca has been given extra time to pursue his plan, mainly because of Black's inexact 8 . . . P–QR3? and 11 . . . R–QB1? The text move admittedly threatens the unpleasant 20 P × KP N × P 21 N–N4, thus forcing . . . P–K3, but as the knight will have to return to Q1, the lost time is too high a price to pay. Correct therefore was 19 P–KR4!

19 . . .	**NP × P**
20 NP × P	**P–K3**
21 P–KR4	**R–N1**
22 P–R5	**R–N3**
23 P × P	**RP × P** *(14)*

The decisive factor here is the asymmetrical placing of the central pawns. Black's QBP guarantees him a certain space advantage on the Q-side, whereas White's KP gives him more space on the K-side. This means that White will advance his K-side pawns (P–KB4, P–KN4, P–N5, P–B5 etc.), in conjunction with his pieces, in order to carry out an attack on Black's king. Black on the other hand will try to exploit his space on the other wing by advancing his QNP to QN5. His bishop on KN2 plays a vital part in this plan, as the pressure on the long diagonal will sooner or later force White to play P–QB3, when Black can open up the QN-file by NP × BP.

It is worth pointing out that both sides have already made slight errors in the execution of their plans. White, for example, has developed his K-side pieces too hastily, whereas we now know that in this variation 5 P–Q3! followed by 6 B–K3 and 7 Q–Q2 or 7 Q–B1 is more exact. In many variations White then has an opportunity of exchanging Black's strong KB by B–KR6.

Black too played the passive 8 . . . P–QR3 instead of the more active 8 . . . R–N1. Both moves are played with a view to 9 . . . P–QN4, but the rook move is the logical preparation for a later opening of the QN-file.

We can see now the results of each side's respective plans. White has already driven a wedge into Black's K-side and only needs to double two of his major pieces on the KR-file to finish the game off. Black has managed to open the QN-file and now plans to double rooks followed by penetration to the seventh rank.

24 N–Q1

An attacking move (freeing KB2 for his queen to reach KR4) and at the same time a defensive one (guarding his QN2 and QBP).

24 ...	N2–K4
25 Q–KB2!	N–KN5
26 Q–R4	N3–K4!

Not 26 ... N×B? 27 N×N Q×BP 28 N–N4 winning.

27 P–Q4?

In his desire to force a quick win, Capablanca underestimates Black's counter-chances. He probably failed to take into account Black's 31st move. It was essential to play the preparatory 27 B–Q2 threatening B–R3. This would force 27 ... R1–N1 28 B–R3 R–N7! 29 N×R R×N 30 B×N! (if *30 B–B1 N–R7!*) 30 ... R×B 31 Q–K1! when White has won the exchange but exposed his position. Black must not then go in for 31 ... Q×BP 32 R–B2 R–B7 33 Q×Q R×Q 34 B–K2 B–N4 35 P–R4 B×QP? (better *35 ... B–B3* and *36 ... N–Q2*) 36 B×B N×B 37

N×N R×N because of 38 R–N1! with the threat of 39 R–N8 followed by 40 R2–QN2 or KR2. However, after 31 ... R–QB7 or 31 ... R×RP a very difficult position arises, which could only be evaluated after thorough analysis.

27 ...	N×B
28 N×N	Q×BP
29 P×N	Q×N+
30 K–R1	

After 30 K–R2 R–N7! Romanovsky gives the following variation: 31 QR–K1 (*31 R–Q1 Q×P*) 31 ... Q–QB6 32 R–Q1 P–B5 33 R–Q3 P×R 34 R–B3 R×B+ 35 N×R Q×P+ 36 N–B4 P–Q7 37 R–KR3 B–R3!

White's king, stripped of his pawn protection, is now in serious danger, as a result of Black's counter-attack which springs in turn from his strategic plan of occupying the QN-file.

30 ...	P×P!
31 R–B3	P×N
32 R×Q	P×R

With his 'sacrifice' of queen for rook, minor piece and two pawns, Black has not only parried all threats to his king, but has also obtained a clearly won position. White is powerless against the entry of the black rooks combined with the advance of the passed QBP e.g. 33 R–K1 R–N7 34 R×P R–Q8+ and 35 ... R8–Q7.

33 Q–K1	R–N7
34 Q×P	R1–Q7
35 B–B3	P–B5
36 P–R3	B–Q3
37 Q–R7	P–B6
0–1	

We have already pointed out that it is often much more difficult to find the correct plan than to calculate a complex series of moves. The following game by Alekhine clearly shows the depth of thought and imagination required to formulate a strategic plan.

10 Alekhine-Chajes

Carlsbad 1923, Queen's Gambit

1 P–Q4 N–KB3 2 P–QB4 P–K3 3 N–KB3 P–Q4 4 N–B3 QN–Q2 5 B–N5 B–K2 6 P–K3 0–0 7 R–B1 P–B3 8 Q–B2 P–QR3 9 P–QR3 R–K1 10 P–R3 P–N4 11 P–B5 N–R4 12 B–KB4! N×B 13 P×N P–QR4 14 B–Q3 P–N3 15 P–KR4! B–B3 16 P–R5 N–B1 17 P–KN3 R–R2 18 N–Q1! B–KN2 19 N–K3 P–B4 20 Q–K2! P–R5 (?) 21 N–B2 R2–K2 22 K–B1 B–B3 23 N–K5 (?) B×N (?) better was 23 … Q–B2! when White would have to continue 24 N–B3 followed by N–N4, B–N1, N–Q3 and N–K5 24 Q×B Q–B2 25 Q–B6! R–B2 26 Q–R4 Q–K2 27 P×P! N×P 28 Q–R5 Q–B3 29 B–K2 R–KN2 30 Q–B3 N–B1 31 Q–K3 R1–K2 32 N–N4 B–Q2 33 B–R5 N–N3 (*15*)

15
W

It is obvious that this position is greatly in White's favour. Black has weak pawns on K3 and KR2, whereas White's position offers no weaknesses which Black can use to obtain counterplay. On the other hand, White cannot carry out a pawn breakthrough, as Black's pieces

have sufficient control of the danger points. After thorough examination of the characteristic features of the given position, Alekhine worked out a plan which he explained as follows in *My Best Games 1908–1923.*

'*1st phase:* Bringing the king to the centre where, after the subsequent exchange of queens and rooks on the KR-file, it will threaten a rapid penetration of the hostile camp via QR5.

'These tactics will logically induce a corresponding displacement of the black king, the more plausible since its presence in the centre will consolidate the weak points . . . QB3 and . . . K3.

'*2nd phase:* Compelling the black pieces to remove themselves in succession from the K-side, by the tactical threats aimed either at the king himself or at the adverse pawns (39th and 41st moves).

'The prospect of the occupation of the square K5 by a white knight, thereby immobilizing the black knight at . . . Q2, increases still more the difficulty of concerted action by the black pieces, which is already difficult enough on account of the limited space available to them.

'*3rd phase:* Finally, at an opportune moment, namely, when the black pieces are at their greatest distance from the K-side, doubling rooks on the KR-file. The rooks, after the forced exchange of queens and bishops, will penetrate into the heart of the hostile position.'

As the game continuation shows, White needed 24 moves to carry out the above plan!

34 N–Q3

It would be a gross tactical error to play 34 K–K1? P–K4! and White is in a hopeless position (35 QP×P N×KP 36 P×N R×KP).

34 ...	B–K1
35 K–K2	K–B1
36 K–Q2	R–N2
37 B–B3	K–K2
38 KR–K1	N–B1
39 N–N4	

Threatening 40 B×P! BP×B 41 N×P+ winning the queen.

39 ...	K–Q1
40 K–Q3	R.KN2–K2
41 Q–Q2	R–R2

And now Black must prevent the threatened 42 N–R6 and 43 Q–R5+.

42 R–KR1	R.K2–QB2

Black intends to use his bishop on KN3 to guard his weak KRP. He rightly sees that he will need his knight on Q2 to prevent the entry of White's knight at K5.

43 R–R2	B–N3
44 Q–K3	K–B1
45 R1–KR1	K–N2
46 K–Q2	R–K2
47 N–Q3	N–Q2
48 B–R5!	

When we later discuss the terms 'good' and 'bad' bishops, the reader will see that White's bishop is better than Black's. However, White is logically pursuing the plan of forcing an entry for one of his rooks. This whole manoeuvre can be called a combination, because the exchange of a 'good' for a 'bad' bishop is a strategic contradiction.

48 ...	R–R1
49 B×B	P×B

Of course 49 ... Q×B? fails to 50 R–R6 Q–N1 51 Q–B3 followed by Q–R5 and the transfer of the knight to KN5, winning the KRP.

50 R–R7	R1–K1
51 N–K5!	

The point of the previous manoeuvre, as Black cannot play 51 ... N×N 52 BP×N Q–B1 53 Q–N5 winning the KNP.

51 ...	N–B1

52 R–R8	R–N2
53 N–B3	R–QN1
54 N–N5	R–K2
55 Q–K5	Q×Q
56 BP×Q (16)	

16
B

White has reached his strategic goal, and there is no defence to doubling the rooks on the eighth rank.

56 ...	K–R1
57 R–N8	P–N5
58 R1–R8	R2–K1
59 P×P	K–R2
60 K–B3	K–R3
61 N–B7	

White could also capture the KP, but he is playing for mate.

61 ...	R–R1
62 N–Q6	R.K1–N1
63 R–R1!	N–Q2
64 R–R1!	1–0

The strategic plan must spring from the nature of the position. A faulty plan can ruin even a clear positional superiority, as the following game shows. White must have thought that any plan would do in order to convert his undoubted space advantage into a win, so he opted for a direct attack on the king. However, such an attack did not correspond to the demands of the position and gave Black the possibility of effective counter-play.

11 Opočensky–Nimzowitsch

Marienbad 1925, Nimzo-Indian
Defence

**1 P–Q4 N–KB3 2 P–QB4 P–K3 3
N–QB3 B–N5 4 Q–B2 P–QN3?
5 P–K4 B–N2 6 B–Q3 N–B3 7
N–B3 B–K2 8 P–QR3 P–Q3 9 0–0
P–K4 10 P–Q5 N–QN1 11 P–QN4
QN–Q2** (*17*).

As a result of extravagant play, the
famous grandmaster had reached a
completely restricted position without prospects. Both his bishops are
badly placed. Freeing moves such
as ... P–KB4 or ... P–QB3 can
hardly be attempted. The former
would take a great deal of time to
prepare and the latter would weaken
the QP. This means that Black is
condemned to a passive game and
it is merely a question of the plan
White should select to convert his
advantage into a win.

The central pawn position indi-
cates that White should simply
prepare for P–QB5. After the correct
12 P–R3 followed by B–K3 and
N–QR4, White would carry out this
advance, without Black having any
prospects of effective counter-action
e.g. 12 P–R3 P–KR3 13 B–K3
P–KN4 14 N–KR2 etc.

Instead of this, White chose a
completely wrong plan. He
developed his QB on N2 with the
intention of opening up the long
diagonal onto Black's king by P–B4
or even by a possible knight sacrifice
on K5. However, one cannot select
at random the place where battle is
to take place, and it is soon Black
who becomes master of the field on
the K-side: **12 B–N2? 0–0 13 N–K2
N–R4 14 Q–Q2 P–N3! 15 P–N4
N–N2 16 N–N3 P–QB3! 17 Q–R6
R–B1 18 QR–B1 P–R3 19 KR–Q1
R–B2 20 P–KR4?** consequential
but bad; correct was 20 P–R3 and
the position is still even **20 ... P×P
21 BP×P** if 21 KP×P N–B3 and
Black has the additional possibility
of a dangerous counter-attack with
... P–QN4 **21 ... R×R 22 R×R
N–B3 23 N–R2 K–R1** preventing 24
P–B4? which would now lose the
queen after 24 ... N–N1 **24 Q–K3
N–Q2 25 N–B3 N–B3 26 N–R2
N–N1 27 P–KN5 P–B3! 28 N–B3
P×P 29 P×P B–B1 30 R–B6!**
White's completely misplaced attack
on the K-side has merely weakened
his own position, and he now tries to
complicate the game by imaginative
play on the other wing. However, it
is already too late to go back to the
one correct plan **30 ... B–Q2 31
B×RP! B×R 32 P×B Q–B2 33
P–N5 P–R3!** giving his king more
space, thus cutting out the possible
complications arising from the sacrifice of White's knight on K5. It
would have been bad, for instance,
to play 33 ... N–K3 34 P–R4 B–Q1
35 B–R3 Q–B2? 36 B×P! Q×N 37
B×P+ N–N2 38 Q×Q R×Q 39
P–B7 etc. **34 P×P N–K3 35 P–R4
B–Q1 36 B–R3 Q–B2! 37 N×P** or
37 B×P Q×N 38 B×P+ K–R2
wins **37 ... P×N 38 B×R Q×B
39 P–R5 N×P 40 P×P N–N5 41
P–B7 N×Q 42 P–B8=Q Q–B6
43 P×N Q×N+ 0–1.**

We have so far considered positions in which there was only one correct strategic plan available. In some cases, however, two or even several plans are possible. For example, in the Sämisch variation of the King's Indian Defence after the moves 1 P–Q4 N–KB3 2 P–QB4 P–KN3 3 N–QB3 B–N2 4 P–K4 P–Q3 5 P–B3 0–0 6 B–K3 P–K4 7 P–Q5 N–R4 8 Q–Q2 P–KB4 (*18*), White can choose between two completely different plans.

18
W

1. He can begin a sharp attack on the king with 9 P×P P×P 10 0–0–0 followed by B–Q3, KN–K2, QR–N1 and P–KN4. Black on the other hand will attack on the other wing with ... P–QR3 and ... P–QN4, after which the game takes on a sharp, two-edged character.
2. He can play 9 0–0–0 P–B5 10 B–B2, allowing Black a space advantage on the K-side which he will try to exploit by playing ... P–KN4–5, whereas White will utilize his advantage on the other wing by advancing his pawns (P–QN4, P–B5) after completing his development.

In the Exchange variation of the Queen's Gambit Declined, after the moves 1 P–Q4 P–Q4 2 P–QB4 P–K3 3 N–QB3 N–KB3 4 B–N5 QN–Q2 5 P×P P×P 6 P–K3 B–K2 7 Q–B2 P–B3 8 B–Q3 0–0 (*19*), White even has three advantageous strategic plans at his disposal.

19
W

1. A K-side attack by 9 KN–K2 R–K1 10 P–KR3 N–B1 11 0–0–0 etc.
2. Central action by P–B3 and P–K4 after 9 KN–K2 and 10 0–0.
3. A Q-side 'minority attack' (see the relevant chapter) by preparing the advance of the QNP to N5 after 9 N–B3 and 0–0.

Such a choice of plan is often possible in the transition stage between the opening and the middle game, and sometimes even occurs at a later stage. One cannot always select the correct plan on the basis of objective factors and it may be necessary to take into consideration subjective factors such as the style of both players, the state of the tournament etc. We shall deal with these aspects in later chapters on style and psychology.

Once we have chosen the correct strategic plan which fulfils the demands of the position, we must logically carry it out with all the tactical means at our disposal. In doing so, it is vital to keep a check on our plan, in view of possible changes in the position. Even a slight alteration may necessitate an immediate change of plan, as the following game shows.

12 Rabinovich–Flohr

Moscow 1939, Ruy Lopez

1 P–K4 P–K4 2 N–KB3 N–QB3 3 B–N5 P–QR3 4 B–R4 N–B3 5 0–0 B–K2 6 R–K1 P–QN4 7 B–N3 P–Q3 8 P–B3 0–0 9 P–KR3 N–QR4 10 B–B2 P–B4 11 P–Q4 Q–B2 12 QN–Q2 BP×P 13 P×P N–B3 14 P–Q5 N–QN5 15 B–N1 P–QR4 16 N–B1 N–R3 (*20*).

20
W

Theory now considers that Black has the best prospects, in view of the open QB-file which ensures him good Q-side play. His usual plan is to play ... N–B4, ... B–Q2 and ... KR–B1, whereas White must remain passive on this wing (B–Q2, B–B2, R–QB1) and try for piece play on the K-side (N–N3, N–R2–N4).

17 P–KN4?

A premature attempt to offset his Q-side disadvantage by preparing a K-side attack. If Black now proceeds with his original plan, White would in fact obtain good attacking chances by 18 N–N3 followed by K–R2 and R–KN1. However, 17 P–KN4

weakens his own king, a factor which Black can exploit only by changing his plan and attacking on the K-side himself.

17 ...	P–R4!
18 N–R2	

No better is 18 P–N5 N–R2 19 P–KR4 P–N3 and Black breaks open the KB-file by ... P–B3, at the same time exposing the weakness of White's KRP.

18 ...	P×P
19 P×P	N–R2!

A typical manoeuvre in such positions. Black exchanges his passive black-squared bishop and opens up a path for his queen to reach the K-side (... KN4 or ... KR5)

20 N–N3	B–N4
21 B–Q3	R–N1
22 B–Q2	N–B4
23 B–KB1	Q–Q1
24 B–N2	P–N3

In order to place a rook on the KR-file later on.

25 B×B	Q×B
26 R–K3	B–Q2
27 N3–B1	

In view of his weakened king's position, White can only wait, as he has no chance of active counterplay. This is why Flohr can prepare his final attack at leisure.

27 ...	KR–B1
28 R–B1	Q–Q1
29 N–Q2	N–N4
30 B–B1	K–N2
31 K–N2	Q–B3
32 B–K2	R–KR1

Threatening 33 ... R×N+! 34 K×R Q×P+

33 N.R2–B3	B×P
34 N×N (*21*)	
34 ...	R–R7+!
35 K×R	Q×P+
36 K–R1	R–KR1+
37 N–R3	B×N
	0–1

THE EQUILIBRIUM OF THE POSITION AND ITS DISTURBANCE

So far we have judged a position according to its strategic character and the correct plan arising from this. An equally important aspect of the analysis of a position lies in the evaluation of the chances for each side. This is especially vital when we wish to calculate a specific series of moves. It is clear that we should only go in for a forced manoeuvre or a combination when we assess the final position as more advantageous than or at least equal to the original one. Hence the importance of being able to evaluate our prospects accurately, for this will also influence our choice of strategic plan.

If both players have equal chances we speak of the equilibrium of the position. As we shall see, this concept has nothing to do with that of a drawn position.

This position arises after the moves **1 P–K4 P–K4 2 N–KB3 N–QB3 3 N–B3 N–B3 4 B–N5 B–N5 5 0–0 0–0 6 B×N QP×B 7 N×P R–K1 8 N–Q3 B×N 9 QP×B N×P 10 B–B4 B–B4** (*22*). The pawn structures are symmetrical, sooner or later the major pieces will be exchanged on the K–file, and there are bishops of opposite colour which is an import-

ant equalizing factor. Neither side has a positional advantage. Assuming that the players are equal in strength and no blunders are made, a draw is almost certain. In other words, we have *an equal position offering no prospects to either side*.

Contrast this next example, arising after the moves **1 P–K4 P–QB4 2 N–KB3 N–QB3 3 P–Q4 P×P 4 N×P N–B3 5 N–QB3 P–Q3 6 B–K2 P–KN3 7 B–K3 B–N2 8 N–N3 0–0 9 P–B4 B–K3 10 P–N4 N–QR4** (*23*). Theory considers this position as even, but it is a totally different type of equality from the one we saw in diagram 22. Far from exhibiting drawing characteristics, the position is extremely complex. White has the advantage on the king's side where he is preparing a violent pawn storm. In addition he plans to castle queen's side after

Q–Q2. Black on the other hand can operate down the QB-file (... R–QB1, ... B–B5 or ... N–B5 etc.) thus instituting a counter-attack on the wing where White intends to castle. Experience tells us that both sides have equal prospects of carrying out their respective plans. The outcome of the game will depend on the skill with which each player pursues his plan and exploits possible inaccuracies on the part of his opponent. Here is, then, an example of *an equal position offering both sides even prospects.*

Our next position comes from a variation of the Evans Gambit: **1 P–K4 P–K4 2 N–KB3 N–QB3 3 B–B4 B–B4 4 P–QN4 B×NP 5 P–B3 B–R4 6 P–Q4 P×P 7 0–0 P–Q3 8 P×P B–N3 9 N–B3 B–N5 10 B–QN5 K–B1 11 B–K3 KN–K2 12 P–QR4 P–QR4 13 B–QB4 B–R4** (*24*).

Theory also considers this position even, although material is unequal. Black has an extra pawn and will try to exchange off into an endgame. His disadvantage lies in the inactive placing of his king's rook. White on the other hand has strong centre pawns and more actively posted pieces which he can use to put pressure on the enemy position and to create tactical threats on the

K-side. In this case, the equilibrium of the position takes on a dynamic character, with material superiority being balanced against different factors such as space advantage and a certain lead in development.

To sum up, the equilibrium of position consists basically of two types:

1. Drawn positions which offer neither side a chance to formulate an effective plan.
2. Positions in which prospects are even, because individual determining factors balance each other out.

How does such an equilibrium come about? As White has the first move in the game, this clearly gives him a lead in development with the possibility of an advantage in space. Theoreticians once argued about whether the advantage of the first move is sufficient to win against exact play, or whether a game free from errors must end in a draw. Such discussions are naturally pointless, mainly because it is by no means possible, especially in the opening, to make absolutely exact moves.

Modern theory has shown that the advantage of the first move is not so great as was once thought, and that during the first 12 to 20 moves Black can generally neutralize White's initial slight advantage. However, one clear fact emerges: the slightest opening inexactitude on Black's part usually leads to an important disturbance of the equilibrium. White on the other hand has more scope and can often allow himself (e.g. for psychological reasons) objectively weaker moves, without risking a serious loss of equilibrium to his disadvantage.

In the first phase of the game

Black is fighting for equality, so must strive to bring about equilibrium. (However, as we have already shown, this in no way means that he is forced to play for a draw). Let us assume, then, that an equal position has been obtained from the opening. How can the further course of the game bring about a disturbance of this equilibrium? Basically, only by a mistake on the part of one of the players. This does not have to be a gross error leading to material loss or clear positional disadvantage. It can be a faulty strategic plan or a series of minor inaccuracies whose individual shortcomings could hardly be demonstrated objectively.

When we maintain that the equilibrium can only be disturbed by a mistake, we do not mean that a player cannot fight to achieve this result. To bring about an advantage, he must create complex strategic and tactical problems for his opponent. Even in so-called drawn positions it is sometimes possible to find a continuation which makes it hard for the opponent to formulate the correct strategic plan, or which even induces a tactical error.

The equilibrium cannot, however, be advantageously disturbed by a sudden attack. That would automatically have the reverse effect, a basic positional rule discovered by Steinitz, the founder of modern chess. Let us illustrate this point with a simple and well-known example:

This position (Meek–Morphy) arose after **1 P–K4 P–K4 2 N–KB3 N–QB3 3 P–Q4 P×P 4 B–QB4 B–B4 5 N–N5?** (*25*) White's 4th move is already an attempt to disturb the equilibrium, for White is ready to sacrifice a pawn in order to

increase his initial lead in development. Indeed if he had continued logically with P–QB3! on move 4 or 5 (in order to bring his QN into play after . . . P×P), a *dynamic equilibrium* would have been brought about (lead in development versus material advantage).

White's last move, however, is an attempt to exploit the weakness of Black's KB2 by a sudden attack. This decision is unjustified, since Black has clearly made no error in his play so far, and the equilibrium has not been sufficiently disturbed for such brutal measures to be effective. Play continued: **5 . . . N–R3! 6 N×BP!? N×N 7 B×N+ K×B 8 Q–R5+ P–KN3 9 Q×B . . .** A beginner would probably enjoy such a 'combination', but in reality White has only succeeded in weakening his own position. His queen is now his only developed piece and will immediately be subjected to attack. Black concluded the game in the following decisive fashion: **9 . . . P–Q3 10 Q–QN5 R–K1 11 Q–N3+?** after 11 0–0! R×P 12 N–Q2 R–K1 13 N–B3 Q–B3, White would have insufficient compensation for the sacrificed pawn, but this was his only chance of avoiding a rapid defeat **11 . . . P–Q4 12 P–KB3 N–R4 13 Q–Q3 P×P 14 P×P Q–R5+ 15 P–KN3 R×P+ 16**

K–B2 Q–K2 17 N–Q2 R–K6 18
Q–N5 P–B3! 19 Q–B1 19 Q×N
R–K7+ 19 ... B–R6! 20 Q–Q1
R–KB1 21 N–B3 K–K1 0–1.

The following miniature illustrates
the same strategic point:

13 Koch–Michel

1935, Bishop's Opening

1 P–K4 P–K4 2 B–B4 N–KB3 3
P–Q3 B–B4 4 N–QB3 P–Q3 5
P–B4 N–N5? 6 P–B5! N–B7 7
Q–R5 Q–Q2? 7 ... 0–0 fails to 8
N–B3 N×R 9 N–KN5 P–KR3 10
N×P R×N 11 Q×R+ K–R2 12
B–KN5!!, but Black might have
saved the game with 7 ... P–KN3
8 Q–R6 N–N5! 9 Q–N7 Q–B3 8
B–K6! N×R or 8 ... Q–K2 9
N–Q5 etc. 9 B×Q+ N×B 10
N–Q5 B×N 11 N×P+ K–Q1 12
N×R P–B3 13 B–Q2 1–0.

Our next example is equally
instructive but much more complex:

14 Szabo–Smyslov

Moscow 1956, Nimzo-Indian
Defence

1 P–Q4 N–KB3 2 P–QB4 P–K3 3
N–QB3 B–N5 4 P–K3 0–0 5 B–Q3
P–B4 6 P–QR3 B×N+ 7 P×B
N–B3 (26)

We shall be dealing with this type

of position more fully in our chapter
on 'The Doubled Pawn'. For the
moment let us give a brief assessment. White has the more active
central pawn position and intends
P–K4. If Black tries to prevent this
with ... P–Q4, then White exchanges this pawn and we have the
Botvinnik–Capablanca game (No.
7). In addition White has the two
bishops which he can exploit if the
position opens up (see 'The Two
Bishops').

The disadvantage of White's
position lies in his doubled QB
pawns which hinder active operations in the centre and offer Black a
point of attack. Black also has a lead
in development, so we might say
that the position is approximately in
equilibrium. We shall discuss the
correct play for both sides at another
time.

In this game Szabo tries to
disturb the equilibrium to his
advantage by instigating a sudden
attack before completing his development. Basically we are dealing with
the same principle as in the preceding game, but White's attempt here
has sounder tactical motivation and
is thus much more difficult to refute.

8 P–K4?!　　　P×P
9 P×P　　　　N×QP
10 P–K5

The purpose of White's pawn
sacrifice is now clear. He hopes to
misplace Black's pieces, increase his
central space advantage and win
back the pawn by B×RP+ and
Q×N. As the further play shows,
Szabo's plan is brilliantly conceived
from a tactical viewpoint. Nevertheless, the deeper logic of chess now
comes to the fore: such a sudden
attack cannot lead to an advantageous disturbance of the equilibrium. Smyslov could now even

play 10 ... N–K1 e.g. 11 B×P+
K×B 12 Q×N P–Q3 13 N–B3
P–B3. Matanovic analyses this as
follows: 14 Q–R4+ (*14 0–0 BP×P
15 N×P Q–B3*) 14 ... K–N1 15
0–0 QP×P 16 N×P P–KN4! 17
Q–N4 (*17 Q–N3 Q–Q5*) 17 ...
N–N2 with an excellent position for
Black. However, after careful consideration Smyslov opts for a more
active continuation which is not
without risk but which offers greater
chances of refuting White's plan.

10 ...	**Q–R4+!**
11 K–B1	**N–K1**

Not of course 11 ... Q×KP? 12
B–N2 and the threat of 13 B×N
Q×B 14 B×P+ wins a piece for
White – the neat tactical point of 8
P–K4?!

12 B–Q2	**Q–Q1!!**

A splendid defensive move. As we
shall soon see, the natural 12 ...
Q–B2? would be a gross error. As in
the last resort Black suffers material
loss after the ... Q–R4–Q1 manoeuvre, it is possible to term it a
combination whose purpose is to
hinder White's development (his
KR!) and then to exploit the
weakness of the QBP.

13 B–N4

Yudovich recommends instead 13
N–B3, giving up the idea of winning
back the pawn, and attempting to
use his two bishops in an attack on
the king. However, in my opinion
after 13 ... N×N+ 14 Q×N
P–B4 Black has a solid set-up and
should be able to consolidate his
advantage once he has completed
his development.

13 ...	**P–Q3**
14 B×RP+	

A highly interesting situation
would arise after 14 P×P B–Q2 15
B–K4 P–K4! 16 B×NP R–N1 17
B–Q5 P–QR4 18 B–QB3 N×P 19

B×N P×B 20 Q×P. We would
then see the disadvantage of White's
lack of development, as 20 ...
N×P! 21 B×N B–N4 wins back the
piece with the better position e.g. 22
Q–B5 Q–B3 and 23 ... KR–B1; or
22 Q–B3 R–B1; or 22 Q–B4 (*22
Q–K4 R–K1*) 22 ... Q–B3! 23
Q×Q B×B+ 24 N–K2 P×Q; or
finally 22 Q–N4 P–R4! 23 Q–K2
Q–Q5 24 R–B1 KR–B1 25 N–B3
Q×B! etc.

14 ...	**K×B**
15 Q×N	**P–R4!**

Forcing White to capture the QP
with the bishop rather than the pawn,
thus exchanging a valuable attacking piece. We now realize the
subtlety of 12 ... Q–Q1!!, for if the
Black queen were on QB2 White
would be able to play 16 P×P with
gain of tempo and a winning
position.

16 B–B3?

This attempt at attack is doomed
to failure. It was essential to play
16 B×QP N×B 17 P×N (*17 R–Q1?
B–Q2 18 Q×N B–R5* with clear
advantage to Black) 17 ... B–Q2 18
N–B3 P–B3, when White has an
extra pawn, but he has difficulty
completing his development, and
his QBP is extremely weak. Black
has a very strong bishop and can
create various tactical threats, so
has a clear advantage. Black also
stands better after the interesting
16 B–B5 B–Q2 17 P×P R–B1! 18
B–N6 Q–B3 19 Q×Q N×Q 20
P–B5 N–Q2.

16 ...	**P–B3**
17 Q–R4+	**K–N1**
18 R–Q1	**Q–B2**
19 R–Q3	

Or 19 P×BP N×P and 20 ...
P–K4 when Black can quickly
exploit his positional superiority.

19 ...	**QP×P**

20 R–R3	P–QN3
21 N–B3	B–R3
22 N–Q2	R–B1
23 Q–R7+	K–B2
24 P–N4	B×P+
25 K–K1	Q–Q3
26 P–N5	Q×P
27 Q–B2	B–Q4
28 R–N1	Q–R8+
29 N–N1	Q–R7
30 P–N6+	

Or 30 Q–R7 P–K5 winning.

30 ...	K–K2
31 Q–B1	N–Q3
32 R–R7	N–B4
33 R–N3	P–N4
34 R–Q3	P–N5
35 R–Q2	Q–B5
36 R–B2	Q–K5+
0–1	

It would be possible to cite numerous other examples to demonstrate that similar attacks, which are begun before the equilibrium has been disturbed, have no chance of success against accurate defensive play. By *attack* we mean direct threats against the enemy position through either a pawn advance supported by pieces or a concentration of pieces aimed at a certain part of the board. In chess as in war, it is important to attack where one is strongest. Beginners already know the basic principle: 'Do not attack where you are weaker, or else it will rebound against you'. To instigate an attack we need either more actively placed pieces or a space advantage, more mobile pawns, weak points in the enemy position and so on. These advantages can only be achieved once the equilibrium has been disturbed. The sole exception to this rule can be seen in positions of dynamic equilibrium like the one in diagram 23, where each side has attacking chances on

one sector of the board but must reckon with his opponent's counter-attack on the opposite wing. We shall discuss this problem later along with other questions of attack and defence.

We now need to examine the consequences of a disturbance of the equilibrium brought about by our opponent's mistakes. This may be sufficient to give us an objectively won position. For example, it is often purely a matter of technique to exploit a material or positional advantage. Or the game may be decided by a successful attack against a weakened king's position.

In most cases, however, a disturbance of the equilibrium does not lead to such dramatic results, because a given advantage may prove insufficient to guarantee a win. We are already acquainted with endings in which even significant material advantage cannot be converted into a win (e.g. bishop plus rook's pawn cannot usually win against a bare king when the bishop does not control the queening square of the pawn; or queen and pawn cannot win against rook and pawn in certain positions). However, such an advantage always gives the stronger side more favourable conditions for carrying out his strategic plan and controlling the course of the game. The opponent is immediately compelled to parry tactical or positional threats, and has no time to pursue an active plan of his own. In other words we possess the *initiative*, a natural consequence of the disturbance of the equilibrium in our favour.

We must be careful not to confuse the concepts of 'attack' and 'initiative'. An attack is only one possible form of the initiative which can assert itself in various ways e.g. exploitation of material superiority, planned simplification and transposition into an advantageous ending, forcing through passed pawns etc. It can even happen that one side has the initiative whilst being attacked. For instance, when we are threatening to exploit a position in which we have won a pawn, our opponent may seek salvation in a desperate attack which must fail because of insufficient preparation. It is clear that the initiative here is not with the player who has been driven to an unsound attack by force of circumstances, but with the player who has material superiority. Basic principles tell us that the initiative must lie with the player in whose favour the equilibrium of the position has been disturbed.

There are not only various forms but also various degrees of initiative. Sometimes we can talk of a *decisive initiative* which leads to a win even against best defence. At other times it is not clear whether the given advantage is enough to win, but our opponent is tied down to defence for a long time if not for the whole game and cannot pursue any active counter-plan. In this case we refer to a *lasting initiative*. And finally, there are occasions when our opponent is compelled to spend some time defending against our threats, but can restore the equilibrium if he succeeds in neutralizing them. In this case we have a *temporary initiative*. We might even view the original position as an example of the temporary initiative which White possesses as a result of the first move.

3 The Value of The Pieces

One of the beginner's first tasks is to become familiar with the power of the individual pieces. Without this knowledge he has no means of deciding which material changes on the board are favourable and which should be avoided. The most usual and simplest method of piece evaluation is to take the pawn as the basic unit and grade the other pieces accordingly. We then have:

Bishop or knight $=3$
Rook $\qquad =5$
Queen $\qquad =9$

We can of course hardly grade the king in this way, as this piece represents an absolute factor in chess, the game being over once it is 'captured'.

The relationship of the pieces to one another is at all events more complicated than this numerical evaluation can express. A beginner may be able to get along for a while on a system that judges exchanges on a purely arithmetical basis, but the advanced player knows that such evaluations are inexact even when comparing minor pieces and rooks. Admittedly a minor piece and two pawns are usually worth a rook $(3+2=5)$, but two minor pieces $(2 \times 3=6)$ are almost always more effective than a rook and pawn $(5+1=6)$, while three minor pieces $(3 \times 3=9)$ are normally at least as strong as two rooks $(2 \times 5=10)$.

This evaluation is at the moment only an abstract idea with no connection to a particular position. It represents the average value of the individual pieces i.e. their mutual relationship in the majority of positions, and is in no way to be taken as absolutely valid for concrete situations.

The value of the pieces is in fact *relative*, depending on the character of the position and on the actual material possessed by both sides. As we shall see later two pawns, especially when passed and connected, are in many cases worth a minor piece. However, in the middle game,

3 The Value of The Pieces

unless the pawns are well advanced, even three pawns do not usually compensate for an actively placed minor piece. Consider the following example, Fischer-Bisguier, Buenos Aires 1970.

The opening moves were: **1 P-K4 P-K4 2 N-KB3 N-QB3 3 B-N5 P-QR3 4 B-R4 N-B3 5 0-0 P-QN4!? 6 B-N3 B-N2 7 P-Q4 N×QP 8 N×N P×N 9 P-QB3! N×P 10 R-K1 B-Q3?** much better is 10 ... B-K2 11 Q-N4 0-0 12 R×N B×R 13 Q×B B-B3 **11 N-Q2! B×P+ 12 K-B1! P-Q4 13 Q-R5!** better than 13 N×N P×N 14 Q-R5 Q-Q3! 15 Q×BP+ K-Q1 **13 ... 0-0 14 Q×B P×P 15 N×N P×N 16 P×P P-QB4** (*27*).

Because Black's pawns are not dangerous, White can easily exploit the superior power of his pieces. The game continued: **17 R-K3! P-B5 18 B-B2 Q-B3 19 R-B3!** not 19 R-R3 P-R3 when 20 B×RP does not work. Black's queen must first be driven to a less favourable square **19 ... Q-K3 20 R-R3 Q-B4** now 20 ... P-R3 21 B×RP! wins **21 B-K3 QR-Q1 22 R-K1 R-Q2 23 B-Q4 R-K1** or 23 ... P-B3 24 R1-K3 and White's reserves come into action **24 R-R5! P-N4** if 24 ... Q-N3 25 R-K3 would again be decisive **25 P-N4 1-0** 25 ...

Q×NP 26 R×RP, or 25 ... Q-N3 26 R-R6.

We shall later consider in detail the relative strength of the knight and bishop, but a minor piece must not be under-estimated when compared with a rook. 'Positional' exchange sacrifices are extraordinarily common in modern chess.

In the game Reshevsky-Petrosian, Candidates 1953, White was here preparing to open up the game for his two bishops by P-K6. Black's defence was highly ingenious (*28*).

| **25 ...** | **R-K3!!** |

26 P-QR4

White intends to weaken Black's pawns before capturing the rook. If now 26 ... P-N5? then 27 P-Q5! R×QP 28 B×R Q×B 29 Q×QBP would give him a clear advantage.

26 ...	**N-K2!**
27 B×R	**P×B**
28 Q-B1	**N-Q4**
29 R-B3	**B-Q6**

The black knight dominates the position and there is no longer a question of a White win. For example, if 30 Q-B2 P-N5 gives Black a clear advantage, so White must aim for the draw. The game ended : **30 R×B! P×R 31 Q×P P–N5!** if 31 ... P×P White would stand better after 32 P–B4 which now fails to 32 ... N–N3 winning the RP **32 P×P P×P 33 P–R5 R–R1 34 R–R1 Q–B3 35 B–B1 Q–B2 36 P–R6 Q–N3 37 B–Q2 P–N6 38 Q–B4 P–R3 39 P–R3 P–N7 40 R–N1 K–R1** if 40 ... R×P 41 Q–B8+ K–R2 42 Q–B2+ etc. **41 B–K1 ½–½.**

15 Domnitz–Pachman

Netanya 1973, Ruy Lopez

1 P–K4 P–K4 2 N–KB3 N–QB3 3 B–N5 P–QR3 4 B–R4 P–Q3 5 P–B3 B–Q2 6 P–Q4 KN–K2 7 B–N3 P–R3 8 QN–Q2 N–N3 9 N–B4 B–K2 10 P×P P×P 11 N–K3 B–N4!? a well-known strategic idea, to exchange Black's passive bishop. Best is now 12 N×B P×N 13 P–N3! N.B3–K2! with approximate equality **12 0–0? B×N 13 B×B Q–B3** threatening ... B–N5 **14 N–Q2 N–B5 15 B×N P×B!** releasing an important central square on K4 for his pieces **16 Q–R5!** otherwise Black would simply castle long and begin a strong attack with ... P–KN4 **16 ... 0–0 17 N–B3 QR–K1 18 KR–K1** (*29*) more exact was 18 QR–Q1 B–B1 19 KR–K1 N–K4! 20 N×N R×N 21 Q–B3 R1–K1 when although Black stands better it is not certain that he can win against best defence.

18 ...   R–K4!
Of course 18 ... N–K4 was also possible, but the text move promises more, as the knight will prove more effective on K4 than the rook. One can hardly talk of forced variations after this exchange sacrifice, for it is based mainly on judgement

of the position. In such cases, we have a *positional sacrifice*.

19 N×R   N×N
Threatening 20 ... B–N5 winning the queen, against which both 20 P–B3 and 20 P–KR3 are insufficient e.g. 20 P–B3 K–R2! threatening 21 ... P–KN3 (winning material); or 20 P–KR3 K–R2 followed by 21 ... P–KN3 and 22 ... P–B6, when White's KRP is a serious weakening of his king's side.

The only forced variation which Black had to calculate when sacrificing the exchange was 20 Q–Q1 P–B6 (threatening both ... *Q–N3* and ... *P×P* followed by ... *B–N5*) 21 R–K3. Now 21 ... P×P would fail to 22 R–N3, but 21 ... Q–KN3! 22 R×P (*22 P–N3 Q–R4 23 P–KR4 P–KN4*) 22 ... B–N5 23 R–N3 (*23 K–R1 Q–R4*) 23 ... B×Q 24 R×Q B×B 25 R–N3 B–K3 would give Black a definite endgame advantage – two minor pieces are almost always stronger than rook and pawn.

20 B–Q1!   R–Q1!
The struggle continues on positional lines, without direct attacking moves.

21 B–K2?
Overlooking the main threat and losing quickly. The best defence lay in 21 Q–K2! when Black has surprisingly no direct win e.g. 21 ...

B–N4 22 Q–B2 P–B6!? hoping for 23 B×P? N×B+ 24 P×N Q–N4+ 25 K–R1 R–Q7 26 Q–B1 Q–B5 27 K–N2 B–Q2! 28 R–Q1 B–R6+! or here 28 R–KN1 B–N5! winning. However, White plays the stronger 23 R–K3! P×P 24 B–K2 etc.

The other possibility is 21 ... P–B6. If then 22 P×P? B–N4 23 Q–K3 R–Q6 24 Q–B1 R×KBP! wins for Black (*25 B×R N×B+ 26 K–N2 N–R5+ 27 K–N3 Q–B6+! 28 K×N P–N4+*). However, 22 Q–K3! is much better e.g. 22 ... B–R6! 23 P–KN3! (*23 B×P R–Q6*) 23 ... B–N7. Now there is a pretty variation after 24 B–B2? Q–K3! (not *24 ... N–N5 25 P–K5! N×Q 26 P×Q · N×B 27 QR–Q1*) 25 Q–B4 R–Q7!! (or the prosaic *25... Q–R6 26 Q–R4 Q×Q 27 P×Q N–N3*) 26 QR–B1 Q–R6 27 Q–B5 Q×Q 28 P×Q N–N5 29 R–K8+ (*29 R.K1–Q1 N×BP!*) 29 ... K–R2 30 P–B6+ P–KN3 31 R–KB8 N×BP 32 R×P+ K–N1 33 R–N7+ K–B1 34 P–KR4 N–R6+ 35 K–R2 B–B8+ 36 K–R1 B–B5! and 37 ... R–N7 winning. Nevertheless, White has an excellent counter in 24 B–N3! N–N5 25 P–K5! or here 24 ... R–Q6 25 Q–B4 Q×Q 26 P×Q N–N3 27 QR–Q1 N×P 28 P–KR4.

All this means that Black must play more quietly after 21 Q–K2! and gradually try to strengthen his position with lines such as 21 ... B–N4 22 Q–B2 B–Q6 23 Q–N3 Q–B3, or 21 ... P–B6 22 Q–K3 B–R6 23 P–N3 P–KN4! in both cases giving White a difficult game.

21 ...   K–R2!

Threatening 22 ... P–KN3 winning the queen. The only defence now is 22 B–Q1 but the gain of tempo allows Black to play 22 ... B–K3 23 Q–K2 P–B6 24 Q–K3 R–Q6 etc.

22 P–KN4	P–B6
23 P–N5	Q–B5
24 B–B1	R–KR1!!
0–1	

There is no defence to Black's surprising and powerful final move which threatens 25 ... P–KN3 26 Q×RP+ K–N1 winning the queen.

In this position (*30*) from Ivkov–Larsen, Beverwijk 1964, the black bishop is clearly a strong piece, controlling the long black diagonal. However, at the moment it lacks support from the other black pieces, and White is also threatening to open lines on the king's side with 21 P–R5.

20 ...   R–B4!

A surprising positional idea, increasing the power of his own bishop by eliminating White's bishop and providing a strong point on ... Q5.

21 B×R	P×B
22 R–Q5	

Winning the QBP but also tying his rook up. However, Black was threatening an immediate 22 ... Q–K4.

22 ...	P–K3!
23 Q×BP	

Black wins easily after 23 R×P Q–B5+ 24 K–B2 Q–K6! 25 P–K5 R–Q1 etc.

23 ...   Q–N6!

He would achieve nothing with 23 ... Q–B5+ 24 R–Q2 B–B6 25 Q–B2, whereas now 24 R–Q2 loses to 24 ... B–R3 25 Q×P Q×NP 26 R1–Q1 Q×P etc.

| 24 R–N5 | Q–B5+ |
| 25 K–B2 | P–B4! |

Not of course 25 ... Q–K6 26 P–K5.

| 26 P×P | KP×P |

White now has rook and pawn for bishop, but his rook is cut off on KN5 and Black's bishop dominates the board. The threat is 27 ... Q–Q5.

| 27 R–Q1 | P–N3 |

So that 28 Q×NP would allow 28 ... Q–K4.

| 28 Q–K7 | Q×RP |
| 29 R–Q7? | |

Settling the fate of the game. There were still some drawing chances with 29 Q–K3 B–B3 30 P–B4 B×R 31 P×B Q–K5+! 32 Q×Q P×Q although the end-game is better for Black.

29 ...	B–B3
30 Q–K6+	K–R1
31 Q–Q6	Q–B7+!

Now Black's pieces combine effectively to finish the game.

32 K–B1	Q–B8+
33 K–B2	Q–K7+
34 K–B1	Q–N7+
35 K–Q1	Q–N8+
36 K–K2	R–K1+
37 K–B2	Q–K8 mate

The value of the queen is also relative. Under normal circumstances it is worth a rook plus a minor piece and two pawns, but there are a fair number of positions in which rook and minor piece work as effectively as the queen.

Consider our next diagram which arose in Ljubojevic–Planinc, Vrsac 1971, after the moves 1 P–K4 P–K4 2 N–KB3 N–QB3 3 B–N5

P–QR3 4 B–R4 N–B3 5 0–0 P–QN4 6 B–N3 B–N2 7 P–Q4 N×QP 8 N×N P×N 9 P–K5 N–K5 10 P–QB3 P–Q6 11 Q×P N–B4 12 Q–N3 N×B 13 P×N Q–K2 14 B–N5 Q–K3 15 P–KB4 P–KB3! Black must solve the problem of his king, and 15 ... B–B4+ 16 K–R1 0–0 fails to 17 B–B6. There is an alternative plan in 15 ... P–R3 16 B–R4 P–N4! 17 P×P R–KN1 e.g. 18 Q–B4 B–K2 wins back the pawn. The text-move is imaginative and original, so much so that at first sight it looks like a blunder! 16 P×P B–B4+ 17 K–R1 P×P 18 R–K1 0–0–0 19 R×Q P×R (*31*)

31
W

We can now see Black's plan. He wins White's bishop and has rook and two powerful bishops for queen and knight. In particular the pressure down the long white diagonal is very embarrassing to White. The open Q-file is also an important factor, allowing effective co-operation between Black's rooks and bishops. In such positions a rook and minor piece are often worth a queen or even superior to it.

20 Q–K1

After 20 N–R3 P×B Black would have the strong threat of 21 ... R–Q7.

| 20 ... | P×B |

21 N–Q2

The win of further material would lead to a rapid decision after 21 P×P KR–N1 22 P–R4 P–R3! 23 Q×P+ K–N1 24 Q×KRP R–Q8+ etc.

21 ...	P×P
22 Q×P+	K–N1
23 N–B3	KR–N1
24 P–B4	P–N5

A strategically important move. Because Black controls open lines in the centre and on the K-side, he must prevent any line-opening on the Q-side!

25 R–KB1	R–N3
26 Q–B5	B–K6
27 P–R3	

Allowing the entry of Black's rook, but there was nothing to be done.

27 ...	R–N6!
28 Q×RP	

Leading to a forced loss. However, passive defence by 28 Q–N1 is equally hopeless.

28 ...	B×N!

Now if 29 P×B R–Q7 followed by 30 ... R6–N7 etc.

29 R×B	R–Q8+
30 K–R2	B–N8+
31 K–R1	R–N2!

A pretty tactical idea, freeing KN6 for his bishop, as 32 Q×R fails to 32 ... B–Q5+.

32 Q–R8+	K–N2
33 R–Q3	R–K8
34 P–N3	

The only way to prevent mate without losing the queen.

34 ...	B–Q5+
35 K–R2	R2–K2!
0–1	

In some exceptional positions even two minor pieces can prevail against the queen. This occurs when the side with the queen is driven back on the defensive, which necessarily limits the queen's powers.

16 Marshall–Halper

New York 1941, Scotch Game

1 P–K4 P–K4 2 N–KB3 N–QB3 3 P–Q4 P×P 4 P–B3 P×P 5 B–QB4 P–Q3 6 Q–N3 Q–Q2 7 Q×BP (?) P–Q4! 8 P×P B–N5 9 P×N B×Q+

10 N×B	P×P
11 0–0	N–K2?

Up till now Black's prospects have been superior, but he needs to play carefully if he is to complete his development and take over the initiative. For instance, 11 ... N–B3 would be wrong because of 12 R–K1+ K–B1 13 B–K3 followed by B–B5+ and R–K7. So Black should play 11 ... Q–B4! preparing to complete his development after 12 R–K1+ B–K3, even if this means the loss of a pawn or two.

12 B×P+!	K–B1

The end-game is better for White after 12 ... K×B 13 N–K5+ winning back the queen. Despite bishops of opposite colour, Black's pawn position would put him at a serious disadvantage.

13 B–N3 (32)

The queen is now no match for White's minor pieces. On the one hand, Black cannot complete his development by connecting his rooks, and on the other, his king will soon be attacked by White's pieces.

13 ...   B–N2
14 B–K3   N–B4

After 14 ... N–Q4 Fine gives the following continuation: 15 B–B5+ K–N1 16 N–K5 Q–K3 17 QR–K1 with decisive positional advantage to White.

15 B–B5+   N–Q3
16 N–Q4   R–K1
17 KR–K1   P–KR4

Even weaker is 17 ... R × R+ 18 R × R P–KR4 19 N–K6+ K–B2 20 N × BP+ etc.

18 N–K6+   R × N
19 B × R

White already has rook and bishop for the queen and his positional superiority fully compensates for his slight material deficiency.

19 ...   Q–Q1
20 R–K5   R–R3
21 R1–K1   B–B1
22 B–N3   B–Q2
23 B–K3!

Black could now resign, as 24 B–N5 is threatened and if 23 ... R–N3 24 R × P N–B2 25 B–B5+ K–N1 26 R–K7 R–B3 27 N–K4 clinches matters.

23 ...   N–B4
24 B × R   P × B
25 N–K4   K–N2
26 N–B5   K–B3
27 N × B   Q × N
28 B–K6   1–0

Three minor pieces are usually stronger than the queen, unless the latter can penetrate into the enemy position attacking weak points and thus tying down his pieces to passive defence. However, if the side with the minor pieces has a solid position he can usually co-ordinate his pieces in an attack.

17 Kmoch–Prins

Amsterdam 1940, Grünfeld Defence

1 P–Q4 N–KB3 2 P–QB4 P–KN3 3 N–QB3 P–Q4 4 N–B3 B–N2 5 Q–N3 P × P 6 Q × BP 0–0 7 P–K4 P–N3? 8 P–K5! B–K3 9 P × N! B × Q 10 P × B K × P 11 B × B *(33)*

33
B

Opening theorists all consider this well-known line as advantageous if not won for White. What is the basis for such a judgement when from a purely materialistic point of view Black has the edge, with queen and pawn against two bishops and a knight, and there are no immediate threats against his position? White's superiority consists in the fact that Black has no chance of active counter-play, whereas passive play will only reveal the static weaknesses created by ... P–QN3 and ... P–KN3. Noteworthy is the rôle played here by White's QP (see the chapter 'The Isolated Pawn') which is by no means weak and is restricting Black's freeing moves ... P–QB4 and ... P–K4.

11 ...   N–B3
12 B–K3   N–N5

Better was 12 ... N–R4 13 B–Q5 P–QB3 14 B–K4.

13 0–0   N–B7
14 QR–Q1   N × B
15 P × N

This exchange would have been good for Black if it did not entail the opening of the KB-file for White's rook. Even if Black were now to protect himself against the following combination, he would stand worse after 16 N–K4.

15 ...	P–QB4?
16 N–KN5	P–K3
17 R×P+!	1–0

17 ... R×R 18 N×KP+, or 17 ... K–R3 18 R×KRP+ K×N 19 P–KR4+ with a quick mate.

We fairly often meet situations in which the queen is fighting against two rooks. The advantage lies almost every time with the rooks, the queen needing at least an extra pawn to hold the balance. The power of the rooks is best shown when they are doubled on open lines or on the 7th or 8th ranks. Once again the queen is then seen as a poor defender.

The queen thrives on weak enemy pawns or an exposed king, but it can also be effective when used with other pieces, even against otherwise solid positions. In conjunction with a knight or even more with a bishop, the queen's power increases noticeably, as it can combine effectively with a minor piece in attacking weak points or the enemy king.

This position (*34*) was reached in

Barcza–Florian, Budapest 1953. Black clearly stands better. His passed pawn is ready to advance, the white rooks cannot co-ordinate their action and the white knight is immobile. It is worth mentioning that the same ending without the minor pieces would be easily won by the two rooks, because the passed pawn would fall and White's pawn majority could gradually come into its own. However, the presence of minor pieces dramatically reverses this situation.

37 ...   B–R6!

Black's winning plan is to prevent the co-ordination of White's pieces by threatening to advance his passed pawn, and then to exploit the weakness of White's king position.

38 R–B7

After 38 R–R1 Black would of course play 38 ... B–B4 and if 38 R1–QB6 then 38 ... B–N7 39 R–Q6 B–Q5 (40 N–K2? Q–N8+ 41 K–R2 B×P).

| 38 ... | B–Q3 |
| 39 R–N7 | |

39 R–Q7? loses to 39 ... Q–Q8+ 40 N–B1 B–R7+, and after 39 R7–B6 Black plays 39 ... B–K4 threatening ... B–Q5 as well as the advance of his passed pawn to the seventh.

39 ...	B–B4!
40 R–QB6	Q–Q5
41 N–R1	P–N5
42 P–N4	

White has no reasonable move, as 42 R7–B7 fails to 42 ... Q–Q8+ 43 K–R2 B–Q3+.

42 ...	Q×KP
43 R6–B7	Q–K8+
44 K–N2	Q–K5+
45 K–N1	Q–B6!

Now if 46 R×BP+ Q×R 47 R×Q+ K×R 48 N–N3 P–N6 49 N–K4 (or K2 or B1) 49 ... B–N5 the pawn cannot be stopped. Meanwhile, Black is threatening . . . P–N6 followed by . . . B–Q5 and . . . P–N7, so the game would have been decided even without the following blunder.

**46 R–N5?   Q–Q8+
0–1**

47 K–N2 Q–Q4+ 48 K–N1 B×P+, or here 48 P–B3 Q–Q7+ etc.

18 Portisch–Fischer

Santa Monica 1966, Nimzo-Indian Defence

1 P–Q4 N–KB3 2 P–QB4 P–K3 3 N–QB3 B–N5 4 P–K3 P–QN3 5 KN–K2 B–R3 6 N–N3 B×N+ 7 P×B P–Q4 8 Q–B3 stronger is 8 B–R3! **8 . . . 0–0 9 P–K4 P×KP! 10 N×P N×N**

11 Q×N   Q–Q2!

Much stronger than 11 . . . N–Q2 12 B–Q3 N–B3 13 Q–R4. The knight is to be used on QR4 to attack the weak QBP.

12 B–R3

It does not matter very much if White takes the rook now or after two forced moves. In both cases the black queen is more active than the two rooks.

**12 . . .   R–K1
13 B–Q3   P–KB4
14 Q×R**

Portisch has been criticized for this move, but after the recommended 14 Q–K2 Black gains the advantage by 14 . . . N–B3 15 0–0 P–K4, or by 14 . . . P–B4.

**14 . . .   N–B3
15 Q×R+   Q×Q
16 0–0   N–R4** (35)

Now the QBP is lost and at the same time White has to give up one

of his bishops. He could try to force opposite coloured bishops by 17 B–N4 B×P 18 B×N B×B 19 KR–Q1, but in this sort of position such an exchange would only help the side with the queen. Black's queen and bishop would then successfully combine to attack White's KN2, against which there is no effective defence.

**17 QR–K1   B×P
18 B×B   N×B
19 B–B1**

Even without his extra pawn Black would now stand better, because his knight is more active than White's bishop. White lacks in particular open files for his rooks and an effective diagonal for his bishop.

19 . . .   P–B4!

Energetic play. White must capture this pawn or else his QP becomes weak and after this capture Black can easily mobilize his K-side pawn majority.

**20 P×P   P×P
21 B–B4   P–KR3
22 R–K2   P–KN4
23 B–K5**

After 23 B–B1 Black plays . . . Q–N4 and . . . P–K4, but even the blockade of Black's KP does not help, as the white pieces lack co-ordination and will soon even become tactical weaknesses.

23 ...	Q–Q1
24 R1–K1	K–B2
25 P–KR3	P–B5

Completely hemming in the bishop which has no moves and must constantly be protected by the rooks.

26 K–R2	P–R3
27 R–K4	Q–Q4
28 P–KR4?	

This move costs the exchange and hastens White's downfall, but equally hopeless would be 28 R4–K2 P–B6 29 P × P N–Q7 etc.

28 ...	N–K6!
29 R1 × N	P × R
30 R × P	Q × RP
31 R–B3+	K–K1
32 B–N7	Q–B5
33 P × P	P × P
34 R–B8+	K–Q2
35 R–QR8	K–B3
0–1	

4 The Minor Pieces

4 The Minor Pieces

As we have already stated, the knight and bishop are approximately equal in value, strange as this may seem when the movement of each piece is so different. The knight is a piece which admittedly cannot move very far, but it can move in all directions, being the only piece which can jump over its own as well as enemy pieces, and has a way of moving which differentiates it from all other pieces. The bishop on the other hand is a long-ranging piece with the peculiarity that its activity is limited to squares of one colour only i.e. half of the chess board. This is a severe limitation which means that it can neither attack nor protect pawns or pieces which are placed on squares of the opposite colour.

The reader may have the impression that we are unnecessarily stating the obvious and that any beginner already knows all this. However, these basic points can lead to complex strategic consequences which we shall encounter again and again.

Let us first deal with each piece separately and then see how it fits in with other pieces and pawns. We divide this chapter into six sections:

The bishop and open diagonals
The 'good' and 'bad' bishop
Bishops of opposite colour
The knight and its operation base
Bishop versus knight
The two bishops

THE BISHOP AND OPEN DIAGONALS

The strategic value of a piece can only be judged when it has reached maximum power. For the bishop this means opening up diagonals along which its long-range power can be put to good effect. The first moves 1 P–Q4 or 1 P–K4 already open up the QB1–KR6 or KB1–QR6 diagonals for the white bishops, and might be termed deployment diagonals. However, these are only ways of allowing the bishops to come into play and do not guarantee permanent pressure. To achieve maximum effectiveness for the bishop, a player must strive to open up and control diagonals along which the enemy position can be threatened.

36
W

Smyslov–Darga (*36*). If Black's knight reaches Q4, he will even stand better, as White's bishop will be condemned to passivity.

18 P–Q5!

A very promising positional sacrifice which Black should accept by 18 ... N–B4! 19 Q–B4 R–Q2. Smyslov had then prepared 20 Q–KN4 P–N3 21 N–K5! R×P 22 N–B6 R×R+ 23 R×R Q–B2 24 Q–B3! R–B1 25 N×B+ Q×N 26 Q–B4. In spite of his pawn minus, White would stand better, but Black could probably draw with best play.

| 18 ... | P×P? |
| 19 R×P | B–B3 |

Black has a simpler idea in mind. He intends to exchange bishops to simplify down to a draw, but White can avoid this by tactical exploitation of the Q-file.

| 20 Q–Q3! | Q–B1 |

White has a clear advantage after 20 ... B×B 21 R×B R–N2 22 Q–Q4 Q–K2 23 R–K3, or 23 N–N5.

21 N–N5	B×N
22 R×B	P–B3
23 R–KR5	P–N3

24 Q–Q5+	K–N2
25 R–R3	N–B4
26 R–K1!	

Cleverly cutting out counter-play by 26 ... N–R5 (again aimed at the strong bishop!) when 27 B–Q2 would be very strong e.g. 27 ... K–R1 28 Q–K4, or 27 ... R–Q1 28 B–R6+ K–R1 29 R3–K3! etc.

26 ...	Q–Q2
27 Q–N5!	K–N1
28 Q–R4	P–KN4
29 R–N3	N–K3
30 Q–QN4	N–N2
31 R3–K3	Q–Q4
32 Q–R3	P–KR4 (?)

Black's position is very difficult, although there are no direct threats at the moment. However, in this attempt to give his king more breathing space he only weakens his position further. Smyslov finished the game prettily as follows: **33 P–KR3 R1–KB2 34 Q–R4 P–R5 35 R–Q1 Q–KB4 36 R–B3 Q–N3 37 R–Q6 N–R4 38 Q–K8+ K–R2 39 R–Q8 Q–N2 40 Q–K4+ K–R3 41 Q–R8 K–R2 42 Q–K4+** repeating moves rather than committing himself before the adjournment **42 ... K–R3 43 Q–R8 K–R2 44 R–B5! R.KB2–Q2 45 R×NP! Q×R 46 R–R8+ K–N3 47 Q–K4+ Q–KB4 48 R–R6+ K×R 49 Q×Q** although Black now has two rooks for the queen, he has too many weak pawns **49 ... R–Q8+ 50 K–R2 R2–Q2 51 B×P N×B 52 Q×N+ K–R4 53 Q–B5+ K–R3 54 Q–B4+ K–N2 55 Q–N5+ K–B2 56 Q×P R8–Q7 57 P–KN4 R–K7 58 Q–R7+ K–K1 59 Q–N8+ 1–0**

Alekhine–Duras, St. Petersburg 1913 (*37*). The pressure exerted by the 'classically' developed bishop against KB7 is the main idea of many old openings. It can also be of decisive strategic significance in the middle-game, as Alekhine shows us here.

16 P–K5! Q–K2 17 KR–K1 R.N1–K1 18 Q–Q2 P×P 19 R×P Q–Q3 20 Q–N5! R×R 21 N×R threatening 22 N×P! **21 ... Q–N3 22 P–N4! B–Q3 23 N×P! R×N 24 Q–KB5!** now the point of 23 P–N4 is clear; Black has no defence to the threat of 25 B×R+ followed by 26 P–N5 **24 ... P–N3 25 Q–K6 K–N2 26 Q×R+ K–R3 27 B–K6! 1–0**

19 Unzicker–Bobotsov

Bamberg 1968, Sicilian Defence

1 P–K4 P–QB4 2 N–KB3 P–Q3 3 P–Q4 P×P 4 N×P N–KB3 5 N–QB3 P–QR3 6 B–K2 P–K4 7 N–N3 B–K2 8 0–0 0–0 9 B–K3 Q–B2 10 P–QR4 B–K3 11 P–R5 Q–B3 11 ... QN–Q2 is better **12 B–B3 R–B1 13 R–K1 QN–Q2 14 R–K2! Q–B2 15 R–Q2 P–R3 16 B–K2 R–Q1 17 P–B3 N–B4 18 K–R1 R–Q2 19 N×N! P×N 20 R×R B×R 21 B–QB4 R–Q1** (*38*)

Once again there is uncomfortable pressure exerted on Black's KB2, but it is not clear how this can be intensified. Which piece can lend support to the bishop?

22 Q–QN1!

The queen is the surprising answer. Black dare not exchange bishops by 22 ... B–K3, for after 23 B×B P×B 24 Q–R2 Q–B3 25 Q–B4 Black has too many pawn weaknesses. As 22 ... B–K1 would lose control of his important Q4 square, Black must defend with his rook.

22 ...   R–KB1
23 Q–R2   B–B3
24 R–Q1   B–Q3
25 Q–R3!

Black's QBP is also a strategic weakness.

25 ...   Q–K2
26 P–R3!

The loophole is essential, as 26 R×B fails to 26 ... Q×R 27 B×QBP Q–Q7 threatening 28 ... Q–K8 mate.

26 ...   R–B1
27 N–K2   N–R4
28 Q–N3   B–B2?

This loses at once because of White's pressure on KB7, but 29 B×KBP+ was the threat and after 28 ... B–K1 29 B–Q5 White would of course stand better.

29 B×QBP!   Q×B
30 B×BP+   K–R1
31 B×N   Q–B7
32 N–B3   Q–B4
33 B–N4   R–B1

34 B–Q7	B×RP
35 B×B	P×B
36 N–K2	Q–B7
37 N–B1	R–Q1
38 N–Q3	Q–N6
39 Q–N7	R–KB1
40 Q×RP	B–Q1
41 Q×P	B–N4
42 R–KB1	R–Q1
43 Q–KN6	R–QB1
1–0	

20 Uhlmann–Osnos

Zinnowitz 1971, English Opening

**1 P–QB4 P–K4 2 N–QB3 N–KB3 3
N–B3 N–B3 4 P–KN3 B–N5 5 B–N2
0–0 6 0–0 R–K1 7 N–Q5 N×N!?**
7 ... B–B1 was safer **8 P×N N–Q5
9 N–K1! B–B1 10 P–K3 N–B4**
11 P–N3   P–B4
12 P–B4!

This pawn will increase the
effectiveness of White's QB on the
long black diagonal.
12 ...   P–Q3
13 B–N2   P–QN3?

A loss of tempo. 13 ... N–R3!
could have removed the sting from
the coming centralization of White's
KB and avoided serious disadvantage.
14 B–K4!   P×P?

Black did not relish the prospect of
weakening his black squares further
by 14 ... P–N3, but this move was
nevertheless correct, as the white
bishops now become very active.
15 R×P   N–R3
16 Q–B2   P–B4
17 B–Q3   P–N3 (?) (*39*)

The ugly-looking 17 ... Q–Q2
was essential to avoid the fatal
weakening of the long diagonal.
18 Q–B3   N–B2
19 P–KN4!

And now it is the turn of the
KB-file. If 19 ... P×P 20 R×N!

K×R 21 Q–R8 Q–R5 22 N–N2
Q–R3 23 R–KB1+ wins. Black
decides to give up a pawn, but his
position cannot be held.

19 ...	N–K4
20 P×P	B–KN2
21 K–R1	P×P
22 B×P	B×B
23 R×B	Q–Q2
24 R–N5	Q–KB2
25 N–N2!	Q–B6

If 25 ... Q×P? 26 P–Q4.

26 Q–B2!	P–KR3
27 R–N3	Q×QP
28 P–K4	Q–B3
29 R–KN1	1–0

In the above game White easily
occupied the long diagonal, but
usually various tactical means have
to be employed to achieve this end.

Alekhine–Alexander, Nottingham
1936 (*40*). Alekhine played **13
P–Q5!**, as Black loses a pawn if he

tries to block the diagonal by 13 . . .
P–K4 14 N–R4 N–N4 15 P–B4. In
the game continuation White's
powerful QB is skilfully used as the
basis for a decisive attack: **13 . . .
P×P 14 P×P N2–B3 15 N–R4!
Q–Q2** 15 . . . N×QP? loses to 16
R×N! B×R 17 Q–Q4 gaining two
minor pieces for a rook **16 B–KR3!
P–N3** 16 . . . N×QP? 17 Q×N!
17 P–B3 N–B4 18 Q–N5 Q–N2 18
. . . N×QP? 19 N×NP! **19 P–QN4
N4–Q2 20 P–K4! N×KP!** still the
best, as if now 21 B×Q N×Q 22
B×R N×B+ 23 K–N2 R×B 24
K×N N–B3 Black obtains some
counterplay. Alekhine has a much
stronger move! **21 Q–B1! N5–B3 22
B×P! K–R1** or 22 . . . P×B 23
N×P Q–R1 24 N–R6+ K–N2 25
Q–N5 mate **23 B–K6 B–R3 24
KR–K1 N–K4 25 P–B4! N–Q6 26
R×N B×R 27 P–N4 1–0.** Black is
helpless against the threatened 28
P–KN5.

21 Najdorf–Minev

Havana Olympiad 1966, Boglojubow
Defence

**1 N–KB3 N–KB3 2 P–B4 P–K3 3
P–Q4 B–N5+ 4 QN–Q2 P–Q4 5
P–K3 0–0 6 P–QR3 B–K2 7 B–Q3
P–QN3 8 0–0 B–N2 9 P–QN4!
P–B4 10 QP×P NP×P 11 P–N5
P–QR3 12 NP×P B×P**
    13 Q–B2   QN–Q2?
After this routine move White
gains the advantage. Correct was
13 . . . N–B3! when White would
have to adopt a different plan, as 14
P–K4 would weaken his Q4.
    14 P–K4   P×KP
It is important to note that 14 . . .
P–Q5 fails to 15 P–K5 and 16
B×P+.
    15 N×P   Q–B2
    16 N×N+!

To allow his QB to control the
long diagonal. This would not be
possible after 16 B–N2 P–R3 17
N×N+ B×N!, or here 17 N–B3
Q–B5! and, surprisingly enough,
Black then has an attack.
    16 . . .   N×N
If 16 . . . B×N 17 B×P+ K–R1
18 R–N1 P–N3 19 B×P P×B 20
Q×P B×P 21 N–N5! B×N 22
Q–R5+ and both black bishops
fall.
    17 B–N2   P–R3 (*41*)

White's QB now controls the
important K5 square and, as we
shall soon see, exerts strong pressure
on Black's KNP.
    18 N–K5   B–Q3
Instead, 18 . . . N–Q2 would have
been somewhat better. After 19
N–N4 (threatening 20 N×P+)
Black has to weaken his position by
19 . . . N–B3 or 19 . . . P–B4, but
this is not fatal.
    19 QR–K1   KR–N1
It is already too late for 19 . . .
N–Q2 20 N–N4! P–B4 21 N×P+
P×N 22 R×P etc.
    20 P–B4   B–QB1
Intending to exert pressure down
the QN-file and threatening . . .
Q–N3 and . . . Q–N6.
    21 R–K3!
Preventing the threat by indirectly
guarding his QN3 square, and at the

same time deploying the rook in his
K-side attack.

21 ...	R–R3
22 Q–K2	R3–N3
23 B–R1	R–N6
24 R–N3	K–B1 (*42*)

25 R×P!!

A typical way of exploiting the
pressure along the black diagonal,
as Black's knight will be pinned.

25 ...	K×R
26 N–N4	K–B1?

Making White's task far easier.
Instead, 26 ... B–K2! was stronger
e.g. 27 N×N B×N 28 Q–N4+
K–B1 29 B×B R×B 30 P–B5!
Despite the reduced material, White
maintains a powerful attack, as
30 ... P×P? fails to 31 Q–N7+
K–K1 32 R–K1+ B–K3 33 R×B+!
etc.

27 B×N	B×P

White was threatening among
other things 28 N×P followed by
29 Q–N4.

28 N–K5	B–N4
29 B×B	P×B
30 R×P+	Q×R
31 N×Q	K×N
32 Q–R5+	

Once again the two rooks are
helpless against a queen, because
Black loses several pawns and his
king is driven across the board. The
game ended: **32 ... K–B3 33**

Q–N6+ K–K4 34 Q×NP+ K–Q5
35 B–B1 R–N8 36 Q–B4+ K–B6
37 Q–K3+ K–N7 38 Q×BP R–N6
39 K–B2 K–R7 40 Q×B 1–0.

In many modern openings the
KB can also exert great pressure
along the KR1–QR8 diagonal,
against the opponent's queen's wing.

Keres–Platz, Budapest 1952 (*43*).
Black has correctly fianchettoed his
QB in order to neutralize White's
powerful KB, but he now commits
a serious blunder and allows White's
KB to come into its own: **13 ...
B–R3?** correct was 13 ... B–B3!
14 N–B4! P×N The queen has no
good retreat, for both 14 ... Q–N2
15 N3–K5 and 14 ... Q–R2 15
N4–K5 are unattractive. **15 Q×Q
N×Q 16 R×B N.N3–Q4 17
B–Q2 N–K5 18 B–R5 P–B6 19
N–K5! N–Q7 20 R–Q1 P–B7 21
R–QB1 N–N6 22 R×BP N×P 23
R–Q2 N–N6 24 B×N! N×R 25
B–N7 1–0** 25 ... R–QN1 26 B–B6+.

22 Najdorf–Pachman

Amsterdam Olympiad 1954, Grünfeld Defence

**1 P–Q4 N–KB3 2 P–QB4 P–KN3 3
P–KN3 B–N2 4 B–N2 P–Q4 5
P×P N×P 6 N–KB3 0–0 7 0–0
P–QB4 8 P×P N–R3 9 N–N5!
N4–N5 10 N–QB3! Q×Q?** The

losing move; it was essential to play 10 ... P–R3 11 N–B3 N×BP 12 B–K3 when White stands better, but not here 11 N5–K4? Q×Q 12 R×Q P–B4! with a good game for Black. **11 R×Q N×BP 12 B–K3 N4–R3 13 QR–B1 P–R3 14 N5–K4 N–B3 15 P–QR3! N–B2 16 P–QN4** (*44*).

44
B

As the further course of the game shows, Black's position already contains the seeds of defeat, mainly because of White's powerful bishops. In particular, his KB exerts great pressure on Black's QNP, and proves to be the decisive factor.

| **16 ...** | **P–R3** |
| **17 N–B5** | **N–K3** |

If 17 ... N–N4 18 N×N P×N 19 N×P! B×N 20 B×N B×B 21 R×B R×P 22 R–N6 wins.

18 N–Q5	**N×N**
19 B×N	**B–N5**
20 K–B1!	**KR–Q1**
21 P–QR4!	

Avoiding the last trap of 21 N×P+ N×N 22 B×N R–K1 23 R–B7 B–KB1! etc., White methodically pursues his plan of driving away the black knight in order to lay bare the QNP.

21 ...	**P–K4**
22 P–R3	**B–K3**
23 P–N5	**P×P**
24 P×P	**B×N?**

This only hastens defeat, but even

after 24 ... N–Q5 25 N–K7+ followed by 26 B×N and 27 B×QNP Black is lost.

25 B×B	**N–Q5**
26 B×NP	**QR–N1**
27 B–R6!	**N–N6**
28 R×R+	**R×R**
29 B–K7!	**R–Q2**
30 R–B8+	**K–R2**
31 P–N6!	**R×B**
32 P–N7	**R×P**
33 B×R	**N–Q5**
34 B–Q5	**P–B3**
35 B–N8+	**K–R1**
36 P–N4!	**1–0**

There is no defence to 37 P–K3 winning the knight. A triumph for White's indefatigable KB.

45
W

Pachman–Vidmar, Spindleruv Mlyn 1948 (*45*). Both queen's bishops are developed on the same square, exerting pressure on the centre, but the other bishops contrast strongly. White's KB exerts latent pressure against Black's Q-side (he can later play P–QN4 and P–QR4), whereas Black's KB is passively placed and must head for KR3.

14 P–Q5!

This blockading move immediately lessens the value of each side's QB. Nevertheless it is the correct strategic plan, because White can exchange his QB for Black's KB when it reaches KR3, whereas Black's QB remains inactive until the end of the game. This factor alone determines the outcome!

| 14 ... | R–B1 |
| 15 N–Q2! | |

Heading for QR5.

15 ...	P–N3
16 P–QN4	B–R3
17 R–B2	Q–N3?

After this error Black is lost. The best is 17 ... N–N3 18 B–B1 followed by 19 N–N3 when White ends up with a strong knight against the badly placed QB.

18 N–N3	R–B2
19 B–B1	B×B
20 Q×B	R1–QB1
21 Q–Q2	N–N5
22 R1–B1	K–N2
23 B–Q3	P–B3
24 P–KR3	N–R3
25 N–R5	B–R1
26 P–QR4!	

It is vital to open up lines against Black's cramped position. The text move involves a pawn sacrifice to take advantage of Black's badly placed bishop.

26 ...	P×P
27 N×P	R×R
28 R×R	R×R
29 Q×R!	

After 29 B×R? Q–B2 Black could hold the game comfortably, whereas now White's queen invades the black position.

| 29 ... | Q×NP |
| 30 Q–B7! | N–B2 |

An interesting situation arises after 30 ... Q×N.5 31 N–B6 N–B2 32 Q×N. None of Black's pieces has a reasonable move and there is nothing to be done against 33 Q–B8 forcing a passed QBP. After the text move, 31 Q×N Q×N.4 gives Black the better game.

| 31 N–B6 | Q–N2 |

If Black won a second pawn by 31 ... Q–K8+ 32 B–B1 Q×KP 33 Q×N Q×N, he would still lose after 34 Q–B8.

32 Q–R5	N–N1
33 N–Q8!	N×N
34 Q×N	Q–N6
35 Q–K7+!	K–N1
36 Q×QP	Q×B
37 Q×N+	

White could have won more quickly and elegantly by 37 N–B5! but was in time-trouble.

37 ...	K–N2
38 Q–R7+	K–R3
39 N–B5	Q–Q5
40 Q–K7	B×P
41 P×B	Q–QN5
42 Q–B8+	1–0

It is not always easy to determine whether or not a bishop is badly posted, as we can see from the following diagram (*46*).

46

White's KB has no good move available, apart from the retreat to R1, and yet this bishop is strong. On the one hand it defends the king's side against attacks such as ... N–R4 followed by ... P–KB4, and on the other hand it protects the KP should White decide to play P–KB4.

In modern openings we often see the bishop playing a relatively modest role in the early stages, with its inherent strength coming to the fore later in the game. For example, after 1 N–KB3 P–Q4 2 P–KN3 N–KB3 3 B–N2, White's KB seems at first sight much more passively placed than the 'Italian bishop' is after 1 P–K4 P–K4 2 N–KB3 N–QB3 3 B–B4. Nevertheless, this bishop on QB4 only gives rise to various tactical threats, whereas the fianchettoed bishop usually determines the strategy of the whole game. The first opening might continue for instance: 3 ... P–K3 4 0–0 P–QB4 5 P–Q4 N–B3 6 P–B4 QP×P 7 Q–R4, when the pressure of White's KB on the long diagonal has become a vital strategic factor.

We can only decide whether or not a bishop is well-placed by relating it to the other pieces and especially to the pawns, and we devote a separate section to the relationship between the bishop and the pawn formation.

THE 'GOOD' AND THE 'BAD' BISHOP

In the following position, Tarrasch–Teichmann (*47*), White is able to force a win in ten moves without Black making any obvious mistake.

47
B

25 ... **B–Q2 26 P–KN4 B–B1 27 P–KR4 P–N3 28 R–R1 K–N2 29 P–R5 R–R1 30 R2–R2 B–Q2 31 P–N5! RP×P 32 BP×P R×P 33 R×R P×R 34 R×P K–B1 35 R–R8+ K–K2** and now White

could have played 36 R–R7 K–K1 37 P–B3 followed by B–K2–R5 when Black is helpless.

The reason for Black's disadvantage lies in the difference between the two bishops. Whilst White's bishop is not hemmed in by his pawns and thus has freedom to attack both wings, his black counterpart is condemned to perpetual passivity because it is blocked in by its own pawns.

In most cases the value of the bishop can be judged according to the following rule: the bishop is 'good' if its own pawns are on squares of the opposite colour and the opponent's pawns on squares of the same colour. We are of course referring to a pawn formation which cannot easily be changed, such as a blocked pawn chain. Consider the following position (*48*):

48

We can class White's bishop as 'good' and Black's bishop as 'bad', although most of White's pawns are on white squares, and most of Black's pawns on black squares. It is only the position of the K-side pawns which is relevant, as White can easily transfer his Q-side pawns to black squares when he wants to, whereas on the K-side this would only be possible after the capture of an enemy pawn.

This evaluation of a bishop is an

extremely important strategic factor, and when an ending arises with only one of the pair of bishops remaining, both sides usually try to post their pawns on squares of the opposite colour in order to blockade the enemy pawns and thus hem in the opponent's bishop.

In other cases, when there is a fixed pawn formation and exchanges are imminent, each side endeavours to hold on to the 'good' bishop and rid himself of the 'bad' one. Let us consider a few examples.

Najdorf–Bronstein (*49*). In this game which was played in the 1950 Candidates tournament at Budapest, Bronstein continued: **26 ... B×B 27 Q×B Q–K4!** and after **28 Q×Q P×Q** a position arose in which the superiority of his 'good' bishop was sufficient to ensure Black a win.

In the French Defence the evaluation of the bishops is often the most important strategic factor. In the variation **1 P–K4 P–K3 2 P–Q4 P–Q4 3 N–QB3 N–KB3 4 B–KN5 B–K2 5 P–K5 N3–Q2 6 B×B** exchanging the 'bad' for the 'good' bishop **6 ... Q×B 7 P–B4 P–QR3 8 N–B3 P–QB4 9 P×P Q×P** White can play **10 Q–Q4** in an attempt to simplify into an ending where the disadvantage of Black's QB would be keenly felt.

This is why in many variations Black tries to fianchetto his QB after exchanging pawns in the centre e.g. **1 P–K4 P–K3 2 P–Q4 P–Q4 3 N–QB3 N–KB3 4 B–N5 P×P 5 N×P B–K2 6 B×N B×B 7 N–KB3 N–Q2 8 P–B3 P–QN3** and **9 ... B–N2.**

Or in other cases Black may successfully exchange his QB for White's KB e.g. **1 P–K4 P–K3 2 P–Q4 P–Q4 3 N–Q2 N–KB3 4 P–K5 N3–Q2 5 B–Q3 P–QB4 6 P–QB3 P–QN3** and **7 ... B–R3.** The solution to the problem of his QB is vital for Black in many systems of the French Defence.

In the Dutch Defence, after the moves **1 P–Q4 P–KB4 2 P–KN3 N–KB3 3 B–N2 P–K3 4 N–KB3 B–K2 5 0–0 0–0 6 P–B4 P–Q4,** Black feared for a long time Botvinnik's manoeuvre **7 P–N3 P–B3 8 B–QR3** (*50*).

White exchanges Black's 'good' bishop which is all the more important because it could be used in the fight for the vital strategic point at White's K5 (see the chapter 'Strategic Points'). Black is left with his 'bad' QB. It was only later that Bronstein demonstrated that this bishop is not condemned to permanent inactivity but can be fianchettoed and used effectively

after ... P–QN3 and ... P–QB4.
Here are two more complex
examples.

23 Kmoch–Alekhine

Kecskemet 1927, Queen's Gambit

1 P–Q4 P–Q4 2 N–KB3 P–QB3 3
P–K3 B–B4 4 B–Q3 P–K3 5 0–0
N–Q2 6 P–B4 KN–B3 7 Q–B2
B×B 8 Q×B N–K5 9 N3–Q2
N2–B3 10 N–QB3 N×N.7 11 B×N
B–K2

   12 P–K4

An understandable attempt to
give his bishop more scope. However, it is a two-edged move, as it
weakens his QP which is on a black
square, and clearly underlines the
difference between the bishops.

12 ...	P×KP
13 N×P	0–0
14 B–B3	Q–B2
15 QR–Q1	QR–Q1
16 R–Q2	Q–B5!
17 N×N+	B×N

Black's bishop is now an attacking
piece whereas the white bishop plays
a purely passive role.

18 R1–Q1	R–Q2
19 Q–N3	Q–B4
20 P–B4	

Defending against a possible ...
B–N4 but placing another pawn
on a black square.

20 ...	R1–Q1
21 Q–K3	P–KR4!

A typical thrust to blockade
White's K-side. If now 22 P–KR3
P–R5 Black also would place one
of his pawns on a black square,
albeit well-protected. However,
much more important is the fact
that White's KBP could not then be
protected by P–KN3. This example
shows us once again that we must
not be dogmatic about the 'good'
and 'bad' bishop.

22 P–QN4? (*51*)

A grave strategic error, leading to
a forced loss and completely going
against the spirit of the rule we
stated earlier.

51
B

22 ...	P–QN4!

A symmetrical answer but with a
great difference! This move fixes
White's pawns on black squares and
at the same time gains Q4 for the
black pieces. The game is already
decided strategically. After 23 P–B5
R–Q4 followed by 24 ... P–KN4
Black would force a quick win, so
White plunges into tactical complications which equally prove
insufficient.

23 Q–B3	P×P
24 Q×BP	Q×P
25 Q×BP	P–K4!
26 Q–K2	P×P
27 R–Q3 (*52*)	

52
B

Hoping to blockade the passed pawn, but Alekhine finds a neat tactical solution.

27 ...	**P × B!!**
28 R × R	**R × R**
29 R × R (?)	

Losing at once, but the main variation given by Alekhine leads to a Black win as follows: 29 Q–K8+ K–R2 30 Q × R Q–K5! 31 Q × BP P–B7 32 Q × RP+ K–N1 wins; or here 31 Q–Q5 Q × Q 32 R × Q P–B7 wins.

29 ...	**B–Q5+**
30 K–R1	**Q–QB8+**
0–1	

24 Keres–Botvinnik

World Championship 1948, English Opening

1 P–QB4 P–K3 2 P–KN3 P–Q4 3 B–N2 P–Q5 4 P–QN4 P–QB4 5 P–N5 P–K4 6 P–Q3 6 P–K3! 6 ... B–Q3 7 P–K4? 7 ... Q–B2 8 N–K2 P–KR4! preventing 9 P–B4 when 9 ... P–R5 would follow **9 P–KR4 N–KR3 10 0–0 B–N5 11 P–B3** a better plan is N–Q2–KB3–KR2 **11 ... B–K3 12 P–B4 B–N5 13 P–B5 N–Q2 14 N–Q2** (53)

14 ...   **P–KN3!**
An unusually fine strategic idea! The central pawns are blocked and

Black has a 'bad' bishop on Q3 and a 'good' one at KN5. However, White is threatening to exchange the latter bishop by N–KB3–R2, so the text-move has a dual purpose: to give the QB a retreat and at the same time to allow the KB to become active via KB1 and KR3.

15 P × P	**P × P**
16 N–KB3	**B–K2**

White was threatening 17 B × N followed by 18 N–N5.

17 R–B2	**Q–Q3**
18 B × N?	

White commits the error of giving up his 'good' bishop, thereby presenting Black with a small but definite positional advantage. According to Keres it would have been better to wait by 18 B–Q2 or 18 N–N5, whereas Sokolsky suggests the best plan of 18 K–R1 with the idea of 19 N2–N1 followed by B–KR3 to exchange his 'bad' bishop.

18 ...	**R × B**
19 Q–Q2	**R–R1**
20 N–N5	**N–B3**

Also possible was 20 ... R–KB1 when White would have continued 21 R1–KB1.

21 R–K1

Threatening the cunning 22 N–B4! which would improve his position considerably.

21 ...	**Q–N3**
22 N–KB3	**N–Q2**
23 N–N5	**R–KB1**
24 R × R+?	

White could still defend with 24 R1–KB1 0–0–0 25 B–B3, whereas now Black's KB quickly reaches KR3 and both bishops soon exert strong pressure. The game concluded: **24 ... B × R 25 P–R4?** better was 25 N–KB3 **25 ... B–R3 26 P–R5 Q–KB3 27 N–B1 0–0–0 28 N–N3 R–B1 29 R–R1 Q–K2 30 Q–B1 K–N1 31 R–R2 R–B2 32**

Q–R3 otherwise Black would play his knight to K3 **32 ... B×N 33 P×B B–Q8! 34 Q–B1 B×N 35 R–N2 B–Q8 36 Q×B Q×P 37 Q–K1 N–B1 38 K–R2 Q–B3 39 B–R3 N–R2 40 Q–Q1 N–N4 41 P–N6 P–R5! 42 Q–N4 KRP×P+ 43 K×P R–B1 44 P×P+ K×P 45 P–R6 N×B! 46 Q×N Q–B5+ 47 K–N2 Q–KB8+ 48 K–R2 R–B7+ 49 R×R Q×R+ 50 K–R1 Q–K8+ 51 K–N2 Q–K7+ 52 K–N1 Q–K6+ 53 Q×Q P×Q 54 P×P K×P 55 K–N2 K–N3 56 K–B3 K–R4 57 K×P K–N5 58 K–Q2 P–N4 0–1.**

In many openings where Black fianchettoes his KB and then plays ... P–K4, his bishop is usually passively placed after White's P–Q5 and can only come into action via KR3. For instance, in the variation **1 P–Q4 N–KB3 2 P–QB4 P–KN3 3 N–QB3 B–N2 4 P–K4 P–Q3 5 N–B3 0–0 6 B–K2 P–K4 7 P–Q5 QN–Q2 8 0–0 N–B4 9 Q–B2 P–QR4** White used to continue **10 N–Q2** but it was discovered that **10 ... B–R3! 11 N–N3 B×B** was favourable to Black. It is more difficult to activate the bishop in this line after **7 ... P–B4 8 B–N5 P–KR3 9 B–R4 Q–B2 10 N–Q2 P–R3 11 0–0**, when Black usually tries ... N–R2 followed by ... B–B3–N4.

The following game illustrates some interesting possibilities of exchanging the 'bad' bishop.

25 Pachman–Fabian

Czechoslovak Ch 1968, Benoni Defence

1 P–Q4 N–KB3 2 P–QB4 P–B4 3 P–Q5 P–K4 4 N–QB3 P–Q3 5 P–K4 B–K2
    6 P–KN3
The usual continuation is 6 N–B3

followed by 7 B–K2, but Black can then try 6 N–B3 B–N5 7 B–K2 0–0 8 0–0 B×N 9 B×B N–K1 followed by 10 ... B–N4 exchanging his 'bad' bishop for White's 'good' one and obtaining good chances with two knights against a knight and a 'bad' bishop.

    6 ...   0–0
    7 B–R3 (*54*)
An idea suggested by grandmaster Taimanov. White is willing to lose time in order to exchange Black's active QB. After 7 B–N2 N–K1 8 KN–K2 it is not good for Black to play 8 ... B–N4 9 P–B4 P×P 10 P×P B–R5+ 11 N–N3 P–B4 12 0–0 P×P 13 N.B3×P when White's QB comes to QB3 with strong pressure. Better is 8 ... P–KN3 9 0–0 N–Q2 10 P–B4 with even chances.

54
B

White will now be left with an active QB against Black's passively placed bishop on K2, and this gives him a permanent strategic advantage. The main question is whether Black can exploit by tactical means this clear loss of time. After 7 ... B×B 8 N×B Q–Q2 9 N–KN5 P–KR3 10 N–B3 Q–R6 White has both 11 Q–K2 N–N5 12 B–Q2 P–B4 13 0–0–0, and 11 N–KR4 N–N5 12 N–B5. However 8 ... Q–Q2! is the correct move, with the idea 9 N–KN5 B–Q1! followed by 10 ...

B–R4 in order to exchange his 'bad' bishop and secure complete equality. Although we are discussing opening theory here, this position arising after 7 moves is most instructive for our theme.

7 ...   P–QR3?

Allowing White to carry out his plan undisturbed.

8 B×B   Q×B
9 Q–K2!

Preventing ... P–QN4.

9 ...   QN–Q2
10 N–B3   N–K1
11 0–0   R–N1
12 P–QR4   N–B2?

A completely unnecessary move. Black should block the queen's side by 12 ... P–QR4. White could admittedly prepare action on the king's side by N–K1–N2 and P–B4 but it is not easy to exploit his space advantage.

13 P–R5!   N–K1

Black decides to play a waiting game, as after 13 ... P–QN4 14 P×Pep N×NP the weakness of his QRP would be more important than the open QN-file.

14 N–K1   B–Q1
15 N–Q3   B–B3

To make it more difficult for White to play P–B4.

16 B–K3   P–QN4

As White's QBP is now unprotected, Black tries out this move. Otherwise White plays 17 KR–N1 followed by 18 P–QN4 with strong Q-side play.

17 RP×Pep   N×P
18 P–N3   P–N3
19 R–R3   N–Q2
20 Q–R2   B–N2
21 P–B3!

A strategically important move (not of course *21 R×P? R×P!*), aiming to consolidate the K-side by K–N2, so that he can carry out his

Q-side attack without any difficulties by P–QN4. White's position is clearly favourable, because his bishop is much more active than Black's.

21 ...   P–B4
22 K–N2   N2–B3
23 R–QN1!

White can afford to ignore Black's K-side play.

23 ...   P×P
24 P×P (*55*)

24 ...   N×KP?

At first sight this combination will appeal to the inexperienced player, for Black regains his piece and wins a pawn in the process. However, it is a poor idea which only helps White to break through. It is often easy to calculate a forced series of moves but much harder to assess the strategic consequences. White now obtains a strong point on K4 along with an advanced passed pawn. Admittedly, there was nothing else to be done on the K-side, for 24 ... N–N5 is answered by 25 B–N1, and 24 ... Q–N5 by 25 N–B2.

25 N×N   Q–B4
26 N3–B2   Q–B6+
27 K–N1   Q×B
28 P–QN4   Q–R3

Not an attractive square for the queen, but after 28 ... Q–Q5 29 R–Q3 it is lost!

29 P×P	R×R+
30 Q×R	P×P
31 P–Q6!	

Much stronger than winning a pawn by 31 R×P allowing 31 ... Q–K6, and 31 N×P fails to 31 ... R×N! 32 K×R B–B1. After the text-move Black is completely helpless against the passed pawn supported by the strongly posted knight. The game ended: **31 ... N–B3 32 Q–Q1! N–Q2 33 R–N3!** preventing any counterplay by ... R–N1 **33 ... K–R1 34 R–N7 N–B3 35 Q–K2 N×N 36 N×N Q–R6 37 R–K7! B–R3** with the powerful threat of 38 ... B–K6+! **38 N–B2 Q–B4 39 P–Q7 B–N2 40 N–K4 B–R3 41 N–Q6 B–K6+ 42 K–N2 Q–B3 43 R–K8 1–0.**

In all the examples we have seen so far, the bishop was evaluated according to the placing of the pawns, and this is of course an important strategic principle. However, it is not valid in all circumstances. For instance, after **1 P–Q4 P–Q4 2 P–QB4 P–QB3 3 P×P P×P 4 N–QB3 N–QB3 5 N–B3 N–B3 6 B–B4 B–B4 7 P–K3 P–K3** we can scarcely describe the two developed bishops as 'bad', even though they are on squares of the same colour as those occupied by their own blocked central pawns. Both bishops are outside the pawn chain and are extremely active. In a game Botvinnik-Trifunovic, Moscow 1947, after **8 Q–N3** Black found the correct defence with **8 ... B–QN5!** giving up his 'good' bishop for White's QN but obtaining a good game because of his actively placed minor pieces.

In the following game Black's QB turns out to be badly placed, not so much because it is restricted by its own pawns but because White's

pawns form a barrier to limit its activity.

26 Capablanca–Lilienthal

Moscow 1936, Réti System

1 N–KB3 P–Q4 2 P–B4 P–QB3 3 P–QN3 B–B4 4 B–N2 P–K3 5 P–N3 N–B3 6 B–N2 QN–Q2 7 0–0 P–KR3 better 7 ... B–K2 at once **8 P–Q3 B–K2 9 QN–Q2 0–0 10 R–B1 P–QR4 11 P–QR3 R–K1 12 R–B2 B–R2 13 Q–R1 B–B1 14 R–K1 Q–N3 15 B–R3 B–QB4 16 R–KB1 B–B1 17 R2–B1 QR–Q1 18 KR–K1 B–QB4 19 R–B1 B–B1 20 B–N2 B–Q3 21 N–K5** according to Capablanca, he allowed the following simplifying exchanges because he could already visualize the position after move 28 as in his favour **21 ... B×N 22 B×B N×B 23 Q×N N–Q2 24 Q–N2 N–B3 25 P–QN4 RP×P 26 Q×P! Q×Q 27 P×Q R–R1 28 R–R1** (*56*)

White has obtained a small but definite advantage. His bishop exerts strong pressure on Black's Q-side pawns and this will be increased if Black plays ... P×P. His knight is heading for QR5 from where it will threaten Black's pawns. If need be, his bishop can switch diagonals as in the line 28 . . . P–K4 29 P–B5! N–Q2 30 B–R3! P–B4 31 P–K4, which means that Black should have played . . . P–K4 whilst his rook was still on Q1.

| 28 ... | N–Q2 |
| 29 N–N3 | K–B1 |

Other moves give Black few prospects e.g.

a. 29 . . . N–N3 30 P–B5 N–Q2 31 R–R5 followed by 32 R1–R1

b. 29 . . . P–QN3 30 P–N5! BP×P 31 P×QP with advantage to White.

| 30 R–R5 | P×P |

If 30 . . . K–K2 Capablanca gives the following plan: 31 R1–R1 R×R 32 R×R K–Q3 33 R–R7 K–B2 34 N–R5 R–QN1 35 P–B5 and White wins by P–Q4, B–B1, P–K3 and B–R6.

31 P×P	N–N3
32 R×R	R×R
33 N–R5	R–R2

Or 33 . . . R–N1 34 R–Q1 and Black has no defence against 35 R–Q6 followed by 36 P–N5.

| 34 R–Q1 | |

Threatening 35 B×P! P×B 36 R–Q8+ K–K2 37 N×P+ Black defends against this, but allows another combination which leads to a won ending for White.

| 34 ... | K–K1 |
| 35 N×NP | R×N |

and the game ended as follows: **36 B×P+ R–Q2 37 P–B5 K–K2 38 B×R N×B 39 P–B6 N–N3 40 P–B7 B–B4 41 R–Q8 P–K4 42 R–QN8 N–B1 43 P–N5 K–Q3 44 P–N6 N–K2 45 P–KB8 =Q! followed by 46 P–N7 would also win 45 . . . B–B1 46 R×P N–Q4 47 R×P N×NP 48 R–R7 N–Q4 49 R×P+ K×P 50 P–K4 N–K2 51 P–B3 K–Q2 52 P–R4 K–K1 53 R–KB6 N–N1 54 R–B6 1–0.**

Almost every beginner knows that bishops of opposite colour are often a saving factor in materially unfavourable positions. They represent the strongest means of obtaining a draw, making it difficult to win with one or even several extra pawns. In this respect, the following study by Chekover is instructive (*57*).

57
W

White draws against three pawns by **1 B–K8! K–B3** or 1 . . . K–N5 2 B×P K–R6 3 B–B5 K–N7 4 B–K6! K–R7 5 B–B7 K–R6 6 B–N6 and Black cannot win **2 K–K2!** not 2 B–B7? P–Q4 **2 . . . B–B8** if 2 . . . K–B2 3 B–B7 P–N7 4 B–N6 draws **3 K–Q1 B–N7 4 K–K2 B–Q5 5 K–Q1 K–Q3 6 B–B7! P–N7 7 B–N6 K–B4 8 K–K2 P–Q4 9 B–B5 K–N5 10 B–N6 K–R6 11 B–N1 K–N6 12 K–Q1 K–B6 13 K–K2 B–B4 14 K–Q1 P–Q5 15 K–K2 K–N6 16 K–Q3 Draw.**

It is clear from this example that the reason for the drawing tendency of opposite-coloured bishops lies in the fact that the passed pawns cannot be advanced over squares controlled by the enemy bishop and king. In addition the bishop of the stronger side cannot attack pawns posted on squares of the opposite colour, giving us drawing positions such as: White king on KN3, bishop on K7, pawns on QR3, KR4; Black king on KB4, bishop on Q4, pawns on QR5, QN4, KN5, KR4.

This drawing tendency (so often desired by the weaker side!) is significantly reduced or even disappears completely when other pieces are on the board as well. In many middle-game situations the presence of opposite-coloured bishops even has the reverse effect and favours the side with the initiative. This stems from the fact that the defending bishop cannot protect points attacked by the opponent's bishop. Consider our next position (*58*).

Although Black is up in material he is powerless against the attack aimed at his KN2. 1 ... K–R1 2 Q–K5 R–N1 3 P–N6! or 1 ... Q–Q2 2 Q–K5 P–B3 3 P×P B–B2 4 P×P KR–K1 5 Q–N3 winning in both cases.

Now let us examine more complex cases of the same idea.

27 Taimanov–Averbakh

Candidates 1953, Nimzo-Indian Defence

1 P–Q4 N–KB3 2 P–QB4 P–K3 3 N–QB3 B–N5 4 P–K3 0–0 5 B–Q3 P–Q4 6 N–B3 P–QN3 7 0–0 B–N2

8 P–QR3 B×N 9 P×B P×P 10 B×BP P–B4 11 B–Q3 QN–Q2 12 R–K1 N–K5 13 B–N2 R–B1 14 P–B4 N2–B3 15 N–K5 R–B2 16 P–QR4 N–Q3 17 P–R5 N–Q2 18 RP×P RP×P 19 Q–R5 P–N3 better 19 ... B–K5! 20 Q–R6 N×N 21 P×N N–K5 (*59*)

22 B×N!

Many chess-players in this situation would probably try to retain the two bishops by 22 QR–Q1 but Black would then continue 22 ... R–Q2 23 B–B2 R×R 24 R×R Q–R1 with a defensible position. Taimanov correctly assesses that bishops of opposite colour will favour him here because of the black square weakness in the enemy camp.

22 ...	B×B
23 R.K1–Q1	R–Q2
24 R–Q6!	B–N2

White wins easily after 24 ... R×R 25 P×R P–B3 26 R–R7.

25 R1–Q1	R×R
26 P×R	P–B3
27 P–Q7!	

This pawn will certainly be lost, but White's attack is decisive. He now threatens 28 Q×R+! K×Q 29 B×P winning. If 27 ... R–B2 28 Q–R3 P–B4 29 Q–R6 R×P? 30 Q–N7+! wins.

| 27 ... | B–B3 |
| 28 P–R4 | B×QP |

29 P–R5   P×P

White also obtains a strong attack after 29 ... P–KN4 30 P–B4.

30 P–K4   P–K4
31 P–B4!

Clearing the path for his bishop which will give Black insoluble problems.

31 ...   P×P
32 R–Q6!   Q–K1
33 B×P   R–B2

Or 33 ... Q–N3 34 Q×Q+ P×Q 35 B–K7 winning.

34 R–Q5   1–0

An instructive example of how to attack with opposite-coloured bishops on the board. It is interesting to note the ineffectiveness of the seemingly active black bishop.

The next position (*60*), Filip–Pachman, Czechoslovak Ch 1953, looks drawish at first sight. The pawns are symmetrically distributed and at least one pair of rooks will soon be exchanged on the K-file. If Black could only exchange queens too, the opposite-coloured bishops would guarantee the draw. However, this will prove impossible, and it is the very presence of opposite-coloured bishops which gives White attacking prospects. For instance, if White had a QB on QB1 instead of his strongly placed KB there would be nothing in it.

29 R–K4!   R–K2
30 R1–K1   B–B1

H could not play 30 ... R1–K1 31 Q×R+ when the two rooks would easily win against the queen.

31 P–R4!   K–N2?

The decisive error. Black intends to prevent his pawns being blockaded on white squares and aims to play later ... P–R3 and ... P–N4. However, the plan leads to a fatal weakness on the white squares. It was essential to play ... P–R4! when Black could just hold out. The game ended: **32 P–R5! R–Q1 33 R×R B×R 34 Q–Q1 R–Q3 35 Q–K2 B–B3 36 K–N2 R–Q2 37 Q–B3 Q–Q3 38 R–K4 P–N4 39 Q–B5 P–R3 40 R–K1?** White could have won more quickly and elegantly by 40 R–K6! P×R 41 Q–N6+ K–B1 42 Q×B+ etc., but even in the longer game continuation Black has no chances **40 ... R–K2 41 B–K4 K–B1 42 R–QR1 R–Q2 R–R5 B–K2 44 B–Q5 B–Q1 45 R–R8 K–N2 46 B–K4 K–B1 47 Q–R7 Q–KB3 48 B–Q5 P–N5 49 R–B8 R–B2 50 R×B+! Q×R 51 Q×RP+ K–K2 52 Q–N5+ P–B3 53 Q×NP Q–KB1 54 Q–N6 K–Q3 55 P–R6 Q–KR1 56 Q–N8! R–KR2 57 Q–K6+ K–B2 58 Q–B6+ K–N1 59 B–K4 P–B4 60 Q–QN6+ 1–0.**

28 Gligoric–Larsen

Havana 1967, Nimzo-Indian Defence

1 P–Q4 N–KB3 2 P–QB4 P–K3 3 N–QB3 B–N5 4 P–K3 P–QN3 5 B–Q3 B–N2 6 N–B3 N–K5 7 0–0 P–KB4 8 B×N? Gligoric later found the promising continuation 8 P–Q5! with the idea of sacrificing a pawn to open up a diagonal for his bishop, either QR1–KR8 or QR3–KB8. **8 ... P×B 9 N–Q2 B×N 10 P×B 0–0!**

11 Q–N4   R–B4!

The respective bishops can already be compared. Black's QB protects the strong KP which is restricting White's position, whereas Gligoric must still solve the problem of his QB on QB1. By the following manoeuvre he opens the long black diagonal for it. He could not play 12 N×P? P–KR4! when his knight is lost.

12	P–Q5	R–N4
13	Q–B4	P×P
14	P×P	B×P
15	P–B4	B–B3
16	N×P	R–N3
17	B–N2	N–R3

A strategically fascinating position. Both bishops are very strong, each commanding a long diagonal, but as we shall see later Black's bishop works more effectively with the other pieces, especially his KR! Nevertheless, White could maintain equality with the immediate 18 N–N3 and 19 P–K4.

18	P–B3?	N–N5!
19	B–B3	N–Q6
20	Q–B5	Q–R5!

Clear proof that a combination is not necessarily linked with a sacrifice. Black allows his pawns to be seriously weakened, in order to launch a strong attack down the KN-file. White should now play the modest 21 N–N3.

21	N–B6+?	P×N
22	Q×N (*61*)	

A superficial glance at the position might lead one to believe that White stands better. His QB attacks Black's weak KBP, whereas Black's QB is biting against granite. Nevertheless, although this bishop does not move for the rest of the game, it plays a decisive part in all that follows.

22 ...   R–R3

61 B

23 P–KR3   K–B2!

It is now impossible for White to avoid his king's position being smashed open. After 24 P–K4 R–KN1 25 K–R1? Q×RP+! 26 P×Q R×P is mate. Or 24 Q–K2 R–KN1 25 K–R1 R–N6 26 R–B2 (*26 P–K4 R×RP+ 27 P×R Q×RP+ 28 K–N1 R–N3+*) 26 ... R×RP+ 27 P×R Q×RP+ 28 R–R2 B×P+ etc.

24	R–B2	R–KN1
25	K–B1	R×P!

A simple effective sacrifice, fatally weakening White's KB3.

26 R×R   Q×RP

Threatening both ... Q×P+ and ... B×P.

27	P–K4	R–N3
	0–1	

28 Q–K2 is answered by 28 ... Q–R8+.

The above examples show us that opposite-coloured bishops do not automatically and in all circumstances guarantee drawing chances. In contrast to the end-game, middle-game positions strongly favour the side with the most effectively placed bishop. If the reader turns back to diagram 37 (Alekhine–Duras) he will see yet another proof of this statement. Black lost because his black-squared bishop could not defend against the white square pressure of Alekhine's bishop on QN3 directed at Black's KB2.

THE KNIGHT AND ITS OPERATION BASE

Because the knight moves in short hops, it can achieve maximum effectiveness only when it has an operation base. By this we mean a square, especially a central one, on which the knight cannot be attacked, particularly by enemy pawns.

As we have already mentioned in the chapter 'The Value of the Pieces', such a centralized knight may sometimes be worth a rook. On the other hand, a badly posted knight is often a decisive weakness. The German saying: 'A knight displaced is a knight disgraced' refers to the fact that a knight utilizes only a part of its power when it is placed on the edge of the board. A centralized knight controls eight squares, a knight in the corner only two. That is why it is vitally important for this piece to be well placed, a strategic factor which we shall now examine more closely with the help of various examples.

29 Ahues–Alekhine

Bad Nauheim 1936, Queen's Gambit Accepted

1 P–Q4 P–Q4 2 P–QB4 P×P 3 N–KB3 P–QR3 4 P–QR4 (?) N–KB3 5 P–K3 B–N5 6 B×P P–K3 7 N–B3 N–B3 8 B–K2 B–N5 9 0–0 0–0 10 N–Q2 better 10 B–Q2 **10 . . . B×B 11 N×B P–K4 12 N–KB3 R–K1 13 B–Q2 B–Q3 14 N–N3 P–K5 15 N–K1** (*62*)

15 . . .   B×N!

At first sight a surprising move, as this bishop would appear to have an important part to play in the

coming attack on the king. Alekhine, however, has correctly perceived that this exchange will render White's K-side pawns immobile, allowing the black knights to occupy splendid posts on Q4 and KN5.

16 RP×B	N–K2!
17 P–QN4	Q–Q2
18 N–B2	N2–Q4
19 N–R3	

White also hopes to obtain a strong point for his knight on K5, but this proves impossible.

19 . . .	P–QN4!
20 P×P	P×P
21 Q–K2	P–B3
22 N–B2	Q–B4
23 KR–B1	P–R3
24 R–R5	QR–B1
25 N–R1?	

Aiming for the strong operation base on QB5, but it is already too late for such a manoeuvre. Black's attack now breaks through, depending mainly on his powerfully posted knights. White had to play 25 P–B3 preventing Black's next move.

25 . . .   N–N5 (*63*)

Black has clearly carried out his plan successfully and now threatens . . . Q–R4.

26 K–B1	R–K3!
27 R×NP	R–B3
28 R5–B5	N×BP
29 K–K1	N–Q6+
30 K–Q1	Q–B8+

31 B–K1   **R–B7!**
0–1

Noteworthy is the difference between the ineffective white knight and the strong black knights, especially the one which remained on Q4 for fully thirteen moves yet successfully immobilized White's position.

30 Botvinnik–Donner

Amsterdam 1963, Catalan System

1 P–QB4 N–KB3 2 N–KB3 P–K3 3 P–KN3 P–Q4 4 B–N2 B–K2 5 0–0 0–0 6 P–N3 P–QN3 7 B–N2 B–N2 8 P×P N×P 9 P–Q4 P–QB4 10 P×P B×P 11 QN–Q2 N–Q2 12 P–QR3 N4–B3? Correct was 12 ... P–QR4 stopping White's Q-side action and ensuring an approximately equal game. **13 P–QN4 B–K2 14 N–Q4! B×B 15 K×B Q–B2** (*64*).

White's plan is based on the great activity of his centralized knight on Q4, which can later obtain a further strong point on QB6 after P–QN5. However, White must first of all stop Black regrouping by ... Q–N2+ and ... QR–B1, when if the worst came to the worst he could prevent the entry of White's knight by playing ... N–QN1.

16 Q–N3!   **KR–B1**
17 KR–B1   **Q–N2+**
18 Q–KB3!

In such situations, simplification is not to be feared, as the ending would only emphasize the weakness of Black's QB3 and the strength of the white knight on Q4. Botvinnik gives the following possible line: 18 ... Q×Q+ 19 N2×Q K–B1 20 N–B6 R–B2 21 R–B2 R1–B1 22 R1–QB1 threatening 23 N×B R×R 24 N×R winning a pawn.

18 ...   **N–Q4**

With the strong threat of 19 ... N–K4 20 Q–K4 P–B4! 21 Q×N.K5 N–B5+ followed by mate.

19 P–K4   **N4–B3**
20 P–N5!   **P–QR3**
21 N–B6   **B–B1**

Black wishes to reserve QB4 for his knight, but 21 ... B–B4 was better.

22 P–QR4   **P×P**
23 P×P   **R×R**
24 R×R   **R–R1**
25 R–Q1!

A sound strategic decision. The player with a space advantage should usually avoid too much simplification, unless he can thereby increase his positional advantage. Exchange of rooks would improve Black's position, because the possible penetration of his queen via QR5 or QR7 is more dangerous than his rook (25 ... R–R7 26 N–B4).

25 ...   **N–K1**

Freeing his knight on Q2 which can now go to QB4.

26 N–B4   **N–B4**

27 P–K5!

Preparing an outpost for his knight on Q6 and clearing a route for his rook to reach KN4.

27 ...   **R–B1?**

Black has almost no good moves, but he could at least wait with 27 ... P–R3. The text-move loses in surprising fashion, because White's rook takes over the QR-file with decisive effect.

28 R–QR1!   **R–B2**

Donner probably missed that 28 ... R–R1 fails to 29 R × R Q × R 30 N–K7+.

29 R–R7   **Q × R**

30 N × Q   **R × N**

31 N × P   **1–0**

The creation of an operation base for the knight is one of the most important motifs in chess strategy and we shall return to this later. For the moment, let us consider whether an unfavourable posting of the knight can be a strategic factor, such as we saw in the case of the 'bad' bishop. Of course this situation does not arise as often, because the knight is not restricted to squares of the same colour and its activity is seldom limited by a pawn chain. Its unfavourable position is usually of a temporary nature. However, in some cases the posting of the knight cannot be improved without great difficulty and it is useful to recognize typical set-ups.

Pachman–Szabo, Hilversum 1947 (*65*). Black clearly stands worse, mainly because of his 'bad' bishop. After the best move 16 ... N–K5 17 P × P KP × P 18 Q–N3 N × N 19 Q × N, this bishop would place him at a permanent positional disad-

65
B

vantage. So Szabo decides to go in for a risky side attack.

16 ...   **N–R6+?**

17 K–R1   **P–KN4**

18 P × QP   **KP × P**

19 Q–B2   **P × P**

Only now does Black realize that after 19 ... P–Q5!? 20 KP × P P × P 21 N–K2! (not *21 P × P? Q–R5!* with a strong attack) 21 ... P × P 22 N × P P–B5 23 N–B5 White captures the KBP and wins comfortably. The only alternative is the text-move which keeps his knight permanently out of play and practically gives White an extra piece. This easily guaranteed the win as follows: **20 KP × P Q–B2 21 N–K2! K–R1 22 N–Q4 R–KB1 23 R.QB1–K1 B–K3 24 Q–B5! R–KN1** if 24 ... P–R3 25 Q–Q6 etc. **25 N × B R × N** or 25 ... Q × N 26 Q–Q6! and after the exchange of queens Black's knight is quickly lost **26 Q × RP Q–R4 27 Q–K3 R–R3 28 Q–K2 Q–K1 29 P–K6! R × NP 30 Q–K5+ K–N1 31 B × P R–N2 32 B × N! R × B 33 R–KN1 1–0.**

In the following game too, the winner bases his plans on the unfavourable position of a knight on R3, this time a white one!

31 Stahlberg–Unzicker

Wilderness, South Africa 1964, Old
Indian Defence

1 P–Q4 N–KB3 2 P–QB4 P–Q3 3
N–KB3 B–N5 4 P–K3 P–B3 5
B–K2 QN–Q2 6 N–B3 P–K4 7
0–0 B–K2 8 Q–B2 0–0 9 R–Q1
Q–B2 10 P–QN3 KR–K1 11 B–R3
B–B1 12 P×P P×P 13 B×B N×B
14 N–KN5?

White plays the first part of the
game very tamely and is clearly
intent on a draw. He could have
achieved this fairly easily with 14
N–K4, but instead he selects a most
unfortunate exchange manoeuvre.

14 ...   **B×B**
15 Q×B?

This move leads to a forced loss.
He had to play 15 N×B, although
after 15 ... P–K5 he would have a
poor position.

15 ..   **P–K5!**

Threatening 16 ... Q–K4 winning
a piece.

16 N–R3   **Q–K4**
17 QR–B1   **N–K3** (*66*)

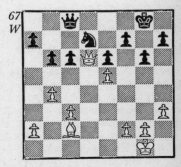

White's KN is completely misplaced. If now 18 K–R1 then 18 ...
P–KR4 threatens 19 ... N–N5. If 18
P–B3 (or 18 P–B4) then White's pawns
are weakened e.g. 18 ... P×P 19
P×P N–N4 20 N×N Q×N.4+
21 K–B2 R–K4! So White hopes to
play his knight to KB4.

18 P–N3   **P–KN4!**
19 N–R4

White could still free his knight by
19 K–N2 but Black would have a
strong attack after 19 ... P–KR4.

19 ...   **Q–KB4**
20 K–N2

If he tries to guard his knight
indirectly by 20 Q–N2 then 20 ...
P–N4! wins a piece.

20 ...   **Q–B6+!**
21 Q×Q   **P×Q+**
22 K×P

It would have been equally hopeless to play 22 K–B1 QR–Q1 23
N–N1 P–N5, when White is practically a piece down. An important
variation! If White's knight remains
on R3, Black frees his knight on K3
either by ... P–KR3 or by playing
his king to KN3. After the text-
move White loses his knight for two
pawns. The game ended: **22 ...
P–N5+ 23 K–N2 P×N+ 24 K×P
N–K5 25 K–N2 QR–Q1 26 P–B3
N5–B4 27 N–N2 P–QR4 28 K–B2
P–R5 29 P×P** if 29 P–QN4 P–R6
**29 ... R×R 30 R×R R–R1 31
R–Q2 N×P 32 N–Q1 N–N3 0–1.**

The displacement of a knight can
of course take on a more subtle
form.

Mohrlok–Gerusel (*67*). The game
continued: **27 B–K4! N–N1** nor
would 27 ... P–QB4 save Black,

after 28 B–B6 N–B1 29 P×P P×P 30 P–QR4! P–B5 31 P–B4 followed by 32 Q–B5 and 33 Q×BP; or here 28 ... N–N1 29 P–N5 **28 P–QB4 P–QR3 29 P–N3 K–N2 30 K–N2 K–N1** Black cannot move his other two pieces e.g. 30 ... Q–B1 31 Q–B7 or 30 ... Q–N2 31 P–N5. **31 P–KR4 P–QN4 32 P×P RP×P 33 P–R3 Q–B1 34 Q–B7 Q–K1 35 B–B3 P–R4** Somewhat better was 35 ... P–R3 36 P–R5 P–N4 when White can further weaken Black's position by 37 B–K4 and 38 P–B4. **36 B–K4 K–N2 37 K–B3 K–R1 38 K–K3 K–N2 39 K–B4 K–R3 40 Q–Q6 K–N2 41 K–K3 K–N1 42 P–B3!** finally the winning plan is discovered: White creates a passed pawn on the K-side **42 ... K–N2 43 K–B4 K–R2 44 P–N4 P×P 45 P×P K–R3 46 B–B3 K–N2 47 P–R5 P×P 48 P×P K–R3 49 K–N3 K–N2 50 K–N4 P–KB4+** to prevent White's queen reaching KN5 **51 P×Pep K×P 52 Q–B4+ K–K2 53 Q–N5+ K–Q3 54 Q–QB5+ K–B2 55 P–R6 P–K4 56 Q–R7+ K–Q3 57 Q–KN7 Q–K3+ 58 K–N3 Q–B4 59 P–R7 Q–B5+ 60 K–N2 Q–Q7+ 61 K–R3 Q–K6 62 Q–B6+ 1–0.**

32 Pachman–Fichtl

Prague 1951, French Defence

1 P–K4 P–K3 2 P–Q4 P–Q4 3 N–QB3 P×P 4 N×P N–Q2 5 N–KB3 B–K2 6 B–Q3 KN–B3 7 N×N+ N×N 8 O–O O–O 9 Q–K2 P–QN3 10 R–Q1 B–N2 11 P–B3 avoiding the line 11 B–KN5 P–KR3 12 B–R4 Q–Q4 followed by 13 ... Q–KR4 **11 ... P–KR3 12 B–KB4 B–Q3 13 N–K5 Q–K2 14 B–N3!** threatening the unpleasant pin 15 B–R4 **14 ... N–Q2 15 R–Q2!**

sooner or later Black will be forced to exchange White's knight on K5, so White doubles his rooks on the prospective open file **15 ... KR–Q1 16 R1–Q1 B×N** not 16 ... N×N? 17 P×N B–B4 18 P–N4 winning, and if Black tries to prepare this by 16 ... P–QR4, White plays 17 P–QR3 when 17 ... P–R5 leads to a weakening of the RP after 18 B–N5. It is also clear that 16 ... P–QB4? fails to 17 N×N R×N 18 B×B R×B 19 P×P followed by 20 B–R7+ **17 P×B N–B4 18 B–B2 R×R**

19 Q×R!

A move which certainly surprised Black, as it allows him to exchange White's 'good' bishop and to leave him with a knight against the 'bad' bishop. A careful analysis of the position shows us, however, that it is precisely this knight which is the source of all Black's troubles. After 19 R×R R–Q1 20 P–B3 R–Q2, White admittedly stands better, but Black can hold the position.

19 ...   **B–K5**

Not of course 19 ... N–K5 20 Q–Q3 winning, and otherwise 20 P–B3 and 21 P–QN4 would drive the black knight to QR3.

20 P–N4!   **B×B**
21 Q×B   **N–N2** (*68*)

If 21 ... N–Q2 22 Q–K4 White

stands better after 22 ... R–Q1 23
Q–Q4, or 22 ... R–K1 23 Q–N7, or
22 ... R–N1 23 Q–Q4 N–B1 24
P–B3. After the text-move, Black is
equally lost, as his knight's mobility
is restricted in a most unusual way.

22 Q–R4   R–Q1

White was threatening 23 R–Q7.

23 R×R+   Q×R

24 P–KR3

If Black now protects his QRP, the
restricted mobility of his knight
proves the decisive factor e.g.

a. 24 ... Q–N1 25 P–KB4 K–B1 26
   B–R4 and White wins because
   Black's knight is completely cut
   off (26 ... N–Q1 27 Q–Q7).

b. 24 ... P–QR4 25 Q–B6 Q–QB1
   26 P–KB4 K–B1 27 B–R4 N–Q1
   28 Q–N5 P×P 29 P×P and
   again Black has no defensive
   possibilities.

This means that Black must give
up a pawn, although even then his
knight cannot be freed in time. The
game concluded: **24 ... K–R2 25
Q×P Q–Q4 26 P–QB4 Q–B3 27
P–N5** 27 Q–N8 would also win
**27 ... Q–K5 28 P–B3 Q–Q5+ 29
B–B2! Q–R8+ 30 K–R2 N–R4** if
30 ... Q×KP+ 31 B–N3 wins the
knight **31 Q×BP Q×RP 32 B×P**
not 32 Q×NP? N×P 33 Q–Q4
N×P! **32 ... N×P 33 B–Q4
Q–K7** or 33 ... N–Q7 34 Q–B3
N–B8+ 35 K–N1 Q–N8 36 Q–R1,
or here 35 ... N–N6 36 Q–N2 etc.
34 P–N6 N–Q7 or 34 ... N–K6 35
B×N Q×B 36 Q–B2+ P–N3 37
Q–N2! **35 Q–B3 P–N3 36 P–N7
N–B8+ 37 K–N1 N–N6 38 P–N8
=Q Q–Q8+ 39 K–B2 N–R8+ 40
K–K3 1–0.**

We shall see examples of favourable knight positions in the next
section and also in the chapters on
'The Battle for Strategic Points' and
'Centralization'.

THE BATTLE OF BISHOP AGAINST KNIGHT

The characteristics of these two
minor pieces are seen most clearly
when they are face to face in an
ending. The evaluation of each piece
is one of the most interesting problems of chess strategy, and it is only
in recent years that definitive con-
clusions have been reached. The last
century produced some experts who
were biased in favour of the bishop,
because of its long-ranging powers
(Tarrasch), and others who plumped
for the knight, because of its ability
to occupy squares of any colour.
People even began to talk of the
'minor exchange' which usually
referred to the superiority of the
bishop but sometimes indicated the
opposite.

It is impossible to give a set
answer to the question of the relative
strength of bishop and knight. We
can logically assume that pieces with
such distinct ways of moving cannot
be equal in all circumstances. At all
events, their respective strength
depends upon the character of each
position and in particular upon the
pawn structure.

The long-range power of the
bishop is seen at its best in open
positions, with mobile pawns on
both wings, or in positions where the
enemy pawns are blocked on the
same colour as the bishop.

The strength of the knight, on the
other hand, comes to the fore in
blocked positions in which its complex way of moving reaches the
desired goal much more effectively
than the straight-line movement of
the bishop. However, it is essential
for the knight to have strong-points

from which it can attack enemy pawns and protect its own.

In order to help the reader evaluate these two pieces in relation to the existing pawn structure, we begin with a few examples from the end-game.

The Superiority of the Bishop
diagrams 69, 70, 71

It is not the place here to examine these end-games in detail, as our main purpose is to show the functions of the two minor pieces.

Stoltz–Kashdan, The Hague 1928 (*69*). **1 ... K–B1 2 K–B1 K–K2 3 K–K2 K–Q3 4 K–Q3 K–Q4 5 P–R4 B–B1! 6 N–B3 B–R3+ 7 K–B3** if 7 K–K3 K–B4 **7 ... P–R3 8 N–Q4 P–N3 9 N–B2 K–K5 10 N–K3 P–B4 11 K–Q2 P–B5 12**

N–N4 P–R4 13 N–B6+ K–B4 14 N–Q7 B–B8 15 N–B8 P–N4 16 P–N3 NP×P 17 P×RP K–N5** and Black won.

Chekover–Lasker, Moscow 1935 (*70*). **1 K–B1 P–N4! 2 K–K1 B–N7 3 P–QR4 P×P 4 P×P K–B3!** if 4 ... K–N3 5 K–Q2 K–R4? 6 K–B2 etc. **5 K–Q2 K–B4 6 N–B3 K–N5 7 N–N5 P–QR4! 8 N–Q6 K×P 9 K–B2 B–K4 10 N×P B×P 11 N–Q8 P–K4** and Black won.

Capablanca–Tartakower, New York 1924 (*71*). **1 P–R5! R–B3 2 P×P P×P 3 R–R1 K–B1 4 R–R7 R–QB3 5 P–N4 N–B5 6 P–N5!** threatening 7 R–R6 followed by 8 P–B5 **6 ... N–K6+ 7 K–B3 N–B4** if 7 ... N–Q8 8 R–R6 K–B2 9 P–B5 R×P 10 P×P+ K–N1 11 K–K2 N–N7 12 B–B5 **8 B×N P×B 9 K–N3 R×P+ 10 K–R4 R–B6 11 P–N6 R×P+ 12 K–N5 R–K5 13 K–B6 K–N1 14 R–N7+ K–R1 15 R×P R–K1 16 K×P R–K5 17 K–B6 R–B5+ 18 K–K5 R–N5 19 P–N7+ K–N1 20 R×P R–N8 21 K×P R–QB8 22 K–Q6 R–B7 23 P–Q5 R–B8 24 R–QB7 R–QR8 25 K–B6 R×P 26 P–Q6 1–0.**

N–Q4 B–R6 21 N–K2 B–B4 22
N–B4 B–N5 23 P–N4 K–Q2 24
K–N6 B–B6 25 K×RP K–B3 26
N×KP 1–0.

*The Superiority of the Knight
diagrams 72, 73, 74*

72
W

(72) 1 N–K1 B–R8 2 N–B3 B–Q5 3
N–R4+ K–B3 4 K–R5 B–N7 5
N–B5 B–B8 6 N–R6! B–N7 7
N–N4+ K–K3 8 K–N6 B–B8 9
N–R6 B–Q7 10 N–B7 B–B5 11
N–N5+! K–Q3 12 K–B6 and White
wins.

73
W

Subarev–Alexandrov, Moscow 1915
(73). 1 K–B2 K–K2 2 K–K3 K–Q1
3 K–Q4 K–B2 4 K–B5 B–B1 5
N–N4 B–N2 6 P–KN3 B–B1 7
N–Q3 B–Q2 8 N–B4 P–N3 9
N–R3! P–R3 10 N–B4 P–N4 11
N–R5 B–K1 12 N–B6 B–B2 13
N–N4! P–KR4 14 N–K3 more
exact would be 14 N–B2 followed by
15 N–R3 14 ... B–N3 15 P–KR4!
P×P 16 P×P B–K5 17 N–B1 B–B6
18 N–Q2 B–K7 19 N–N3 B–N5 20

74
B

Capablanca–Reshevsky, Notting-
ham 1936 (74). 1 ... P–N4 passive
defence would not help Black, as the
following analysis by Fine shows: 1
... K–B2 2 N–N4 B–N2 3 N–B2
B–B3 4 N–Q4 B–Q2 5 K–K2 K–K2
6 K–Q3 P×P 7 P×P K–Q3 8
K–B3 K–B4 9 P–QN4+ K–Q3
10 N–K2 K–K4 11 N–B1 B–
B3 12 N–Q3+ K–Q3 13 K–Q4
B–K1 14 N–B4 B–B2 15 N–K2 B–K1
16 N–B3 B–B3 17 P–N4 P–N4 18
P–R5 P–R3 19 P–B4 P×P 20 P×P
winning 2 RP×P BP×P 3 N–N4
B–N2 4 P–N4! K–N2 5 K–K2
K–N3 6 K–Q3 P–R4 7 KNP×P+
K×P 8 K–Q4 K–R5 9 N×P
K–N6 10 P–B4 P–KN5 11 P–B5
B–B1 12 K–K5 B–Q2 13 P–K4
B–K1 14 K–Q4 K–B6 15 P–K5
P–N6 16 N–K3 K–B5 17 P–K6
P–N7 18 N×P+ K×P 19 K–Q5
K–N5 20 N–K3+ 1–0.

We can draw the following con-
clusions from the above six examples:
As a rule the bishop is stronger than
the knight in positions such as
diagrams 69, 70 i.e. positions with
mobile pawns on both wings. In
such positions the possessor of the
bishop only needs a small positional

advantage in addition (mobile king) in order to swing the balance over to him and guarantee the win. The bishop is equally effective in positions where the enemy pawns are on the same colour as it and thus offer a welcome target (see diagram 71). Here the bishop is attacking Black's K-side whilst protecting White's position on the opposite wing, whereas the short-hopping knight cannot operate on both wings at the same time.

Three further diagrams (72 to 74) clearly show us the superiority of the knight in blocked or semi-blocked positions in which the enemy pawns are on the same colour as his bishop which has no points of attack. Diagram 72 is a simple and instructive example of the powerlessness of a bishop against a mobile knight. The last two diagrams also illustrate the active knight versus the 'bad' bishop. These six examples point to the basic principles which govern bishop versus knight endings. The side with the bishop must try to maintain the mobility of the pawns on both wings, while the side with the knight must strive to fix the enemy pawns on the same colour as the bishop and to manoeuvre his knight in order to attack weak points. These principles should be enough to guide the reader when he has to make decisions about whether to exchange knight for bishop, or vice versa.

Finally, let us consider a few games in which we can see the above principles applied.

33 Najdorf–Stahlberg

Candidates 1953, Queen's Gambit

1 P–Q4 N–KB3 2 P–QB4 P–K3 3 N–QB3 P–Q4 4 B–N5 B–K2 5 P–K3 QN–Q2 6 N–B3 0–0 7 R–B1

P–B3 8 B–Q3 P×P 9 B×BP N–Q4 10 B×B Q×B 11 N–K4 P–K4!? The usual move is 11 ... N4–B3. **12 0–0 P×P 13 Q×P N2–N3 14 B–N3 B–N5 15 N–N3! B×N 16 P×B Q–B3 17 Q×Q N×Q 18 N–B5 QR–Q1 19 KR–Q1 N–B1 20 K–B1 KR–K1 21 K–K2 K–B1 22 R×R R×R 23 R–KN1 N–K1 24 R–N4 N–K2 25 N×N K×N** (75)

75
W

At first sight it seems that Black has few difficulties to face after all these simplifying exchanges. However, we already know that the bishop is superior to the knight when there are mobile pawns on both wings. Nevertheless, White's task is made more difficult because of his doubled pawns on the K-side.

26 R–K4+	**K–B1**
27 R–QR4	**P–QR3**
28 R–KB4	**P–B3?**

As a general rule the side with the knight should place his pawns on squares not controlled by the bishop. However, every rule has its exceptions, and ... P–KB3 here increases the activity of the bishop and later allows White to create a passed pawn. For this reason 28 ... N–Q3 was better.

29 R–KR4	**P–R3**
30 R–R5!	

Stopping Black's pawns from becoming active by ... P–QB4.

30 ...	N–B2
31 P–B4	K–K2
32 R–QB5	R–Q3
33 R–B1?	

White ought to play 33 P–B5! immediately. Black could now considerably reduce White's advantage on the K-side by playing 33 ... P–KB4, a move once again contrary to general principles but showing the creative undogmatic approach that chess requires.

33 ...	P–QN3?
34 P–B5!	

This move has a dual purpose, to restrict the activity of Black's knight and at the same time prepare the advance of the K-side pawns.

34 ...	P–B4
35 P–B4	R–B3
36 P–QR4!	

Sooner or later Black will have to play ... P–QN4 in order to mobilize his Q-side pawns, but then White can open the QR-file when necessary.

36 ...	P–QN4
37 B–B2!	

A very strong move which compels Black to move his knight and allow the bishop to reach an extremely advantageous position. White threatens to win a pawn after 37 B–K4, and 37 ... P–B5 equally loses a pawn to 38 B–K4 R–Q3 (QN3) 39 P–N3 etc.

37 ...	N–K1
38 B–K4	R–B2
39 B–Q5 (76)	

White's powerfully centralized bishop can now support his own pawn advance in the centre whilst keeping an eye on Black's Q-side pawns.

39 ...	P–B5

Otherwise White's king would reach Q5 after P–K4–K5, K–K3–K4 and B–K6.

40 P–K4	N–Q3

76
B

41 P×P	P×P
42 K–K3	R–R2

Apparently activating his pieces, but White's next two moves force him back onto the defensive.

43 R–KN1	K–B1

He cannot play 43 ... N–K1? as 44 B–B6 wins a pawn.

44 K–Q4	R–QB2
45 R–QB1	N–N2!

In order to parry 46 P–N3 with 46 ... N–B4

46 R–QR1!	N–B4
47 R–R8+	K–K2
48 P–K5	N–N6+
49 K–B3	N–B8

Other defences are equally insufficient:

a. 49 ... R–B4 50 R–R7+ K–Q1 (if *50 ... K–B1 51 R–Q7*, or *50 ... K–K1 51 B–B7+ K–B1 52 P–K6*) 51 B–K4 P×P 52 R×P N–Q5 53 P–B6! N–K3 54 B–B5 winning.

b. 49 ... P×P 50 P×P R–B4 51 R–R7+ K–K1 (*51 ... K–B1 52 R–Q7 K–K1 53 P–K6*) 52 B–B7+ K–B1 53 P–K6 R×P 54 B–N6 R–K4 55 R–KB7+ winning.

50 R–KN8	N–K7+
51 K–Q2	N×P
52 R×P+	K–Q1
53 P×P!	R–Q2

Or 53 ... N×B 54 R–N8+ and 55 P–B7 wins.

54 R×R+	K×R

55 B–B6+! 1–0

White wins both Q-side pawns, as
55 ... K×B loses to 56 P–B7.

34 Fischer–Spassky

6th match game, Reykjavik 1972,
Queen's Gambit

**1 P–QB4 P–K3 2 N–KB3 P–Q4 3
P–Q4 N–KB3 4 N–B3 B–K2 5
B–N5 0–0 6 P–K3 P–KR3 7 B–R4
P–QN3 8 P×P N×P 9 B×B Q×B
10 N×N P×N 11 R–B1 B–K3 12
Q–R4 P–QB4 13 Q–R3 R–B1 14
B–N5 P–R3?** 14 ... Q–N2! is
better. **15 P×P P×P 16 0–0 R–R2**
after 16 ... Q–N2 17 B–R4! White
maintains his advantage **17 B–K2
N–Q2 18 N–Q4! Q–B1** if 18 ...
N–B3 19 N–N3! N–K5 20 P–B3;
or here 19 ... R2–B2 20 B×P R–R1
21 R×P **19 N×B P×N** (*77*)

20 P–K4!

In the struggle of bishop against
knight, the owner of the bishop must
strive to open up the position or fix
the enemy pawns on the same colour
as his bishop. The first aim would
be achieved immediately after 20 ...
P×P, so this move can be discarded.
The second aim is achieved after 20
... N–B3 21 P–K5 N–Q2 22 B–N4
Q–K2 23 P–B4, when White undoubtedly stands better. Black's best

chance lay in 20 ... Q–Q3 which
still offered many defensive possibilities.

20 ... P–Q5?

Admittedly, Black now has a
protected passed pawn but this
counts for little compared with the
fact that White's bishop can occupy
the QR2–KN8 diagonal.

21 P–B4!

Threatening 22 B–B4 followed by
23 P–B5.

**21 ... Q–K2
22 P–K5**

Fixing Black's KP and threatening
23 P–QN4!

**22 ... R–N1
23 B–B4 K–R1**

The threat was 24 P–B5, and 23
... N–N3 would lose a pawn at
once to 24 Q–QN3!

24 Q–R3	**N–B1**
25 P–QN3	**P–QR4**
26 P–B5	**P×P**
27 R×P	

White has opened up the game to
his advantage, and has a passed
pawn plus strong pressure down the
KB-file.

27 ... N–R2

Preventing 28 R–B7 when 28 ...
N–N4 wins the exchange.

**28 R1–B1 Q–Q1
29 Q–N3**

Either here or on the next move
29 P–K6 would also be very strong.

**29 ... R–K2
30 P–KR4**

Now threatening 31 R–B7.

**30 ... R1–N2
31 P–K6 R.N2–B2**

Not of course 31 ... P–Q6 32
R–Q5! followed by 33 R×QP. This
means that Black cannot use his
only trump card and is therefore
condemned to passive defence.

32 Q–K5 Q–K1 (*78*)

Again 32 ... P–Q6 would lose a

pawn after 33 R5–B3 P–Q7 34 R–Q3.

33 P–R4

One of those moves which do not have any direct threat but serve to impress upon the opponent the unpleasant situation he is in. There is no way for Black to improve his position e.g. 33 ... N–B3 34 R×N P×R 35 R×P, or 33 ... K–N1 34 R–B7!

33 ...	Q–Q1
34 R1–B2	Q–K1
35 R2–B3	Q–Q1
36 B–Q3	Q–K1

If 36 ... R–B3 37 Q–K4! threatening the rook as well as 38 R–B8+. The same move also proves decisive in the game continuation.

37 Q–K4!	N–B3
38 R×N!	P×R
39 R×P	K–N1
40 B–B4	K–R1

Otherwise 41 R–B7 wins.

41 Q–B4	1–0

35 Ivkov–Wade

Havana 1963, Sicilian Defence

1 P–K4 P–QB4 2 N–KB3 N–QB3 3 P–Q4 P×P 4 N×P P–K3 5 N–QB3 Q–B2 6 B–K3 P–QR3 7 B–K2 N–B3 8 P–QR3 B–Q3!? intending to exchange this bishop

against White's QB, as usually after ... B–K2 and ... P–Q3 it stands rather passive **9 Q–Q2** after 9 P–KN3 N×N 10 B×N P–K4 11 B–K3 B–B4 12 Q–Q3 B×B 13 P×B! we have a position similar to the one in the game **9 ... N×N 10 B×N B–B5 11 Q–Q3 P–K4** 11 ... B–K4 was worth consideration **12 B–K3 B×B 13 P×B!** after 13 Q×B? 0–0 and 14 ... P–Q3 Black would have a good game in view of his 'good' bishop **13 ... P–Q3 14 0–0–0 K–K2 15 P–KN4!**

With the immediate threat of 16 P–N5 followed by 17 N–Q5+, but the main purpose is to activate his bishop.

15 ...   P–R3?

This is already the decisive strategic mistake. Black should maintain his king's side intact by playing 15 ... B–K3 at once. The text-move leads to the opening of the KR-file which is the main cause of Black's defeat.

16 P–KR4	B–K3
17 P–N5	P×P
18 P×P	N–Q2
19 B–N4!	QR–Q1
20 N–Q5+	B×N
21 P×B (79)	

White has skilfully changed the pawn structure to favour his bishop.

He now threatens mainly 22 P–N6, but Black should not make White's task easier by giving up the KR-file next move. He should play 21 ... R.Q1–KB1.

21 ...	R × R(?)
22 R × R	N–B1
23 R–B1!	

The final decision will come about via the KR-file, but White first wants to force ... P–B3 to increase the activity of his bishop.

| 23 ... | K–K1 |

23 ... N–N3 fails to 24 R × P+! K × R 25 B–K6+ K–K2 26 Q × N R–K1 27 Q × P+ K–Q1 28 Q × Q+ K × Q 29 P–N6; or here 26 ... K–B1 27 Q–R7 Q–R7 wins.

| 24 P–N6! | |

A neat breakthrough. Black cannot play 24 ... N × P 25 B–K6! which forces him to give up the exchange by 25 ... R–Q2, as 25 ... N–R1 fails to 26 Q–R7 K–K2 27 Q × P etc. Similarly, after 24 ... P × P 25 B–K6 Black must again play 25 ... R–Q2 to prevent 26 R–B7.

| 24 ... | P–B3 |
| 25 R–R1! (*80*) | |

The black knight is now tied to KB1 and White can calmly strengthen his position by R–R8–N8 and Q–B5.

| 25 ... | K–K2 |

26 R–R8	R–K1
27 Q–B5	K–Q1
28 P–K4	

Cutting out even the slightest counterplay that 28 ... P–K5 may offer.

| 28 ... | P–N4 |

A remarkable position in which none of Black's pieces can move e.g. if 28 ... N–Q2 29 R × R+ K × R 30 Q–K6+ wins, or if 28 ... Q–N3 R × N wins.

| 29 R–N8 | P–R4 |
| 30 K–N1! | |

An important preparatory move, as after the immediate 30 R × P Q × R 31 Q–B8+ K–K2 32 Q–B7+ N–Q2 33 B × N K–B1 34 Q–B6 Q × P Black would be threatening perpetual check!

30 ...	P–N5
31 P × P	P × P
32 R × P!	Q × R
33 Q–B8+	K–K2
34 Q–B7+	N–Q2
35 B × N!	K–B1
36 Q–B6!	

Much stronger than 36 Q × P+ Q–K2 37 Q × Q+ R × Q etc. After the text-move the black rook must remain on K1 e.g. 36 ... R–Q1 37 Q × P+ Q–K2 38 P–N7+; or here 37 ... K–N1 38 B–K6+ etc.

| 36 ... | Q × P |
| 37 B × R | Q × P |

A desperate try, but after 37 ... Q × B 38 Q × P+ the queen ending is hopeless. The game finished: **38 B–Q7 P–N6 39 Q × P+ K–N2 40 Q–K7+ K–N3 41 B–K8+ K–N4 42 Q–KN7+ K–B5 43 Q–R6+ K–N6 44 Q–N6+ 1–0.**

36 Lilienthal–Bondarevsky

Moscow 1940, French Defence

1 P–K4 P–K3 2 P–Q4 P–Q4 3 N–QB3 P × P 4 N × P N–Q2 5 N–KB3

B–K2 6 B–Q3 KN–B3 7 N×N+
B×N 8 0–0 P–B4 9 P–B3 P×P 10
P×P 0–0 11 Q–B2 P–KN3 12
B–KB4 N–N3 13 B–B7 Q–K2 14
B–K4! beginning a series of simplifying exchanges which give White a
small but permanent positional
advantage 14 ... N–Q4 15 B×N
P×B 16 B–K5! B–B4 16 ... B–N4
17 KR–K1 B–K3 18 B–Q6! Q×B
19 N×B would lead to a position
similar to the one that arises in the
game 17 B×B Q×B (81)

With the centre pawns blocked
in this way, Black's bishop has no
points of attack, whereas the white
knight can manoeuvre freely. However, although the knight is stronger
than the bishop here, this advantage
would be insufficient for winning
purposes, if White did not succeed in
forcing weaknesses on Black's Q-
side in the further course of the game.

18 Q–N3   B–K5

19 N–K5

Threatening 20 Q×NP, 20 P–B3
or 20 N–Q7.

19 ...   Q–N3!

20 Q×Q   P×Q

21 KR–B1

Not of course 21 N–Q7 KR–Q1
22 N×P? R–R3 and the knight is
lost.

21 ...   KR–B1

22 P–QR3   B–B4

23 P–KN4!   B–K3

24 P–R3(?)

White places his pawns on the
same colour as the bishop, but this
is important in order to limit its
activity. If now 24 ... R×R+
25 R×R R–QB1 26 R×R+B×R
Black would have far the worst of
the end-game. However, stronger
than the text-move would be 24
P–B3, when after the above exchange of rooks White could win
easily by 27 P–N5!

24 ...   P–B3

25 N–Q3   P–KN4

26 P–B3   K–B2

27 K–B2   K–K2

28 K–K3   K–Q3?

The decisive error. It was essential to play 28 ... P–R4! followed
by ... K–Q3 and ... P×P. In
this way he could have stopped
White's rook penetrating down the
KR-file.

29 R×R!   R×R

30 P–KR4!   P–R3

Even weaker is 30 ... P×P 31
R–R1 P–B4 32 P–N5.

31 P×P   RP×P

32 R–R1   R–K1

33 K–Q2   B–Q2

34 R–R6   R–KB1

If 34 ... K–K3 35 P–B4! R–KN1
36 P–B5+ follows.

35 N–K1   K–K2

36 N–B2   R–B2

37 N–K3   B–K3

38 K–B3   K–Q3

39 K–N4   B–Q2

40 N–B5+!   K–B2

After 40 ... B×N Lilienthal
gives a quick win as follows: 41
P×B K–B3 42 P–R4! R–B1 43
R–R7 R–Q1 44 R–KB7 R–Q3 45
P–N3 P–N4 46 P–R5 P–N3 47 P–R6
winning.

41 P–R4   B–K3

42 N–N3   B–Q2

43 N–R5!   **P–B4**
44 N–B6!

The point of White's seven move manoeuvre in which his knight has demonstrated great mobility. Black now loses a pawn, the game ending as follows: **44 ... P×P 45 N×QP+ K–N1 46 P×P B×NP 47 N×P R–B7 48 P–N3 B–Q8 49 P–Q5 K–B2** 49 ... R–B6 50 P–Q6 R×P+ 51 K–R5 **50 P–R5 R–Q7 51 R–R7+ K–N1 52 P–Q6! R–Q5+ 53 K–B5 R–KR5 54 P–Q7 K–B2 55 P–Q8 =Q+ K×Q 56 R–Q7+ 1–0.**

37 Smyslov–Rudakovsky

Moscow 1945, Sicilian Defence

1 P–K4 P–QB4 2 N–KB3 P–K3 3 P–Q4 P×P 4 N×P N–KB3 5 N–QB3 P–Q3 6 B–K2 B–K2 7 0–0 0–0 8 B–K3 N–B3 9 P–B4 Q–B2 10 Q–K1 N×N 11 B×N P–K4 12 B–K3 B–K3? better 12 ... B–Q2 and 13 ... B–B3 **13 P–B5 B–B5?** 13 ... B–Q2 was still essential giving a sharp game, with better prospects to White, after 14 P–KN4 B–B3 15 B–B3 P–Q4!? 16 P×P P–K5 17 N×P N×QP. **14 B×B Q×B 15 B–N5!** *(82)*

82
B

The decisive move from a strategic point of view. Black cannot prevent the exchange of his knight for the bishop, after which we have a typical position with the centralized knight on Q5 proving much stronger than Black's bishop which remains inactive for the rest of the game.

15 ...   **KR–K1**
16 B×N   **B×B**
17 N–Q5!

There is no need to waste time by guarding the BP, as 17 ... Q×BP would lose the exchange after 18 R–B2 Q–B4 19 R–QB1 followed by 20 N–B7.

17 ...   **B–Q1**
18 P–B3   **P–QN4**
19 P–QN3   **Q–B4+**
20 K–R1   **R–QB1**
21 R–B3   **K–R1**

This was Black's last chance to prolong his resistance with 21 ... P–B3. White would then have a choice between attacking the K-side with all his heavy pieces (22 R–R3 P–QR4 23 Q–R4 P–R3 24 Q–N4 K–R1 25 R–KB1 followed by Q–N6 and R1–B3) and adopting the equally strong plan of opening the QR-file by 22 P–QR4. After the text-move, White decisively weakens Black's king position.

22 P–B6   **P×P**
23 Q–R4   **R–KN1**
24 N×P   **R–N2**
25 R–N3!

Threatening both 26 Q×P+! and also 26 R×R K×R 27 Q×P+ K×N 28 R–KB1+.

25 ...   **B×N**
26 Q×B   **R1–KN1**
27 R–Q1   **P–Q4**
28 R×R   **1–0**

38 Filip–Barda

Bucharest 1953, English Opening

1 P–QB4 N–KB3 2 N–QB3 P–Q4 3 P×P N×P 4 P–KN3 P–K4 5 B–N2 N–N3 6 N–B3 N–B3 7 0–0 B–K2 8 P–Q3 B–K3 9 P–QR3 0–0

10 P–QN4 P–B4 11 B–K3! better
than 11 B–N2 **11 . . . B–B3 12 R–B1
N–Q5 13 N–Q2 P–B3 14 B×N!**
P×B 14 . . . Q×B! **15 N–R4 N×N
16 Q×N B–Q4 17 R–B5 B×B
18 K×B** (*83*)

White clearly stands better already. His knight is mobile and can
go to QR5 or QB5 via QN3, whereas
the black bishop is restricted by his
QP. However, Black's next move is
a grave strategic error, as it gives
White's knight an unassailable
strong-point at K4. 18 . . . B–K2
was essential.

18 . . .	Q–K1?
19 Q–N3+	**K–R1**
20 R×KBP!	

White sees that the attack by the
black queen in no way compensates
for the permanent positional advantage which possession of K4
gives him.

20 . . .	Q×P
21 N–K4	**QR–K1**
22 P–R3	**B–K2**
23 R–K5	**Q–B6+**
24 K–N1	**B–Q1**
25 R×R	**R×R**

Both Black's QP and his weakened
K-side now offer objects of attack.

26 Q–B4	**P–KR3!**

Black would willingly give up his
QP to eliminate the white knight.
After 27 Q×QP B–N3 28 Q–B4 (*28*

N–B5 R–Q1 and *29 . . . B×N*) 28
. . . R–Q1 29 N–B5 B×N 30 Q×B
R×P 31 Q×RP P–QN4 he could
still manage to save the game.

27 P–N5!	**P×P**
28 Q×NP	**R–B1**
29 Q–B4	**B–N3**
30 P–QR4!	

Black's bishop can find no security
on QN3 either, as White now prepares P–R5 to remove the defence
of the QP.

30 . . .	Q–B4
31 Q–N4!	**R–B1**
32 K–N2	**Q–Q4**
33 R–QN1	**R–B2**
34 Q–N5!	**R–Q2**
35 P–B4	**R–Q1**
36 R–N2	**Q–N1?**

Hastening his defeat, but after
36 . . . R–Q2 White would play 37
P–N4 and 38 P–B5, when Black
would have no good moves.

37 Q–KR5

Threatening 38 N–N5 R–Q2 39
Q–N6! P×N 40 Q–R5+ Q–R2 41
Q–K8+ winning.

The game concluded: **37 . . . Q–K1
38 Q×Q+ R×Q 39 R–N5 R–QB1
40 P–R5 B–Q1 41 R×P B×P 42
R×RP B–Q7 43 P–B5 B–K6 44
K–B3 R–B1 45 K–N4 K–N1 46
K–R5 R–B2 47 R–R8+ K–R2 48
P–N4 B–N8 49 R–Q8 B–K6 50
P–R4 B–N8 51 N–N5+ 1–0.**

THE TWO BISHOPS

Almost every chess-player has heard
of the importance of the two bishops,
and has read in thousands of notes
to master games how they are
superior to bishop and knight. We
sometimes even see a pawn being
sacrificed with the sole purpose of
maintaining the bishop pair. Again
and again we come up against the
assertion that the two bishops are an

absolute advantage, irrespective of the placing of the other pieces and pawns. In the present chapter we shall examine wherein this advantage lies, in which positions it comes to the fore, and how it must be utilized.

In the previous chapter we were concerned with the strategic principles arising from the different movements of the bishop and knight, and we demonstrated that the bishop is usually superior to the knight in fluid, open positions. The disadvantage of the bishop lies in the fact that it can only control squares of one colour i.e. half the board. As a result, squares of the opposite colour tend to become weak (the chapter on 'Weak Squares in the Pawn Chain' will deal with this aspect more fully) and prove ideal for enemy pieces. Even his king can utilize them. The extra bishop greatly reduces this disadvantage, because the two bishops control squares of both colours. In open positions their effectiveness is an extremely important factor, as is shown by our next clear-cut example.

39 Botvinnik–Euwe

The Hague 1948, Queen's Gambit

1 P–Q4 P–Q4 2 P–QB4 P–K3 3 N–KB3 N–KB3 4 N–B3 P–B3 5 P–K3 QN–Q2 6 B–Q3 B–N5 7 P–QR3 B–R4 8 Q–B2 Q–K2 9 B–Q2 P×P 10 B×BP P–K4 11 0–0 0–0 12 QR–K1 a very strong alternative is 12 B–R2! when 12 . . . B–B2 fails to 13 N–QN5 **12 . . . B–B2 13 N–K4 N×N 14 Q×N P–QR4?** better is 14 . . . K–R1 or 14 . . . N–B3 15 Q–R4 P–K5 16 N–K5 B–K3 **15 B–R2 N–B3 16 Q–R4 P–K5 17 N–K5!** *(84)*

A strong move which Botvinnik

had probably already envisaged on his 13th move. White offers a pawn in order to gain the two bishops which more than offset this slight loss of material as they exert pressure along the open diagonals against Black's K-side. For this reason, Black should decline the offer by 17 . . . B–K3 18 B–N1 B–Q4, giving him good defensive chances, even though White maintains some initiative after 19 P–B3 or 19 P–B4.

17 . . .	**B×N?**
18 P×B	**Q×KP**
19 B–B3	**Q–K2**
20 P–B3!	**N–Q4**

After 20 . . . P×P White continues 21 B–N1! P–R3 22 R×P N–Q4 23 R–N3! winning. The best move is 20 . . . B–K3 and after 21 P×P! B×B 22 R×N! followed by 23 Q–N5 White has a sharp attack in an unclear position.

21 Q×Q	**N×Q**
22 P×P *(85)*	

We have now reached an interesting ending (or to be more exact a middle-game without queens, in view of the material left on the board) in which White has a doubled KP but two powerful bishops. An important tactical factor is that Black cannot exchange one bishop by 22 . . . B–K3? 23 B×B P×B 24 R×R+ K×R 25 R–

85
B

KB1+ K–N1 26 R–Q1 when he cannot stop White's rook reaching the seventh rank. In this difficult position, Euwe commits another error which leads to a rapid loss. The best defensive chance lay in active counterplay: 22 ... B–N5! 23 R–B4 B–R4 24 P–KN4 B–N3 25 R–Q1 QR–Q1! 26 R×R R×R 27 B×RP R–Q8+ etc.

22 ...	P–QN3?
23 R–Q1	N–N3

It was probably only now that Black realized that 23 ... R–R2 loses to 24 R×P!

24 R–Q6	B–R3
25 R–B2	B–N4
26 P–K5	N–K2
27 P–K4!	P–QB4
28 P–K6	

This is much better than 28 R×NP B–B3.

28 ...	P–B3
29 R×NP	B–B3
30 R×B!	N×R
31 P–K7+	R–B2
32 B–Q5	1–0

In the above game the two bishops worked most efficiently along the open diagonals attacking various points in the enemy position. For example, White's bishop on QB3 was eyeing both the KNP and QRP. Similarly the strength of the bishop pair made itself felt in the further course of the game, when another advantage cropped up: the possibility of purposeful simplification. In certain positions the correct plan is to exchange an actively placed minor piece of the opponent. If you possess the two bishops you have a far better chance of bringing about such an exchange than, for example, trying to exchange your own knight for an enemy bishop. The following game shows how the bishop pair can be used to bring about such simplification.

40 Barcza–Pachman

Prague 1954, Sicilian Defence

1 N–KB3 P–QB4 2 P–KN3 N–QB3 3 P–Q4 P×P 4 N×P P–KN3 5 B–N2 B–N2 6 N–N3 P–Q3 7 N–B3 N–B3 8 0–0 0–0 9 P–K4 B–Q2 We now have the Dragon variation with White playing P–KN3 and B–KN2 **10 N–Q5 N×N 11 P×N N–K4 12 N–Q4 Q–N3 13 P–QB3 QR–B1 14 P–KR3 Q–B4! 15 Q–K2 KR–K1 16 R–Q1 N–B5**
    17 B–K3(?)

After 17 P–N3! N–N3 18 B–N2 N×P 19 P–QB4 the game would be even. White was afraid that Black might build up a powerful position in this variation, so deliberately gives his opponent the advantage of two bishops, relying on his strongly placed knight on Q4.

17 ...	N×B
18 Q×N	Q–N3!
19 Q–Q2	R–B5! (*86*)

This is played with the idea of undermining the position of the centralized knight. The threat is 20 ... B×N weakening White's pawns and taking control of the vital QB-file. If now 20 B–B1 R–B4 21 B–N2 R1–QB1, Black has doubled his rooks with gain of time. However, the game continuation (P–N3)

weakens the QBP and once this advances to QB4 White's knight is no longer protected by a pawn.

20 P–N3   **R–B2**
21 QR–B1   **P–QR4!**

This is better than 21 ... R1– QB1. As White will sooner or later be forced to advance his QBP, Black immediately prepares to open a further line on the Q-side.

22 P–QB4   **P–R5**
23 R–N1   **R–R1!**

There is no need to fear 24 P × P, because after 24 ... Q–B4 25 N–N5 R2–B1 White's pawns are desperately weak.

24 B–B1   **P × P**
25 P × P   **R2–B1**
26 Q–K3

Black is intending to strengthen his position by ... R–R6 followed by doubling rooks on the QR-file. So White prepares to exchange queens, calculating that he can allow penetration by the black rooks, because his one weakness, the QNP, is easily defensible.

26 ...   **R–R7!**
27 N–B5   **Q × Q**
28 N × Q   **P–R4**
29 R–Q3   **P–QN4**
30 P × P   **B × NP**
31 R3–Q1   **R–N1!**

The first offer to exchange minor pieces. After 32 B × B R × B Black would easily be able to exploit

White's weakened QNP and QP e.g. 33 R–Q3 R4–R4 34 N–B4 R– R8 35 R × R R × R+ 36 K–N2 K– B1 and Black's king penetrates down the Q-side.

32 N–B4   **B–B6!**

Heading for QB4 from where he can attack White's weak point at KB2.

33 R.N1–B1   **B–N5**
34 R–R1   **R1–R1**
35 R × R   **R × R**
36 R–N1   **B–R3**

Now this bishop heads for QN2 to attack White's QP. White has no effective defence, as after 37 N–K3 B × B 38 K × B K–N2, the entry of Black's king is decisive.

37 R–N2   **R–R8**
38 R–B2   **B–N2**
39 N–K3   **B–B4!**

White cannot prevent the exchange of his knight and with it the loss of at least one pawn. It is interesting to note that through the threat to exchange white-squared bishops (move 31) Black first of all drove White's pieces into passive positions and now concludes the game by exchanging his other bishop. In other words, the bishop pair is not just a static factor but on the contrary can be exploited dynamically to bring about favourable exchanges.

40 R–Q2   **B × N**
41 P × B   **B–R3**

Of course, 41 ... R–N8 would also win.

42 R–KB2   **K–N2**
43 K–N2

Or 43 P–QN4 B–B5 44 P–K4 B–Q6 etc.

The game ended: **43 ... R × B 44 R × R B × R+ 45 K × B K–B3 46 K–K2 K–K4 47 K–Q3 K × P 48 P–QN4 K–B3 49 K–B4 P–Q4+ 50 K–Q4 K–Q3 0–1.**

With the two bishops the aim is always to open up the position.

In general a centralized knight can forestall this attempt, because it hinders the mobility of at least one of the bishops. Nevertheless, in our next example White managed to exploit the bishop pair by opening up the position on the Q-side. Pachman–Kotov, Sarajevo 1966 (*87*).

18 Q–R5	**R2–B1!**

Indirectly defending his QRP, as 19 Q×RP? loses to 19 ... R–R1 20 Q×P KR–N1 winning the queen.

19 P–B5!	**P–N3**
20 P×NP	**BP×P**

Black could not improve by 20 ... RP×P when his QBP remains weak.

21 Q–R6

If Black now tries to simplify the position by exchanging rooks, he has great problems after 21 ... R–B1 22 R–B1 because White is threatening 23 B×N P×B 24 R–B6! In such a position the bishops of opposite colour would only help White, as we have already seen, for he has a strong point on QB6 and his bishop is more active than Black's. Black therefore decides to exchange queens but White's remaining material of two rooks and two bishops is particularly well suited to this type of position.

21 ...	**Q–N4**
22 Q×Q	**N×Q**
23 R–B1	**R–B1**
24 R–B6	

A good alternative was 24 P–QR4 N–Q5 25 B×N P×B 26 R–B6, but I saw that the text-move would soon net a pawn.

24 ...	**R×R**
25 P×R	**K–B2**
26 P–QR4	**N–B2**

And now 26 ... N–Q5 loses at once to 27 B×N P×B 28 P–B7 R–B1 29 R–B1 P–Q6 30 B×QP B–Q5+ (*30 ... B×P 31 B–R6*) 31 K–B1 B–B4 32 P–QN4.

27 P–R5!	**P×P**

If 27 ... P–Q4 then of course 28 P×P follows.

28 B×RP	**P–Q4**
29 B–N6!	**P×B**
30 P×P+	**K–K3**
31 B×N	

But not 31 R×R? B×R 32 B×N B–B4+ and 33 ... P–R5. After the text-move, White's material advantage should win for him, but it is not easy to exploit this, as Black's rook can become active.

The game concluded: **31 ... R–B1 32 B×RP R×P 33 B–B3 R–B5 34 R–K1 B–B3 35 K–B2 P–R4 36 K–K3 R–R5! 37 R–Q1 B–N4+ 38 K–B3 B–K2 39 R–Q5 B–Q3 40 K–K3 R–R8 41 R–Q2 P–N4 42 P–R3 P–N5 43 P×P P×P 44 K–B2 R–R5 45 R–K2 K–B3 46 P–QN3 R–R6 47 R–N2 K–N4 48 K–K3!?** in his haste to advance his QNP White allows Black's king to penetrate via KB5. Safer was 48 P–N3 **48 ... B–B4+ 49 K–Q3 K–B5 50 K–B4 B–R2 51 P–N4 B–K6 52 R–K2 P–N6?** this loses quickly; Black should play 52 ... B–R2 **53 B–N2! R–R1 54 B×P+ K×B 55 R×B**

R–QB1+ 56 K–N3 K–B5 57 R–K2
K–K4 58 R–K3 K–B5 59 R–KB3+
K–N5 60 P–K5 R–B8 61 R–K3
K–B5 62 R–K2 R–KB8 63 P–K6
R–B7 64 R–K1 1–0.

Those variations of the Ruy Lopez
in which White plays B×QN
provide us with a most interesting
strategic problem. White gives his
opponent the two bishops in order
to obtain the better pawn structure,
and Black must find an active plan
before White can simplify into a
superior end-game.

41 Dückstein–Unzicker

Munich Olympiad 1958, Ruy Lopez
1 P–K4 P–K4 2 N–KB3 N–QB3
3 B–N5 P–QR3 4 B–R4 N–B3 5 0–0
N×P 6 Q–K2 N–B4 after 6 ...
N–B3 the game is equal, but Black
is trying for a strategically more
complex position 7 B×N QP×B
8 P–Q4 N–K3 9 P×P N–Q5 10
N×N Q×N 11 P–KR3 after 11
R–Q1 B–KN5 12 R×Q B×Q 13
N–B3 B–R4 Black has a somewhat
better ending 11 ... B–K3 12 R–Q1
Q–QB5 13 R–Q3 B–K2 14 P–
QN3 Q–KR5 15 N–Q2? 15 B–R3!
was the correct move after which
Black cannot maintain his bishop
pair e.g. 15 ... P–QB4 16 N–B3
and the threat of N–Q5 forces ...
P–B5 15 ... 0–0 16 N–B3 Q–R4
(*88*).

Black already has a clear advantage. White's knight has no suitable
outpost and his bishop is restricted
by the pawn on K5 (if this pawn
were on K4, B–B4 would be attacking the QBP). In addition, Black can
easily mobilize his Q-side pawn
majority, as White's pawn on QN3
helps Black to eliminate his doubled
pawns by ... P–QB5.

17 B–B4   P–QB4
18 Q–K3   P–KR3

Preventing 19 B–N5 exchanging
the black-squared bishops.

19 R1–Q1   Q–N3
20 N–K1

Black was threatening to win a
pawn by ... B×RP or ... B–KB4.

20 ...   B–B4
21 R3–Q2   Q–QB3
22 Q–N3   QR–Q1
23 K–R2   R×R
24 R×R   R–Q1

Otherwise the possession of the
Q-file gives White chances. Black
has no need to fear simplification
as queen and two bishops give him
excellent attacking chances.

25 R×R+   B×R
26 N–Q3   K–R2

Threatening 27 ... P–B5 which
at the moment fails to 27 P×P
Q×BP 28 B×P.

27 Q–K3   B–K2

Or 27 ... P–B5 28 N–N4 Q–N4
29 P–N4 B–N3! is also possible.

28 P–KN4   B–K3?

As we shall soon see, this natural
move is in reality a serious loss of
time. 28 ... B–QB1! was the best
after which White cannot prevent
... P–B5, as 29 P–QB4 allows 29
... P–QN4 threatening both ...
B–K3 and ... P×P followed by ...
Q–R5.

29 B–N3!   P–B5
30 N–B4!   P×P
31 Q–Q3+   K–N1

32 RP×P	B–QB1
33 N–Q5	B–B1
34 B–R4	P–QN4!

Preventing the exchange of his KB, as White cannot play either 35 N–K7+? B×N 36 B×B B–N2 or 35 B–K7 B–K3! 36 B×B B×N 37 B–N4 B–R8 38 Q–Q8+ K–R2 39 Q–Q3+ B–K5; or here 38 Q–N3 Q×P! 39 K×B Q–K5+.

35 P–QB4?

Balancing out Black's mistake on move 28. White could centralize his pieces by 35 Q–K4! forcing 35 ... K–R1.

35 ...	B–N2
36 P–B4	P×P
37 P×P	Q–B4!

Giving White no further chances, as the advance of the QRP is now decisive.

38 B–N3	P–QR4
39 P–B5	B–R3
40 N–K3	Q–R6
41 Q×Q	B×Q
0–1	

The bishops can also prove most effective in exploiting a space advantage.

Unzicker–Pomar, Tel Aviv Olympiad 1964 (*89*).

Play continued: 19 P–B4! N×N after 19 ... N–N6 20 R–QN1 N×B 21 P×N BP×P 22 N–Q2, or here 21 KR×N N–B2 22 N–Q6, White has the advantage. That is why he did not worry about losing his bishop pair. 20 Q×N N–B2 21 P–QN4 Q–Q5 if 21 ... R–Q5? 22 B–K3! R×Q 23 B×Q wins **22 B–K3 Q×Q 23 B×Q** a typical position in which White has a clear advantage because of Black's passively placed knight **23 ... P–KB4** otherwise White will obtain a bind on the K-side with P–KN4 and P–KB5 **24 P×Pep B×BP 25 QR–Q1 N–K1 26 B–QB5 P–QR3 27 B–QN6 R–Q3 28 B–B3!** not at once 28 P–QB5 R×R 29 R×R B–N7 when 30 R–Q7 fails to 30 ... N–B3 etc. **28 ... K–B2 29 P–N4** 29 P–QB5 was also very strong **29 ... B–K2 30 B–K2 N–B3 31 B–B7 R×R 32 R×R R–QB1 33 B–N6 K–K1 34 P–KN5 N–Q2 35 B–Q4 P–KN3 36 P–QB5!** of course this move is only possible when Black's knight cannot reach Q4 **36 ... R–Q1 37 B–QB3 N–B1 38 R–K1!** his winning chances would disappear if rooks came off **38 ... K–B2 39 B–B4 P–QR4 40 P×P** surprising, but well thought out, as White must now obtain a distant passed pawn **40 ... B×BP 41 R–QN1 R–Q2 42 P–QR4 K–K1 43 K–N3 K–Q1 44 P–R6 P×P** if 44 ... P–N3? 45 R–Q1! wins **45 R–N8+ K–K2 46 B–B6+ K–B2 47 B×RP B–K2 48 B–B3 R–Q8** or 48 ... R–R2 49 R–N7! R×B 50 B–B6 etc. **49 R–N7 N–Q2 50 B–K2 R–Q4 51 K–B3 N–B4 52 R–R7 R–Q2 53 R×R N×R** such positions, with each side having a passed pawn, are especially suitable for the two bishops. The rest is fairly simple despite its length **54 P–R5 B–B4 55 B–B4 K–K2 56 P–R4 K–Q3 57 P–R6 B–R2 58 B–N4+ P–B4 59 B–B3 N–N3 60 B–K5+ K–K2 61 B–Q3 N–Q4** or 61 ... P–B5 62 B–K2 followed by

63 B–Q4 62 P–R5 K–B2 63 P×P+ P×P 64 B–Q6 N–N5 65 K–K2 N–B3 66 K–Q2 K–K1 otherwise White's king penetrates via the Q-side **67 B×NP+ K–Q2 68 B–K4 K×B 69 B×N K–K2 69 ... K×B 70 P–N6 wins 70 B–K4 B–N1 71 K–B3 K–Q3 72 K–B4 B–R2 73 K–N5 K–Q2 74 P–N6 K–K2 75 K–B6 1–0.**

In the examples we have seen so far, the two bishops have been used actively to ensure an advantage. However, they may also be used as an equalizing factor when fighting against a disadvantage. Consider our next position from Smyslov–Pachman, Moscow–Prague match 1946 (*90*).

90
B

Black's position is somewhat uncomfortable. His pieces have no strong points and White threatens to play P–K5 after due preparation (KN–K2, R–K1, P–R3, P–B4; or P–R3, P–B4, N–B3). Therefore, Black decides to sacrifice a pawn with a view to obtaining two active bishops.

20 ...	P–QR4!
21 R×P	N–R3
22 K–Q1	N–QN5
23 B–N1	B–QB1!

Threatening ... B–QR3 and at the same time freeing Q2 for the knight.

24 KN–K2	N–Q2
25 P–QN3	N–K4

The black knights are now so active that White must exchange at least one of them.

26 B–R3	N4–Q6
27 B1×N	N×B
28 K–B2	N–N5+
29 B×N	R×B
30 R–QN1	

White now threatens 31 N–N5 B–Q2 32 N2–B3 when Black would be forced to relinquish one of his bishops without sufficient compensation for the pawn.

30 ...	R5–N2
31 N–B1	B–K4
32 P–R3	K–N2?

An inexactitude in time-trouble allowing White to gain the advantage by 33 N–Q3 B–B3 34 P–B4 e.g. 34 ... K–N1 35 N–K2!, but not 35 P–K5 B–R5 36 N–K2 B–B4! 37 P–N3? B×NP! 38 N×B B×N+ 39 K×B R×P+ etc. with a position similar to the one we later see in the game.

33 R1–R1	B–Q2
34 R–R8	R×R
35 R×R	B–Q5
36 N1–K2	B–KB3
37 R–R5	P–N4!

The threat was 38 P–B4 and 39 P–K5.

38 R–R6	B–K4
39 N–R4	B–K1

In order to obtain counterplay after 40 N–N6 P–K3.

40 P–N3	B–Q2
41 P–B4	P×P
42 P×P	B–KB3 (*91*)

We can now see what an equalizing factor the two bishops represent. White can, in fact, win another pawn by 43 P–K5! B–R5! 44 P×P P×P 45 R×P but after 45 ... B–B4+ followed by 46 ... R–K2

91
W

Black's counter-play is so strong that he has the better prospects.

43 P–B5   B×N!

Once again the two bishops can be used to bring about necessary simplification just when White was hoping to exploit the blocked position by playing N–N6 and bringing his other knight to QN5, Black's KB (the so-called 'bad bishop') controls the situation so well in its duel with the knight that it completely compensates for the pawn minus.

44 R×B   B–K4
45 R–R8

There is no time to prepare a Q-side break-through as Black's king is ready to launch a dangerous attack on the K-side.

45 ...   P–K3
46 BP×P   P×P
47 P×P   K–B3
48 R–KB8+

Or 48 R–K8 R–KN2 with sufficient counter-chances.

48 ...   K×P
49 N–B4+   B×N
50 R×B   K–K4
51 R–R4   R–N2
½–½

So far we have seen the two bishops working together effectively and choosing the appropriate moment to exchange themselves for an enemy piece. However, this simple method does not work in some simple positions of an open nature with symmetrical pawn structures. Steinitz demonstrated the very important strategic plan to be followed in such cases: by advancing the pawns gradually, take away squares from the enemy knight (or knights), drive it into an unfavourable position, then exploit this by a timely break-through.

In his book *Masters of the Chess Board*, Réti quoted two fine examples from the play of Steinitz, illustrating the new method of the first World Champion who introduced for the first time into chess literature the concept of the 'advantage of the two bishops'.

42 Rosenthal–Steinitz

Vienna 1873, Three Knights Game

1 P–K4 P–K4 2 N–QB3 N–QB3 3 N–B3 P–KN3?! 4 P–Q4 P×P 5 N×P B–N2 6 B–K3 KN–K2 7 B–QB4 a very good plan is 7 Q–Q2 and 8 0–0–0 **7 ... P–Q3 8 0–0 0–0 9 P–B4? N–R4! 10 B–Q3 P–Q4 11 P×P** if 11 P–K5? P–QB4 wins a piece **11 ... N×P 12 N×N Q×N 13 P–B3 R–Q1** threatening ... P–QB4 **14 Q–B2** so as to answer 14 ... P–QB4 with 15 B–K4 **14 ... N–B5! 15 B×N Q×B 16 Q–B2** (*92*) the threat was 16 ... B×N 17 B×B R×B!

We have reached a typical set-up in which the black bishops have no direct threats. The main object is to limit the activity of the white knight. This game has great historical interest in that it is the first example of the method used by Steinitz to exploit the advantage of the two bishops.

16 ...   P–QB4

92
B

The first and most vital strong-point (Q4) is taken from the knight.

17 N–B3   P–N3

And now Black's Q-side pawns present a barrier to the white bishop, completely cutting down its mobility. This points to the dubious nature of White's 9th move which prevents his bishop from becoming active on the K-side.

18 N–K5   Q–K3
19 Q–B3   B–QR3
20 KR–K1   P–B3!
21 N–N4   P–R4!
22 N–B2   Q–B2

Directed against the threatened P–B5 and preparing ... B–N2 aiming at White's weak KN2. Already White is at a clear dis-advantage, as both his minor pieces are passively placed. His next move quickly loses a pawn which only hastens the end.

23 P–B5?   P–KN4
24 QR–Q1   B–N2
25 Q–N3   R–Q4!
26 R×R   Q×R
27 R–Q1   Q×BP
28 Q–B7   B–Q4
29 P–QN3   R–K1
30 P–B4   B–B2
31 B–B1   R–K7
32 R–B1   Q–QB7

Threatening 33 R×N.

33 Q–N3   Q×RP
34 Q–N8+   K–R2

35 Q–N3   B–N3
36 P–R4   P–N5
37 N–Q3   Q×P
38 Q–B7   Q×N
0–1

It is clear that White's 9 P–B4? and 23 P–B5? made it very easy for Black, so the next game, played ten years later by Steinitz, is even more interesting.

43 Englisch–Steinitz

London 1883, Ruy Lopez

1 P–K4 P–K4 2 N–KB3 N–QB3 3 B–N5 P–KN3 4 P–Q4 P×P 5 N×P? it was not until later that the strong move 5 B–N5! was discovered **5 ... B–N2 6 B–K3 N–B3 7 N–QB3 0–0 8 0–0 N–K2** preparing ... P–Q4; White should play 9 P–K5 N–K1 10 B–KB4 which would give him some space advantage **9 Q–Q2 P–Q4 10 P×P N2×P 11 N×N Q×N 12 B–K2 N–N5 13 B×N B×B**

14 N–N3   Q×Q

More exact was 14 ... Q–B5! 15 P–QB3 QR–Q1. After the text-move Black has only a slight advantage, but this fact makes the rest of the game all the more instructive.

15 N×Q   QR–Q1!

Not at once 15 ... B×P 16 QR–N1, but now he threatens 16 ... B×P 17 QR–N1 B–Q5! when White loses a piece if he tries to regain his pawn.

16 P–QB3   KR–K1
17 N–N3 (*93*)
17 ...   P–N3!

Setting up the same pawn struc-ture as in the previous game, in order to limit the mobility of the white minor pieces and in par-ticular to deny White the use of his Q4 square.

18 P–KR3   B–K3
19 KR–Q1   P–QB4
20 B–N5   P–B3
21 B–B4   K–B2

Here is another common element in this kind of ending. The side with the two bishops can bring his king to the centre more easily under their protection, whereas the enemy king would then be open to checks (e.g. 22 K–B1 B–B5+).

22 P–B3   P–KN4!

In the previous game White's bishop was hemmed in by his own pawn on KB4, and here Steinitz achieves a similar effect by advancing his KNP. If White now wishes to maintain his bishop in the centre, he must relinquish the Q-file, as otherwise he loses a piece after 23 B–K3 R×R 24 R×R B×N.

23 R×R   R×R
24 B–K3   P–KR3
25 R–K1   P–B4
26 P–KB4

If White allows . . . P–B5, he will be completely shut in. However, the presence of this pawn later gives Black an opportunity to open up the game to his advantage (see move 30!).

26 . . .   B–B3
27 P–N3   P–QR4!

Threatening 28 . . . P–R5 29 N–B1 P–R6 shattering White's Q-side pawn formation. With this move, Black completes the restriction of White's knight.

28 N–B1   P–R5
29 P–R3   B–B5
30 K–B2 (*94*)

Black has achieved his objective of tying down White's knight, but now he has the serious problem of converting this positional advantage into a win. White's position seems extraordinarily solid, as his bishop guards the most important points. This fact provides Black with his plan; he must use his two bishops in order to exchange White's best piece.

30 . . .   P×P
31 B×KBP   B–KN4!

Threatening 32 . . . B×B 33 P×B R–Q7+. If now 32 K–K3, then 32 . . . R–K1+ 33 K–B2 R×R 34 K×R B×B 35 P×B K–K3 followed by 36 . . . K–Q4 wins.

32 B×B   P×B
33 K–K3   K–B3
34 P–R4

Or 34 R–R1 K–K4 followed by . . . P–B5+ and Black's rook reaches Q7.

34 . . .   P×P
35 P×P   R–K1+
36 K–B2   R×R
37 K×R   K–K4
38 N–K2   B×N
39 K×B   K–B5

Although White has an outside passed pawn, the strong position of Black's king ensures the win.

| 40 P–B4 | K–N5 |
| 41 K–K3 | P–B5+! |

Not of course 41 ... K×P 42 K–B4 which would even win for White!

42 K–K4	P–B6
43 K–K3	K–N6
0–1	

In these two games and the other examples we have quoted, the two bishops proved so effective because they had open lines whereas the enemy knights lacked an operation base. It is only in these circumstances that we can talk about the advantage of the two bishops. Basically, therefore, the bishop pair is strong in positions where a single bishop is stronger than a knight. In other words the two bishops in themselves do not constitute a positional advantage but simply increase, in certain situations, the advantage of the single bishop versus the knight. We logically conclude from this that the bishops can no longer be viewed as an advantage in positions whose nature favours the knight rather than the bishop i.e. mainly blocked positions. However, in such cases the extra bishop helps by preventing the enemy king from using the otherwise weak squares of a certain colour. For example, the position in diagram 73 would be equal if we placed a white bishop on K3 and a black bishop on ... K2. The same applies to diagram 74 if we add a white bishop on K2 and a black bishop on ... Q3.

All this means that when we are facing the two bishops it is essential to block the position as much as possible and to secure strong points for our knight. Here is a good example of such play: 1 P–Q4 N–KB3 2 P–QB4 P–K3 3 N–KB3 P–Q4 4 N–B3 B–N5 5 Q–R4+ N–B3 6 N–K5 B–Q2 7 N×B Q×N 8 P–QR3 B×N+ 9 P×B P–K4 10 P–K3 0–0 11 B–Q3 R–K1 12 0–0 P–K5 13 B–B2 P×P 14 Q×BP N–Q4! 15 B–Q2 N–R4 16 Q–R4 Q×Q 17 B×Q P–QB3 (95)

The knights are just as strong as the bishops, one of them occupying a splendid post on ... Q4 whilst the other will play to ... QB5 after ... P–QN4. Moreover, Black can choose an even sharper continuation in this variation by 9 ... 0–0 (instead of 9 ... P–K4) 10 P–K3 P–QR3! 11 B–K2 P–QN4! 12 P×NP P×P 13 Q×P KR–N1 14 Q–Q3 N–R4 (96).

The active black knights along with the strong point on ... QB5 give Black sufficient compensation for his pawn. Our next game is also a good example of how powerless two bishops can be.

44 Kliavin–Ragozin

Riga 1952, Ruy Lopez

1 P–K4 P–K4 2 N–KB3 N–QB3 3 B–N5 P–QR3 4 B–R4 N–B3 5 0–0 B–K2 6 Q–K2 P–QN4 7 B–N3 P–Q3 8 P–B3 0–0 9 P–QR4 N–QR4 even better is 9 . . . P–N5 **10 B–B2 B–K3 11 P×P P×P 12 N–R3** White ought to play 12 P–Q4 B–B5 13 B–Q3 **12 . . . N–B5 13 P–QN3 N×N 14 B×N P–B4!** to prevent the opening of the game by 15 P–Q4 when 15 . . . P–N5! 16 P×KP R×B 17 R×R P×R 18 P×N B×BP gives Black a clear advantage **15 B–N2 P–B5 16 R×R** better is 16 P×P P×P 17 N–N5 Q–B2 18 N×B P×N 19 P–Q4 BP×Pep 20 B×P P–Q4 **16 . . . Q×R 17 R–R1 Q–N2 18 P–QN4 R–R1 19 P–Q4 R×R+**

20 B×R   B–N5!

Correctly evaluating that the two bishops have no meaning here, Black aims to eliminate the active white knight.

21 P–Q5?

A tactical mistake, after which there is no saving the game. It was essential to play 21 B–N2 Q–R1 22 B–N1 to prevent the entry of Black's queen down the QR-file.

21 . . .	**Q–R1**
22 B–N2	**B×N**
23 P×B	

Forced, as after 23 Q×B Q–R7 is decisive.

23 . . .	**N–R4**
24 B–B1	**Q–R8**
25 Q–K1	**B–N4!**
26 B–Q2	**Q×Q+**
27 B×Q	**B–B8!** (97)

This is a drastic example of how powerless the two bishops can be

when trapped behind their own blocked pawns. The game concluded: **28 B–Q1 N–B5 29 B–B2 P–B3 30 K–B1 K–B2 31 B–Q1 K–N3 32 B–B2 K–N4 33 B–N1 K–R5 34 B–B2 K–R6 35 K–N1 P–R3 36 B–N1 P–R4 37 B–B2 N–Q6 38 K–B1 K×P 39 K–K2 K–N7 40 B×N P×B+ 0–1.**

There are of course few examples of the bishop pair being so helpless, but we frequently meet situations in which two well-posted knights can neutralize two relatively good bishops. Consider our next position from Pachman–Louma, Prague 1943 (*98*).

20 R–QB1 QR–B1 21 R2–B2 B–K4 22 R–B5 B–N1 23 R×R R×R 24 R×R+ B×R 25 N–QB3 P–B4 26 N–Q5! K–B2 27 K–B2 B–Q2 28 P–KN3 ½–½ The centralized knights are just as strong as the bishops.

The following game is a much more complex example of the same theme.

45 Sokolsky–Kotov

Moscow 1949, Sicilian Defence

1 P–K4 P–QB4 2 N–KB3 P–Q3 3 B–N5+ N–QB3 4 0–0 P–QR3 better 4 ... N–B3 **5 B×N+ P×B 6 P–Q4 P×P 7 Q×P P–K4 8 Q–Q3 N–B3** (*99*). An extremely interesting variation. Black has two bishops and a strong pawn centre. Nevertheless he does not stand better, because White can advantageously post his knights to prevent the advance of Black's centre pawns.

9 R–Q1   B–K2
9 ... P–R3 would lose a tempo after 10 P–QN3 followed by 11 B–R3.
    10 B–N5   0–0
    11 QN–Q2
Not 11 N–R3? P–Q4 12 N×P Q–B2; or here 12 B×N B×B 13 P×P P–K5! 14 Q×KP B×P etc. In the game Szabo–Kotov, Budapest 1950, White chose a good alternative plan: 11 B×N P×B 12 N–R4 K–R1 13 N–Q2! B–N5 14 R–K1 P–Q4 15 N–B1 R–KN1 16 N–K3 B–K3 17 P–QB3 Q–R4 18 N4–B5 with good play for White because of the strong-point on KB5.
    11 ...   Q–B2

12 N–B4   R–Q1
13 N–K3   B–K3
14 P–B4 (*100*)

White's plan is now clear. He has prevented ... P–Q4, reduced Black's KB to passivity and practically rendered the two bishops harmless for a long time to come. In addition he can later play P–QB5 weakening Black's pawn structure.

    14 ...   QR–N1
    15 Q–B2   R–N2
    16 QR–B1   Q–N1
    17 P–QN3   P–R3
    18 B–R4   P–N4
A significant weakening of his K-side but after other moves such as 18 ... P–QR4 White would continue 19 P–B5! P–Q4 20 P×P P×P 21 B–N3.
    19 B–N3   N–Q2
The obvious 19 ... N–R4 fails to 20 P–B5! N×B 21 P×P B×QP 22 RP×N with clear advantage to White.
    20 P–KR4   P–B3
    21 N–K1
White plans to play this knight to Q3 in order to threaten P–QB5.
    21 ...   N–B4
    22 N–Q3!   Q–R2
If 22 ... N×KP 23 N×P! QP× N (*23 ... N×B 24 N×P Q–B2 25 N×R wins the exchange*) 24 Q×N B–B2 25 Q×BP is good for White.

23 N×N	Q×N
24 Q–K2!	

There is nothing much more to be accomplished on the Q-side but White has other weaknesses to attack on the K-side. His knight controls KB5 and his queen heads for KR5.

24 ...	B–KB1
25 Q–R5	K–R2

Not 25 ... B–B2 26 Q–B3 B–N2 27 N–N4.

26 N–N4

An inexactitude! White should play 26 Q–B3 at once, followed by 27 N–B5.

26 ...	B–N2
27 N–K3	

Only now does White realize that 27 P×P BP×P 28 B×P fails to 28 ... B×N. Meanwhile Black threatens 27 ... B–B2.

27 ...	P–R4
28 Q–B3	P–R5

Helping White's attack, as the loss of time entailed in recapturing the pawn will give White a chance to occupy the QN-file.

29 NP×P	R–QR1

After 29 ... R–N7 Sokolsky gives 30 R–N1 R1–QN1 31 R×R R×R 32 N–B5 B–KB1 33 N×QP! B×N 34 Q×P winning.

30 N–B5	B–KB1
31 R–N1	R–KB2
32 P–QR5!	R×P

If 32 ... K–N3 Sokolsky gives 33 P–R6 R×P 34 R–N8 R×P 35 R×P! B×R 36 R–KR8! winning.

33 R–N8	P–Q4
34 Q–R5	P–Q5

This is forced as can be seen from the following variations:

a. 34 ... Q×QBP 35 R×B!
b. 34 ... R×P 35 BP×P BP×P 36 KP×P B×P 37 R1×B! Q×R 38 R×B!
c. 34 ... P×KP (or *34 ... P×BP*) 35 N×P! transposing to the game position.

35 R1–N1	R–Q2

This hastens defeat but there was no real defence to White's strong threats.

36 N×RP!	B×N
37 R–KR8+!	K×R
38 Q×B+	R–KR2
39 Q×BP+	R–KN2
40 R–N7	1–0

5 The Rooks

This chapter is one of the most comprehensive and at the same time one of the most important in the whole volume, not only because the rook, after the queen, is the strongest piece on the board, but also because its way of moving stamps it as a piece whose handling requires the greatest knowledge of strategy. If we examine the way that beginners play, it is clear that most of them operate solely with the queen and minor pieces. Often the rooks remain on their original square and take no part in the action. It is easy to understand why this is so. The rooks are the most difficult pieces to bring into the game and beginners often fail in this task which calls for carefully planned pawn advances, well-chosen exchanges, timely castling, etc.

We divide this chapter into five sections:

The creation and significance of open lines.
The use of open lines in attacking the king.
The use of open lines in the centre and on the Q-side.
The seventh and eighth ranks.
Active rooks in front of the pawn chain.

THE CREATION AND SIGNIFICANCE OF OPEN LINES

In contrast to the minor pieces, much greater preparation is required in order to bring the rook into play. The knight can be developed without any preparatory pawn moves, and the bishop only needs one pawn move (1 P–K4, 1 P–Q4, 1 P–QN3 or 1 P–KN3) before it can come out. However, the rook cannot show its full power after a single pawn move. For example, after 1 P–R4 on either wing the rook's action is not increased overmuch, as the RP stands in the way. The rook's vertical movement requires files that have been cleared of pawns, especially its own. This can happen in a variety of ways, as the following simple examples make clear.

Line-opening by pawn exchanges, especially in the centre

1 P–K4 P–K3 2 P–Q4 P–Q4 3 P×P P×P (*101*)

101
W

Both sides have an open file.
Or **1 P–K4 P–QB4 2 N–KB3 N–QB3 3 P–Q4 P×P 4 N×P** (*102*)

102
B

White has the open Q-file and Black the QB-file.

Line-opening by exchange of pieces protected by pawns (doubling of pawns)

1 P–K4 P–K4 2 N–KB3 N–QB3 3 B–B4 B–B4 4 N–B3 N–B3 5 P–Q3 P–Q3 6 B–K3. Now if **6 ... B×B 7 P×B** White has the open KB-file, but Black has better in **6 ... B–N3**

when **7 B×B RP×B** (*103*) gives him an open QR-file.

103
W

Or consider the position arising after **1 P–K4 P–QB3 2 P–Q4 P–Q4 3 N–QB3 P×P 4 N×P N–B3 5 N×N+** (*104*)

104
B

Black has the choice between opening the K-file by **5 ... KP×N** or the KN-file by **5 ... NP×N**. In both cases the result is one open file for White and two for Black. However, we must point out that the significance of open lines must not be exaggerated. Because Black has two open files in this case, it would be completely wrong to conclude that he has better prospects as a result. The position must be judged as a whole, with open files being viewed as one important factor which is variable according to the specific use which can be made of them.

Line-opening by a pawn advance against the enemy pawn chain

1 P–Q4 N–KB3 2 P–QB4 P–KN3 3 N–QB3 P–Q4 4 P×P N×P 5 P–K4 N×N 6 P×N B–N2 7 B–QB4 0–0 8 N–K2 P–N3 9 P–KR4!? (*105*)

105
B

White plans to open the KR-file by P–R5×NP.

Or **1 P–K4 P–K4 2 N–KB3 N–QB3 3 B–B4 B–B4 4 P–Q3 P–Q3 5 N–B3 N–B3 6 B–K3 B–N3 7 Q–Q2 0–0 8 0–0–0 P–KR3? 9 P–KR3!** (*106*)

106
B

This prepares P–KN4–N5 opening the KN-file against the enemy king.

Line-opening by combinational means

107
W

From the diagram position (*107*), Geller–Spassky, both sides strive to open lines against the enemy king, sacrificial play being essential to break through the opposing pawn chain. **22 P–N6 P–N6 23 BP×P QRP×P 24 R–QB1** if 24 RP×P R–R8+! 25 K×R Q–B7 and the open QR-file brings an immediate decision **24 ... NP×P+ 25 K–R1 Q–Q2 26 P×BP+** if 26 P×RP+ K×P 27 B–B1 R–KN1 28 Q–N6+ K–R1 **26 ... K–B1!** note that here and on White's 25th move, both kings use the enemy pawn as protection from the attack of the major pieces down the file **27 R.N1–Q1 R.Q1–QB1 28 R×R+ Q×R 29 Q–N3** if 29 N×QP N–B4! 30 Q–N3 Q–N5! wins **29 ... Q–B7 30 R–K1 K×P 31 N×QP+ K–N1 32 P–R6 Q–Q7 33 P–B4 KP×P 34 Q–QB3 Q×N 35 Q–QN3 B–B1 36 R–Q1 R–N1 0–1.**

This example shows how difficult it can be to open up lines effectively when the enemy pawns are on their original squares. The reader will see many more examples of line-opening in the remaining sections of this chapter.

Most text-books distinguish between two types of file, those on which no pawns are placed and those on which only enemy pawns are to be found. In the first case they talk of open files, and in the second case they usually refer to half-open files. We do not intend to differentiate in this way, as the distinction seems artificial. The significance of open lines lies in the fact that they offer active play to the major pieces. Only one's own pawns present an absolute barrier to these pieces which often exert against enemy pawns a pressure which is a much more important factor than mere occupation of the file. On the other hand, there is no doubt that a well-protected enemy pawn which blocks a file is a great obstacle to our using this. However, in most cases we can remove this obstacle, as seen in our next example of a basic pawn structure (*108*).

108

Black's QBP, guarded by the QNP, blocks the open QB-file but can soon be removed by preparing P–QN5 or P–Q5. In the same way the KB-file can be cleared by preparing P–KN5.

An enemy piece may also reduce the value of a file, as in the following diagram (*109*).

Black's knight is just as effective as a pawn in blocking the open QB-file. It is therefore illogical to talk

109

of an open file in one case and of a half-open file in another.

We can treat as special cases those occasions when a protected enemy pawn is not easy to remove from the open file, as in our next example taken from *My System* by Nimzowitsch (*110*).

110
W

To quote Nimzowitsch: 'If White now proceeded to attack Black's QP by R–Q2 and R1–Q1, not only the reader but the QP itself would deride him. Let us then stick to the rule that we should first undermine the QP by preparing P–K5 ... If this attempt fails, we begin to look round for some other operation base but are wholly wrong in so doing, for the Q-file can indeed be exploited in this position. The key is **1 N–Q5** utilizing the Q5 square. We term this an outpost by which we mean a piece, usually a knight, established on an open file in enemy territory and protected by a pawn. This knight, guarded and supported as it is, exerts uncomfortable pressure because of its increased range of action. If Black then drives it away by ... P–QB3, he will weaken his position on the Q-file.'

This definition lucidly presents a most important strategic idea. Nimzowitsch also uses the same terminology for positions like the one in our next diagram (*111*), taken from *My System*, p. 24.

111
W

White plays **1 R–N6!** exploiting the fact that Black dare not exchange rooks (1 ... R×R 2 RP×R with a strong protected passed pawn) in order to double rooks on the KN-file. As Nimzowitsch points out, 1 N–N6 leads to nothing because of the knight's limited activity on the side of the board.

However, I consider the use of the word 'outpost' in this case to be unsuitable, along with the explanation given. From the point of view of utilizing an open file by occupying a certain square (here White's KN6) then doubling rooks, this can be applied just as logically to a central file. To place a knight on this square would not achieve the same result as in diagram 110, as it is not a case of provoking a weakening

move which will help us to exploit the open file. In other words, if a knight were to be posted on this square, it would not matter whether the KN-file were open or, for example, a white pawn stood on KN4. It seems better to refer to KN6 in diagram 111 as a 'strongpoint' i.e. a square on an open file protected by pawns and allowing the doubling of rooks.

Let us now examine a few games which illustrate the points arising from the last two instructive examples.

46 Botvinnik–Lilienthal

Moscow 1936, Réti System

1 N–KB3 N–KB3 2 P–B4 P–QN3 3 P–KN3 B–N2 4 B–N2 P–B4 5 0–0 P–N3 6 P–Q4 P×P 7 N×P B×B 8 K×B B–N2 9 N–QB3 0–0? correct was 9 ... Q–B1 10 P–N3 Q–N2+ 11 P–B3 P–Q4 **10 P–K4! N–B3 11 B–K3 Q–B1 12 P–N3 Q–N2 13 P–B3 KR–Q1 14 R–B1 QR–B1 15 Q–Q2 P–QR3 16 KR–Q1 N×N 17 B×N P–Q3** if 17 ... P–QN4 18 P×P P×P 19 B×N B×B 20 N–Q5 **18 P–QR4!** it is vital to prevent the freeing move ... P–QN4 **18 ... N–K1 19 N–Q5!**

White occupies this important outpost with gain of tempo, attacking Black's QNP.

19 ...	**R–B3**
20 B×B	**N×B**
21 P–R4!	

A characteristic move in such positions. White prepares to open the KR-file by advancing this pawn, should Black try to eliminate White's strong knight with ... N–K3–B2. This K-side activity is therefore closely linked with the possession of an outpost on Q5.

21 ...	R–K1
22 R–B3	N–R4
23 Q–Q4 (*112*)	

The white knight dominates the board. If Black tries to drive it away by 23 ... P–K3 then 24 N–K3, with the threat of 25 N–N4, forces 24 ... P–K4 weakening the QP and giving White complete control of Q5. Black's best defence is 23 ... N–B3! when 24 N×N+ P×N 25 Q×BP? fails to 25 ... P–Q4 with counterchances. White can still keep the better game by playing 24 R1–QB1 N×N 25 BP×N R×R 26 Q×R, or here 25 KP×N R–B4 26 P–QN4 R–B2 27 P–KR5. More forceful freeing moves lead to a lost endgame.

23 ...	P–QN4?
24 BP×P	P×P
25 R1–QB1!	

White decisively takes over the QB-file. It is interesting to note that his powerful knight is instrumental in allowing him this, as 25 ... R1–QB1?? loses to 26 R×R R×R 27 R×R Q×R 28 N×P+.

25 ...	R×R
26 R×R	P×P
27 R–B7	Q–N4
28 P×P!	

This is much more exact than 28 N×P+ R×N 29 R×R P×P etc.

28 ...	Q–K7+

29 Q–B2	Q×Q+
30 K×Q	P–K3

White's passed pawn now wins the game easily for him, as follows: **31 N–N6 N–B3 32 P–QR5 R–N1 33 R–B8+! R×R 34 N×R N–K1 35 P–R6 N–B2 36 P–R7 N–R1 37 N×P K–B1 38 P–K5 K–K2 39 K–K3 P–B3 40 K–B4 P–R3 41 N–B8+ K–B2 if 41 ... K–Q2 42 P×P! 42 K–K4 K–N2 43 K–Q4 N–B2 44 K–B5 1–0.**

Fischer–Reshevsky, US Ch 1962–3 (*113*). White has an open file on which there is even a weak black pawn. Nevertheless, Black would have few worries if he could play 13 ... B–K3 followed by ... Q–B2 and ... R–Q1. The game continued: **13 B–N4! B×B** 13 ... Q–K2 is better **14 P×B Q–B1 15 Q–Q1! N–Q5?** and here Black ought to try 15 ... Q–K3 followed by ... 0–0–0 **16 P–QB3 N×N 17 P×N Q–K3 18 R–QR5 P–B3 19 Q–Q5! Q×Q 20 R×Q K–Q2 21 P×P B×P 22 P–N5 B–K2 23 K–K2** White now has a clear advantage. He can begin positional manoeuvring to exploit his pressure on the open KR-and Q-files, whereas Black can find no points to attack. It is instructive to see how Fischer sets about his task: **23 ... QR–KB1 24 B–K3 R–B1 25**

P–N4 P–N4 creating another weakness, his QRP, and giving White three points of attack, but otherwise White plays K–Q3 followed by P–QB4 and P–N5 **26 R5–Q1 K–K3 27 R–R1 R–B3 28 R–KR3!** we can now see the significance of open files. White threatens to double rooks on the KR-file, winning the RP. He can switch from one weakness to the other, whilst tying Black down to passive defence **28 ... B–B1 29 R1–R1 R–B2 30 R–R4!** all at once Black has run out of waiting moves, since any move of his rook on QB2 along the rank loses his QRP after 31 R–R1 **30 ... P–Q4 31 R–R1! R–B3 32 P×P+ K×P 33 R–Q1+ K–K3 34 R–Q8 K–B4 35 R–R8 R–K3 36 R–R3** decisive, for the threat is 37 R–B3+, and after 36 ... K–K5 37 R–B3 White's rook penetrates to KB7 **36 ... B–N2 37 R×R B×R 38 R×P R–K1 39 R–KB7+ K–N5 40 P–B3+ K–N6 41 K–Q3?** 41 K–B1! and 42 B–B2+ wins at once **41 ... P–K5+ 42 P×P R–Q1+ 43 B–Q4 K–N5 44 R–B1 B–K4 45 K–K3 B–B2 46 R–KN1+ K–R5 47 K–B3 R–Q2 48 P–K5 R–B2+ 49 K–K4 R–B4 50 P–K6 B–Q1 51 B–B6! B×B 52 P×B R×P 53 K–Q5 R–B7 54 R–K1 1–0.**

My opponent committed an instructive error in the following position; Stahlberg–Pachman, Amsterdam Olympiad 1954 (*114*).

21 P–K5?	**N–Q4**
22 B×B+	**K×B**
23 N×N	**BP×N**
24 Q–N5	**R–B3**
25 P–N3	**Q–B2**
26 P–R5	**K–N1!**

Care is required, since after 26 ... R–B1? 27 P×P R×P 28 Q–Q3+ and 29 P–N5, or here 27 ... Q× NP 28 Q×Q R×Q 29 P–N5,

Black's rook is trapped on QN3, giving White a win in both cases.

27 P×P	**R×P**
28 Q–R5	**R–B3**
29 Q×Q	

If the queen retreats, Black plays 29 ... R–B5 and 30 ... Q–N3 winning easily.

29 ...	**R×Q**

Despite the simplification and balanced material, this position must be viewed as a win for Black. This is due to the slight difference in the respective placing of the Q-side pawns. If White's pawn were on QN2 or Black's on QN4, the game would be drawn! However, Black has a strong-point on his QB5, whereas White cannot exploit his own QB5, as the following variation shows: 30 KR–B1 R1–B1 31 R–B5 P–QN3! and 32 R–N5 places the white rook in the same trapped position that we mentioned in our note to move 26. As he cannot avoid the loss of a pawn, White now makes a desperate attempt at counter-play, but 30 KR–Q1 R–B5 followed by ... R–R1–R5 would be equally hopeless for him.

30 R–R1	**R–B5**
31 KR–Q1	**R1–B1!**

It is more important to maintain control of the QB-file than to capture the pawn at once, as the latter will not run away. The game ended: **32**

R.Q1–QN1 R×QP 33 R–R7 R–N1 34 P–N5 R–K5 35 R–QB1 P–Q5 36 R–Q1 R×P 37 R×QP R×P 38 R–Q7 P–N4 39 K–N2 P–R4 40 R–B7 K–N2 41 R–R4 K–N3 42 P–R4 P–N5 43 R–R7 R–N7 44 R–K7 and White resigned without waiting for a reply.

To conclude this section, we give a highly instructive position (*115*) culled from Euwe's *Strategy and Tactics in Chess*.

115
W

Material is even, yet White can obtain a decisive advantage by opening the QR-file: **1 P–QR4!** **K–Q2** this is the only way to hold the file, since 1 . . . R–QN1 2 P×P P×P 3 R–R7 would give White all the advantages, even though the win still requires exact play **2 R–R2!** an important tactical point is that it is best to double on the file before opening it, and in fact White achieves nothing with the immediate 2 P×P P×P. Dr Euwe now gives two main lines:

A 2 . . . K–B2 3 R1–QR1 K–N2 4 K–B3 P–B3 Black would have slightly better defensive chances by transposing to variation B with 4 . . . P×P **5 P–K4 KR–Q1** if 5 . . . QP× P+ 6 K×P White threatens 7 P×P P×P 8 R×R R×R 9 R×R K×R 10 P–B4 and 10 P–Q5 winning **6 RP×P RP×P 7 R×R R×R 8**

R×R K×R 9 P×P P×P 10 K–B4 P–N3 11 P–N4 P–R3 12 P–R4 K–N2 13 P–R5 and White wins easily.

B 2 . . . P×P 3 R×P K–B2 4 R1–QR1 K–N2 5 R–R5 KR–QB1 6 K–B3 R–Q1 7 P–K4 P×P+ 8 K×P R.Q1–QB1 9 R–K5 R–B3 10 R1–R5 R1–QB1 11 P–Q5! P×P+ **12 R.R5×QP R3–B2 13 K–Q4 K–N3** preventing R–QB5 **14 P–B4 R–B3 15 P–N3 R1–B2 16 P–R4 R–B1** or 16 . . . R–N3 17 R–KN5 R×R 18 R×R P–N3 19 R–Q5 **17 P–R5 R1–B2 18 P–N5 P×P 19 R×P+ K–R3 20 R.K5– QB5** and White wins by capturing the QBP.

In the first variation White exploited his pressure down the QR-file by forcing the black pieces into passive positions then penetrating with his king. In the second variation Black's pieces were again driven to passive positions in order to defend the weak QRP, then White used the open file as a spring-board to establish his rooks on the fifth rank and finally win the QBP.

THE USE OF OPEN LINES IN ATTACKING THE KING

From a strategic point of view, line-opening is the simplest method of attacking the enemy king, as the rooks are the most effective pieces in such attacks. Pawns are used to open the files, as the following relatively simple example illustrates.

47 Pachman–Runza

Czechoslovak Ch 1946, Ruy Lopez

1 P–K4 N–QB3 2 N–KB3 P–K4 3 B–N5 P–QR3 4 B–R4 N–B3 5 O–O B–K2 6 R–K1 P–QN4 7 B–N3 P–Q3 8 P–B3 N–QR4 9 B–B2 P–B4

10 P–Q4 Q–B2 11 P–KR3 N–B3 12 QN–Q2 B–Q2? a weak move and loss of time, after which Black can no longer deploy his forces successfully 13 P×BP P×P 14 N–B1 R–Q1 15 Q–K2 P–R3 to avoid the line 15 ... B–K3 16 N–K3 followed by 17 N–N5 **16 N–K3 B–K3 17 P–QR4!** after the immediate 17 N–B5 B–B5 is awkward **17 ... P–B5 18 P×P P×P 19 N–B5 0–0** (*116*) there were better defensive chances with ... B–KB1 followed by ... P–N3 and ... B–N2.

20 P–KN4

The beginning of a typical attack in which White intends to open the KN-file after K–R2, R–KN1 and P–KN5. Black tries to prevent this by guarding his KN4 square with pieces, but this only leads to the opening of the KR-file which is equally dangerous.

20 ...   N–KR2
21 P–R4   R–R1
22 R–N1

The exchange of rooks would also have been advantageous, but White wishes to use his QR for the K-side attack. This move does not involve loss of time, for Black has to move his KR to free the KB1 square.

22 ...   KR–Q1
23 K–N2

The final preparation for the attack. Black's counter-action comes a move too late.

23 ...   P–N5
24 P–N5!

Utilizing the fact that Black cannot reply ... P–R4 because his QBP is weak e.g. 24 ... P–N6 25 B–Q1 P–R4 26 N–Q2 P–KN3 27 N–R6+ K–N2 28 N×QBP N–Q5 29 P×N B×N 30 Q–B3 R×P 31 B×P B×B 32 Q×B B–N5 33 R–Q1 and 33 ... R×P fails to 34 Q–Q5. If Black had not played 23 ... P–N5, White would have had to prepare P–KN5, otherwise the reply ... P–R4 would keep the files blocked on the K-side.

24 ...   RP×P?

There were more chances for Black in the line given in the previous note. The text-move loses quickly.

25 N3×NP

A surprising move, as one would have expected the capture with the pawn. However, this move is much stronger, since it opens the way for White's queen to join in the attack. Black is forced to exchange the knight on KN5, otherwise 25 N.N5 ×B and 26 Q×P follows.

25 ...   N×N
26 P×N   P–N6 (*117*)

27 Q–R5!

White can seize the open KR-file

without loss of time, as 27 ... P×B loses to 28 R–KR1 P–B3 29 Q–R8+ K–B2 30 P–N6+! etc.

27 ...   P–N3
28 Q–R4   P–B3

Again the only move. Black hopes to escape after 29 R–KR1? K–B2.

29 B–Q1!

Preventing the black king's escape. If now 29 ... K–B2 30 Q–R7+ K–K1 31 N–N7+ followed by 32 N×B and 33 B–N4+ wins. Or 29 ... P×P 30 Q–R6! wins e.g. 30 ... P×N 31 Q×B+ K–N2 32 P×P B–B3 33 B×KNP! etc. The exchange sacrifice 29 ... R×B is also unavailing after 30 R×R P×N 31 R–KR1 K–B2 32 P–N6+; or here 31 ... K–B1 32 NP×P etc.

29 ...   P×N?
30 R–KR1   K–B2
31 B–R5+   K–B1

Only now does Black realize that 31 ... K–N2 32 B–K8!! gives mate in three moves.

32 B–N6   B–B4
33 NP×P   1–0

48 Korchnoi–Fischer

Herceg Novi 1970, King's Indian Defence

1 P–Q4 N–KB3 2 P–QB4 P–KN3 3 N–QB3 B–N2 4 P–K4 P–Q3 5 B–K2 0–0 6 N–B3 P–K4 7 0–0 N–B3 8 P–Q5 N–K2 9 N–Q2 P–B4

10 P–QR3

White intends to open the QN-file by P–QN4 and he has no better plan at his disposal. However, experience tells us that White's chances on the Q-side are no greater than Black's counter-chances on the other wing.

10 ...   N–K1

Black can also simplify on the Q-side by 10 ... P–QR4 11 R–N1 N–K1 12 P–QN4 RP×P 13 P×P P–N3 14 Q–N3 P–B4 15 NP×P NP×P etc., with a probable draw, but such a peaceful set-up is hardly to the liking of the World Champion.

11 P–QN4   P–N3
12 R–N1   P–B4
13 P–B3

There is no need to hurry with this move. As long as it is not played, Black's ... P–KB5 is bad because White can exchange Black's 'good' bishop e.g. 13 NP×P NP×P 14 R–N3 P–B5? 15 B–N4 with a good game. Black can of course first play ... N–KB3 but then ... R–B3–KN3, as in the game, will not be possible.

13 ...   P–B5!

Very strong here. Opening the KB-file by ... P×KP gives Black nothing, so he plans to use the KN-file as the basis for his attack.

14 P–QR4

Too slow. White should open the QN-file at once.

14 ...   P–KN4!
15 P–R5   R–B3!
16 NP×P?

And this is completely illogical, simply leaving a weak QRP on the board. White still has equalizing chances with 16 RP×P RP×P 17 P×P NP×P 18 Q–N3 followed by Q–N6.

16 ...   NP×P
17 N–N3   R–N3
18 B–Q2   N–KB3
19 R–R1 *(118)*

In order to continue with a later P–R6 and at the same time freeing his knight on QN3 from the defence of the QRP.

19 ...   P–N5
20 P×P   N×NP
21 R–B3   R–R3!

The rook forces a weakening of White's castled position then returns to its natural post on KN3.

118
B

22 P–R3	N–KB3
23 R–N1	N–N3
24 B–K1	N–R1!

An excellent manoeuvre to bring the knight to ... KN4 where it will strongly threaten White's position. Instead, 24·... N–R5 25 B×N R×B would give Black two bishops but make White's task easier.

25 R–Q3	N–B2
26 B–B3	N–N4
27 Q–K2	

It is difficult to find anything better. Black is threatening to win a pawn by 27 ... B–R3, and 27 P–R4 fails to 27...N×B+ 28 P×N N–R4! followed by ... N–N6.

| 27 ... | R–N3 |
| 28 K–B1? | |

This loses at once, but White's king is in just as hopeless a position after 28 K–R2 e.g. 28 ... Q–Q2 29 Q–B1 P–R4! threatening ... N–N5+.

28 ...	N×RP!
29 P×N	B×P+
30 K–B2	N–N5+
31 B×N	B×B
0–1	

32 ... Q–R5+ leads to a quick mate.

49 Barcza–Filip

Bucharest 1953, Sicilian Defence

1 P–K4 P–QB4 2 N–KB3 P–Q3 3 P–Q4 P×P 4 N×P N–KB3 5 N–QB3 P–KN3 6 B–K3 B–N2 7 P–B3 0–0 8 N–N3 8 Q–Q2 is better 8 ... N–B3 9 Q–Q2 B–K3 10 N–Q5 B×N 11 P×B N–K4 12 0–0–0? He should play 12 B–K2 followed by 0–0. After 12 P–QB4 Filip gives 12 ... R–B1 13 R–B1 P–QN4! 14 P×P R×R+ 15 N×R Q–R1. 12 ... Q–B2 13 K–N1 KR–B1!(*119*)

119
W

The correct rook, as the QR will later be required on the open file. It is often a very difficult tactical problem to know which rook should occupy an open file. Before making our decision we must carefully examine all future possibilities. Black now threatens the piece sacrifice 14 ... N×QP! 15 Q×N Q×P+ 16 K–R1 N–Q6. So White must play P–B3, if he wishes to avoid the passive R–B1, and this gives Black a chance to open another line onto the king.

14 P–B3	P–QR4
15 N–Q4	N–B5
16 B×N	Q×B
17 N–B2	P–QN4!
18 Q–Q3?	

This loses very quickly. White had better prospects of a successful defence by 18 N–R3 Q–QR5 19 Q–QB2 reducing Black's attacking chances by exchanging queens.

18 ...	Q–B2!
19 KR–K1	

If 19 Q×QNP QR–N1 20 Q–B6 Q–Q1 Black soon wins by pressure down the open lines.

19 ...	P–N5!
20 B–Q4	

If 20 P×P Black replies 20 ... N×P!

20 ...	P×P
21 B×P	QR–N1
22 K–R1	

White's bishop now blocks the open lines in place of the QBP, but Black will soon remove this obstacle as well.

22 ...	N×P!
23 B×B	K×B
24 Q×N	Q×N
25 Q–Q2	P–K4! *(120)*

120
W

Preventing check by Q–Q4, so threatening 26 ... R×P.

26 P–QN3	P–R5!

Opening the QN-file completely. White could already resign.

27 P×P?	R–N7?

There was an immediate win by 27 ... R–N8+

28 Q×Q	R1×Q
29 R×QP	R×RP+
30 K–N1	R.B7–N7+
0–1	

The above game is particularly noteworthy for the way that Black exploited the open lines, culminating in penetration to the seventh rank on which the two rooks were doubled. This is a very important strategic goal when the heavy pieces have occupied an open file, as we shall see in our later examples of using lines in the centre and on the Q-side.

White produced a similar result in the following game which is all the more instructive because the attack is not carried out until after the exchange of queens, with much less material on the board.

50 Botvinnik–Vidmar

Groningen 1946, Catalan System

1 P–Q4 P–Q4 2 N–KB3 N–KB3 3 P–B4 P–K3 4 P–KN3 P×P 5 Q–R4+ Q–Q2 6 Q×BP Q–B3 7 QN–Q2 Q×Q 8 N×Q B–N5+? 8 ... B–K2 or 8 ... P–B4 is better 9 B–Q2 B×B+ 10 N3×B! N–B3 11 P–K3 N–QN5 12 K–K2 B–Q2 13 B–N2 B–B3 14 P–B3 N–Q2 15 P–QR3 N–Q4 16 P–K4 N4–N3 17 N–R5 B–N4+ 18 K–K3 0–0–0! *(121)* Black's only weaknesses, QN2 and QB2, lie on the Q-side, so his king is an important defensive piece (see the chapter 'The King').

121
W

19 KR–QB1!
Once again the correct rook. White intends to attack on the Q-side, so his QR will be needed to support the advance of his QRP.

19 ...   N–N1

In order to exchange White's powerful knight on QR5.

20 P–N3   B–Q2

Not of course 20 ... N–B3? 21 P–QR4 N×N 22 P×B winning a piece.

21 B–B1   N–B3
22 N×N   B×N
23 P–QR4   B–K1!

Another vital retreat, as White was threatening to push his pawn to QR6, weakening the black pawns and opening the QR-file.

24 P–R5   N–R1!

Stronger than 24 ... N–Q2 after which Botvinnik gives 25 P–R6 P–QN3 26 R–B3 K–N1 27 R1–B1 R–QB1 28 N–B4 (threatening N–Q6!) 28 ... R–Q1 29 N–R3 R–QB1 30 N–N5 winning.

25 P–R6   P–QN3
26 P–QN4   K–N1
27 R–B3

Nothing is gained by 27 P–N5 P–QB3! 28 P×P R–Q3 29 B–N5 N–B2 30 P–K5 R–Q1 31 B–B1 N–Q4+ and 32 ... R–QB1.

27 ...   P–QB3
28 R1–B1   P–B3

To prevent the white knight reaching K5.

29 N–N1   B–Q2
30 N–R3   N–B2

After 30 ... P–QN4 White's knight would proceed to QB5 with decisive effect.

31 P–N5!

A typical pawn sacrifice to clear the file for the rook to penetrate to the seventh rank.

31 ...   N×P
32 B×N   P×B
33 R–B7   R–QB1

Black must prevent the doubling of White's rooks on the seventh rank, but the best way of doing so is 33 ... B–B1 34 N×P B×P 35 N×P

B–N2 36 N–N5 with a clear advantage to White. A pretty exchange sacrifice now brings about the decision.

34 R–N7+   K–R1 (122)

122
W

35 R×B!

A characteristic set-up with the dominant rook on the seventh more than outweighing the loss of the exchange.

35 ...   R×R
36 N×P   R1–QB1

The threat was 37 R×RP+ K–N1 38 R–N7+ K–R1 39 N–B7+, but now the black rooks are tied to the QB-file.

37 R×NP   P–R3
38 R×P+   K–N1
39 R–QN7+   K–R1
40 R–QR7+   K–N1
41 R–QN7+   K–R1
42 P–N4   P–K4

Otherwise White wins by creating a passed pawn on the K-side.

The game ended: 43 P–Q5 R8–B4 44 R–QR7+ K–N1 45 R–QN7+ K–R1 46 R×P R–QN1 47 R×R+ K×R 48 P–R7+ K–N2 49 N–Q6+ K×P 50 N–K8 K–N3 51 N×P R–B6+ 52 K–B2 R–B2 53 P–R4 R–B2 54 N–R5 K–B2 55 P–N5! P×P 56 P×P R–R2 57 N–B6 R–R7+ 58 K–N3 R–R1 59 P–N6 1–0.

THE USE OF OPEN LINES IN THE
CENTRE AND ON THE Q-SIDE

More difficult strategic problems
arise when we try to exploit open
lines on the Q-side and in the centre.
Our aims may be summarized as
follows:

a. Penetration of the rook into the
   enemy position, especially the
   seventh and eighth ranks.
b. Winning a pawn by pressure
   down a file.
c. Restricting the mobility of the
   enemy pieces.

Rather than try to formulate
abstract rules, let us illustrate the
above aims with practical examples.

51 Stahlberg–Taimanov

Candidates 1953, Queen's Indian
Defence

**1 P–Q4 N–KB3 2 P–QB4 P–K3
3 N–KB3 P–QN3 4 P–KN3 B–R3
5 Q–R4 B–K2 6 B–N2 0–0 7 N–B3
P–B3 8 N–K5** better 8 B–B4 P–Q3
9 0–0 as in Guimard–Rossetto,
Argentine Ch 1953 **8 ... Q–K1 9
0–0 P–Q4 10 R–K1?** 10 P×P
BP×P 11 Q×Q with equality
10 ...   P–QN4!

Black forces open the QB-file
under favourable circumstances and
soon makes his presence felt on the
Q-side.

**11 P×NP   P×P
12 Q–Q1**

More active was 12 Q–N3.

**12 ...   P–N5
13 N–N1**

A time-consuming manoeuvre to
play the knight to KB3. 13 N–QR4
N–B3 14 N×N Q×N 15 B–K3
was slightly better.

**13 ...   N–B3
14 N×N   Q×N**

15 N–Q2   Q–N3

Preventing 16 P–K4, White's
only freeing plan.

**16 P–K3   QR–B1
17 B–B1   R–B3**

Black completes his domination
of the open file and soon places
White in a strait jacket.

**18 B×B   Q×B
19 N–B3   R1–B1
20 Q–N3   N–K5
21 N–Q2   R–B7!**

Black would also have good winning chances after 21 ... R×B 22
R.K1×R R×R+ 23 R×R N×N,
with two pieces for a rook. However,
this would give White some chances
on the open file, so the text-move is
the correct and logical way to
proceed.

**22 N×N   P×N
23 P–QR3   P–R4
24 P–Q5   R1–B5!** (*123*)

123
W

The black rooks have taken up
typically instructive positions. One
is on the seventh rank, preventing
the development of White's bishop,
and the other is played to shut out
the white queen. White's game is
already hopeless e.g. 25 QP×P
Q×KP 26 K–N2 (the threat was
... R×B!) 26 ... P–R5 etc.

The continuation was **25 R–Q1
KP×P 26 B–Q2 Q–KB3 27 QR–
N1 P–R5 28 Q–R4 Q–B4 29 Q×RP**

B–B1 30 Q–N8 P–N4 31 NP×P KNP×P 32 Q–B4 Q×Q 33 P×Q P–Q5 34 P–N3 R–B3 35 P×P P–B4 36 P–R3 R–QR3! 37 R.N1–B1 R×R 38 R×R R–R7 39 B–K1 R–N7 40 K–N2 R×NP 41 R–B8 R–N8 42 B–Q2 P–K6 0–1.

52 Pachman–L. Steiner

Budapest 1948, Queen's Gambit

1 P–Q4 P–Q4 2 N–KB3 N–KB3 3 P–B4 P–K3 4 B–N5 B–K2 5 N–B3 P–KR3 6 B–R4 0–0 7 P–K3 P–QN3 8 P×P P×P 8 ... N×P is better and more usual **9 N–K5 B–N2** not 9 ... B–K3 10 B–QN5 **10 R–B1** it would be more exact to play 10 B–K2 N3–Q2 11 B×B Q×B 12 N–Q3! **10 ... QN–Q2 11 N×N** not 11 P–B4 N×N 12 QP×N N–K5, or here 12 BP×N N–Q2 13 B×B Q×B 14 N–N5 Q–R5+! **11 ... Q×N 12 B–Q3 P–R3?** a faulty plan; better was 12 ... N–K5 or 12 ... P–B4 13 Q–B2! and White's advantage is problematical

**13 0–0   Q–K3
14 Q–N3!**

Black's last two moves indicate that he intends to remain passive on the Q-side and prepare ... P–KB4. White's chances lie on the QB-file, so this move both prepares to double the rooks on the open file and at the same time prevents ... P–QB4 which Black could suddenly decide to play.

**14 ...   QR–Q1
15 B–N3   B–Q3
16 N–K2   N–K1**

Black cannot play 16 ... N–K5 because of 17 B×N P×B 18 Q×Q P×Q 19 B×B P×B 20 N–B4 e.g. 20 ... KR–K1 21 R–B7 followed by 22 N–R5.

**17 R–B3   B×B
18 RP×B!**

After 18 N×B P–KB4 19 Q–B2 P–N3 then ... R–Q2–KB2, Black would have some attacking chances.

18 ...   P–KN4

Denying the white knight use of KB4 and preparing a K-side pawn advance. However, Black's KB4 is weakened, allowing White a decisive break-through.

19 Q–B2   P–KB4 (124)

At first sight Black's position seems solid enough, with his only serious weakness at QB2 well protected. Nevertheless, White manages to capture the QBP by means of a tactical stroke on the K-side.

20 P–KN4!   P×P

The pawn has to be accepted, as 20 ... P–B5? fails to 21 P×P P×P 22 B–B5 winning a pawn.

21 N–N3   N–N2

We now see the point of White's 20th move. Black must surrender his QBP, for if 21 ... B–B1 then 22 B–N6 follows, and if 21 ... P–B3 22 B–B5 and 23 B×P would gravely weaken Black's K-side.

**22 R×P   R–B1
23 R×R   R×R**

The capture of Black's QBP has created significant weaknesses in his position. His occupation of the QB-file is only temporary, as the rook will soon be forced to defend the K-side.

| 24 Q–K2 | P–KR4 |
| 25 B–N1! | |

Not of course 25 B×P? B×B 26 Q×B R–B7 when Black's rook on the seventh rank would be worth far more than the pawn sacrificed.

| 25 ... | R–B1! |

Forced! If 25 ... P–R5 26 Q–Q3! Q–R3 27 N–B5 N×N 28 Q×N P–N6 29 Q–K5 P×P+ 30 R×P, or 25 ... Q–R3 26 N–B5 N×N 27 B×N R–B1 28 B–Q3 P–R4 29 R–B1, with decisive advantage to White in both cases.

After the text-move White's queen uses the open file to penetrate into the enemy position.

| 26 Q–B2! | Q–R3 |
| 27 Q–B7 | B–B1 |

Or 27 ... P–R5 28 N–K2 B–B1 29 Q–K5 etc. Not however 28 Q×B? P×N 29 Q×QP+ K–R1 30 P×P R×R+ 31 K×R Q–R8+, nor 28 N–B5? N×N 29 Q×B Q–K3 when Black suddenly has a dangerous attack.

| 28 Q–K5 | P–R5 |
| 29 N–K2 | Q–R4? |

This removal of the queen from the main theatre of operations only hastens the inevitable end. Perhaps Black now expected 30 Q×QP+? B–K3 followed by 31 ... P–N6 with a strong attack.

| 30 N–B3 | P–N6! |
| 31 P–B3! | |

Simplest and best. After 31 P×P R×R+ 32 K×R P×P 33 Q×NP.3 Q–R8+ Black draws, and if 31 N×P P×P+ 32 K–R2 he can sacrifice the exchange by 32 ... P–N5! with good attacking chances.

| 31 ... | R–K1 |

Or 31 ... B–K3 32 N×P Q–B2 33 B–N6! wins.

| 32 Q×QP+ | B–K3 |

33 Q–Q6	B–B5
34 N–Q5	R–K3
35 Q×R+!	N×Q
36 N–B6+	K–B2
37 N×Q	B×R
38 K×B	1–0

53 Pachman–Korchnoi

Havana 1963, Nimzo-Indian Defence

1 P–Q4 N–KB3 2 P–QB4 P–K3 3 N–QB3 B–N5 4 Q–B2 P–Q4 5 P×P P×P 6 B–N5 P–KR3 7 B×N Q×B 8 P–QR3 B×N+ 9 Q×B 0–0 10 P–K3 P–B3 11 N–B3 N–Q2 he should first play ... B–B4 12 B–K2 R–K1 13 0–0 P–QN3? (*125*) and here 13 ... N–B1 or 13 ... Q–K2 followed by 14 ... N–B3 is better. Now Black stands worse, because White can play the so-called 'minority attack' which we shall discuss later.

125
W

14 KR–B1!

Once again, the QR is needed to support the advance of the QRP.

14 ...	B–N2
15 P–N4	Q–K3
16 Q–N2!	P–KB4!?

As Black would have no counter-chances with quiet play, he weakens his K-side in an attempt to begin his own minority attack.

17 B–Q3   P–KN4
18 R–B3!

This move has a dual purpose, to double the rooks when necessary and at the same time guard K3, the importance of which we shall see later. It is sometimes effective to overprotect even those points which are not yet threatened, but more about this in the chapter about prophylactic defence!

18 ...   Q–B3
19 P–QR4!

Choosing the favourable moment for this advance, when Black cannot counter with 19 ... P–QR4 (20 R1–QB1 P×P 21 Q×P threatening the unpleasant 22 N–K5!).

19 ...   P–N5
20 N–Q2   P–B5

White still has the advantage after 20 ... P–QR4 21 P×P R×RP 22 N–N3.

21 P–R5!   QR–Q1?

He could not play 21 ... BP×P 22 BP×P R×P? 23 B–R7+ (White's rook on QB3!), and the threat was 22 P–R6 B–B1 23 R1–QB1 or 23 Q–B2. Black must of course free QR1 for his bishop, but the correct move is 21 ... QR–N1! in order to defend the bishop (not yet attacked!) and saving a tempo. Perhaps Korchnoi felt that clarification of the position on the Q-side would lighten his defensive problems.

22 RP×P   RP×P
23 R–R7 (*126*)

The culmination of the file-opening, with the white rook reaching the seventh rank. Although this rook remains here quietly for the next 17 moves, its latent power makes it a strong attacking piece for the whole of that time!

23 ...   R–N1
24 N–B1   N–B1

25 Q–B2   N–K3

Black does not want to make a premature capture of the KP, in order to retain the possibility of ... P–B6. Normally good tactics, but incorrect in this position, even though White still stands much better after 25 ... P×P 26 P×P.

26 B–B5!   P×P
27 B×N+   R×B
28 R×KP!

Having done its main job on the QB-file, this rook now eliminates Black's active rook, thus removing an important piece from the defence of the king.

28 ...   R×R
29 N×R!   Q×QP

After 29 ... P–R4 White can reach a won ending if he wishes by 30 Q–KB5! Q×Q 31 N×Q R–R1 32 R×R+ B×R 33 N–K7+ K–B2 34 N–B8 P–N4 35 N–N6 B–N2 36 N–Q7 etc.

30 Q–N6+   Q–N2
31 Q–K6+   Q–KB2
32 Q×RP!   R–K1

If 32 ... R–R1 the simplest way to win is 33 Q–N5+ K–B1 34 R×R+ B×R 35 Q–Q8+ Q–K1 36 Q×NP etc.

33 Q–N5+   K–B1
34 P–R3!   P×P
35 N–B5!

Threatening N–Q6, and if 35 ...

R–K3 36 Q–Q8+ R–K1 37 Q–Q6+.

35 ...	R–K8+
36 K–R2	Q–B2+
37 P–N3	R–K3
38 N–R6	K–K1
39 Q–N8+	K–Q2
40 N–B5	R–K7

Otherwise 41 Q–B7+ wins the rook.

41 R×B! **1–0**

After 41 ... Q×R Black loses the queen to 42 Q–B7+ K–B1 43 N–Q6+.

54 Karpov–Spassky

Moscow 1973, Ruy Lopez

1 P–K4 P–K4 2 N–KB3 N–QB3 3 B–N5 P–QR3 4 B–R4 N–B3 5 0–0 B–K2 6 R–K1 P–QN4 7 B–N3 P–Q3 8 P–B3 0–0 9 P–KR3 N–N1 10 P–Q3 B–N2 11 QN–Q2 QN–Q2 12 N–B1 N–B4 13 B–B2 R–K1 14 N–N3 B–KB1 15 P–N4 N4–Q2 16 P–Q4 P–R3 17 B–Q2 N–N3 18 B–Q3 P–N3 19 Q–B2 N.B3–Q2 20 QR–Q1 B–N2 21 P×P P P×P (*127*) better was 21 ... N×P.

127
W

Black has nearly equalized, and if he were given time to play ... Q–K2 and ... P–QB4 there could be no talk of a white advantage. For this reason, White himself must act first on the Q-side.

22 P–B4 **P×P**

After 22 ... P–QB4? Karpov gives 23 BP×P! P–B5 24 B×BP R–QB1 25 B×BP+! K×B 26 Q–N3+ etc., a promising piece sacrifice.

23 B×BP **Q–K2?**

Spassky thinks ... P–QB4 will give him the best chance to equalize, but White's bishop now becomes strong. After 23 ... N×B 24 Q×N the bishop pair would be some compensation for the weakness of his QBP.

24 B–N3 **P–QB4**

25 P–QR4!

This move ensures White a strong initiative. If 25 ... P×P 26 P–R5 N–QB1 (*26 ... QR–QB1 27 Q–R2 N–R1 28 B×NP!*) 27 B×NP! Q×B 28 R×N R–K2 29 R1–Q1 or 29 R–Q8+ followed by 30 R1–Q1, and the unexpected domination of the Q-file wins for White. However, the text-move involves the sacrifice of the exchange, when the open Q-file again plays a vital part.

25 ...	P–B5
26 B–R2	B–QB3
27 P–R5	B–R5
28 Q–B1	N–QB1

Or 28 ... B×R 29 R×B N–QB1 leading to the same position as in the game, for Black cannot improve here with 29 ... N–R5 30 B×RP B×B 31 Q×B e.g. 31 ... N–B6? 32 B×P threatening 33 Q×P+, or 31 ... N–B1 32 R–QB1 etc.

29 B×RP	B×R
30 R×B	N–Q3?

After this the pressure of White's single rook on the Q-file proves decisive. Black should not attempt to guard his QBP but rather protect his vital Q2 square by 30 ... R–R2! White would have a promising game after 31 B×B K×B 32 Q×P, with two pawns for the exchange, but there would be no clear win.

31 B×B   K×B
32 Q–N5!

Spassky was prepared for 32
Q–Q2? QR–Q1! when 33 Q×N?
loses to 33 . . . N–B1. The text move
forces a decisive weakening of
Black's K-side, because 32 . . . Q×Q
33 N×Q wins a piece e.g. 33 . . .
QR–B1 34 R×N N–B3 35 N–K2
P–B6 36 B×P etc.

32 . . .   P–B3
33 Q–N4

Threatening 34 R×N followed
by 35 N–B5+.

33 . . .   K–R2
34 N–R4   1–0

If 34 . . . N–KB1 35 N×P! N×N
36 Q–R5+ ˙K–N2 37 R×N! wins.
Or 34 . . . R–KN1 35 B×P R–N2
36 R×N Q×R 37 N4–B5! wins.

THE SEVENTH AND EIGHTH RANKS

We have already seen in the previous section of this chapter that one
of the most important strategic aims
in exploiting an open file is to obtain
an entry point in the enemy position, in particular on the seventh or
eighth ranks. This penetration usually results in material gain or a bind
on the enemy pieces, as there are
normally, on such a rank, a few
pawns which are under attack by
major pieces. When these pieces
reach the eighth rank, they spell
danger to the enemy king. An
example of this is the well-known
back rank mate with rook or queen,
which not only often surprises the
beginner but can also give rise to
many interesting tactical points and
beautiful combinations.

The power of a rook on the
seventh rank is most clearly seen in
the end-game or in transposing
to an end-game. This can be a
decisive factor even when material

is equal and greatly reduced, as in
the following position (*128*).

128

White wins because after 1 R–Q7
R–QB1 2 K–B3, or here 1 . . . P–B4
2 K–B3, his king strolls up the
board whilst Black's pieces are tied
to the defence of the pawns.

Exchange of material, linked with
this seventh rank control, is therefore a frequent strategic goal which
can lead to a decisive advantage.
Our next game shows Black exchanging material at every opportunity, but then heedlessly allowing
White's rook to penetrate to the
seventh rank, after which the ending
is already decided.

55 Stahlberg–Szabados

Amsterdam 1950, English Opening

1 P–QB4 N–KB3 2 N–KB3 P–B4
3 P–KN3 P–QN3 4 B–N2 B–N2 5
0–0 P–K3 6 N–B3 B–K2 7 P–N3
0–0 8 B–N2 P–Q4 9 P×P N×P 10
N×N B×N 11 R–B1 B–KB3 12
Q–B2 B×B 13 Q×B N–Q2 14 P–
Q3 Q–B3
     15 Q–R3

This completely equal position is
the result of a correctly played
opening. The only way for White to
obtain active play is to prepare P–
QN4 in order to open the QB-file,
and obtain a central pawn majority.

Black should anticipate this plan by playing ... Q–K2 now or on the next two moves, followed by ... KR–QB1.

15 ...	**KR–Q1**
16 N–Q2	**B×B**
17 K×B	**N–K4(?)**
	(129)

Black intends to post his knight on the strong ... Q5 square, but White's next move thwarts this plan.

129
W

18 P–QN4!	**P×P**

Not of course 18 ... N–Q2? 19 N–K4 etc.

19 Q×NP	**R.Q1–QB1?**

This apparently logical rook move, retaining the QR on R1 to guard the RP in case of Q–R3 or R4, gives White an opportunity to seize the open QB-file. The correct move was 19 ... QR–B1 20 Q–R3 N–B3 with only a slight advantage to White.

20 Q–K4!

This move ties Black's rook on QB1 to the defence of his other rook, thus gaining time to double rooks.

20 ...   **N–N3**

If 20 ... QR–N1 21 Q–N7! Q–Q1 22 Q×RP R–R1 23 Q–N7 R.B1–N1 24 Q–K4 R×P 25 Q×N R×N 26 R–B7 threatening R1–B1 followed by R×P e.g. 26 ... Q–Q4+ (*26 ... R×KP! – Translator's*

note) 27 Q×Q P×Q 28 R1–B1 K–B1 29 R–Q7! R×KP 30 R1–B7 wins.

21 R–B4!	**Q–K4?**

It is this error which finally loses the game for Black. Rather than strive for more simplification, he could still hang on with 21 ... Q–K2 22 R1–B1 Q–Q2 e.g. 23 R–B7 R×R 24 Q×R+ N–B1 etc.

22 R1–B1	**Q×Q+**
23 N×Q	**R×R**

Apparently Black intended 23 ... N–K2 then saw 24 R–B7 K–B1 25 R1–B3! R–Q1 26 R–N7 N–Q4 27 R–R3 P–QR4 28 N–N5 winning.

24 R×R	**K–B1**
25 R–B7	*(130)*

130
B

A typical position, with the rook on the seventh completely paralysing Black's game and giving White an easy win.

25 ...	**N–K2**
26 R–N7	

Preventing 26 ... P–QR3.

26 ...	**P–B3**
27 N–Q6	**N–B3**
28 N–N5	

Winning a pawn, as Black has no defence to the threat of 29 R–QB7. The rest is a matter of technique for a player of Stahlberg's class, and the game concluded: **28 ... R–N1 29 R–QB7 N–Q1 30 R×RP R–N2 31 R–R8 K–K2 32 P–B4 R–Q2 33 K–B3 N–B3 34 K–K3 N–N5 35**

P–QR3 N–Q4+ **36** K–Q2 P–B4
37 R–KN8 K–B3 **38** R–N8 P–K4
39 N–B3 P×P **40** P×P N×P **41**
R×P+ K–N4 **42** P–QR4 R–R2 **43**
R–N2 N–K3 **44** R–R2 N–B4 **45**
R–R3 K–B3 **46** K–K3 P–N4 **47**
P–R5 P–R4 **48** N–Q5+ K–K3 **49**
N–N4 P–B5+ **50** K–B3 N–Q2 **51**
P–R6 K–B4 **52** R–R5+ K–B3 **53**
N–B6 R–B2 **54** P–R7 N–N3 **55**
N–N4 R–B1 **56** R–R6 K–B4 **57**
R×N P–N5+ **58** K–B2 P–R5 **59**
R–N5+ K–N3 **60** R–N8 1–0.

Various tactical manoeuvres and
combinations linked with control of
the seventh or eighth ranks are outside the scope of this work and are
treated fully in my *Modern Chess
Tactics*.

Let us now examine a few strategic
problems that arise in the struggle
for control of the seventh and eighth
ranks.

56 Alekhine–Yates

London 1922, Queen's Gambit

1 P–Q4 N–KB3 **2** P–QB4 P–K3 **3**
N–KB3 P–Q4 **4** N–B3 B–K2 **5**
B–N5 0–0 **6** P–K3 QN–Q2 **7** R–B1
P–B3 **8** Q–B2 R–K1 **9** B–Q3 P×P
10 B×BP N–Q4 **11** N–K4 P–KB4?
an anti-positional move, later allowing White to occupy K5 with a
knight. 11 ... P–B3 or 11 ... B×B
were better **12** B×B Q×B **13** N4–
Q2 P–QN4? and now a similar
error on the other wing, weakening
Black's QB4 square. Alekhine uses
both these weaknesses to post his
pieces actively. **14** B×N BP×B **15**
0–0 P–QR4 **16** N–N3 P–R5 **17**
N–B5 N×N **18** Q×N Q×Q.

19 R×Q

Showing sound positional judgement. Alekhine is not afraid of
exchanges, as these only highlight
his advantages – control of the QB-
file and a strong-point for his knight
at K5.

19 ...	P–N5
20 R1–B1	B–R3
21 N–K5	R.K1–N1

Black dare not exchange rooks,
for he loses a pawn after 21 ...
R.K1–QB1 **22** R×R+ R×R **23**
R×R+ B×R **24** N–B6 P–N6 **25**
P×P P×P **26** N–R5. This ensures
White permanent control of the
QB-file and his strategy is clear: to
double rooks on the seventh, thus
pinning down Black's K-side, and
then carry out a mating attack with
the help of his knight and king.
Alekhine executes this plan in
impressive fashion.

22 P–B3	P–N6
23 P–QR3	P–R3

Once again 23 ... R–QB1 fails
to **24** R×R+ R×R **25** R×R+
B×R **26** N–Q3 and **27** N–B5
winning either the QRP or KP.
Even without this, White would win
by playing his king to QN4.

24 K–B2	K–R2
25 P–R4	R–KB1
26 K–N3	R.B1–QN1

Black is reduced to passivity and
must wait and see what his great
opponent has in store for him.

27 R–B7	B–N4
28 R1–B5	B–R3
29 R5–B6	R–K1
30 K–B4	K–N1
31 P–R5! (*131*)	

White has now carried out all the
stages of his plan, except doubling
rooks on the seventh. Once this is
achieved, the game will be over in a
few moves.

31 ...	B–B8
32 P–N3	B–R3
33 R–B7!	K–R2
34 R6–B7	R–KN1
35 N–Q7!	

Threatening 36 N–B6+, and as

131
B

will be seen, Black has no real answer
to this threat.

35 ...	K–R1
36 N–B6!	R.N1–KB1
37 R×P!!	R×N
38 K–K5!	1–0

After either rook to KB1 White
mates in two moves by 39 R–KR7+
and 40 R.B7–KN7 mate, as the
black rook blocks the king's flight
square.

This example shows us how control of an open file ties down the
enemy pieces and can be converted
into control of the seventh rank.
Our next game is a more complex
illustration of the same theme.

57 Pachman–Sefc

Trenčianske Teplice 1949, Queen's
Gambit

1 P–Q4 N–KB3 2 P–QB4 P–K3 3
N–QB3 P–Q4 4 B–N5 B–K2 5 N–
B3 0–0 6 P–K3 N–K5 7 B×B Q×B
8 R–B1 P–QB3 9 B–Q3 P–KB4(?)
10 0–0 N–Q2 11 Q–B2 Q–B3 12 P–
QN4 P–KN4 13 P×P KP×P 14
P–N5 P–N5 15 N–Q2 N–N3 16
P×P P×P

| 17 N–K2 | Q–R5! |

After 17 ... B–Q2 18 N–QN3
White has a positional advantage by
blockading the backward QBP.
However, the text-move offers Black
excellent counter-play, the im-

mediate threat being ... R–B3–R3.

| 18 B×N? | |

White plans a combination involving an exchange sacrifice but
overlooks a subtle zwischenzug. He
should be content with a slight plus
after 18 P–B3.

| 18 ... | BP×B |
| 19 Q×BP | B–Q2! |

A surprise for White who had
expected 19 ... B–R3 20 Q–K6+
K–R1 21 Q–K5+ R–B3 22 N–
KB4! B×R 23 R×B with at least
three pawns for the exchange, and a
winning position. As we shall see,
there is a vital difference to this line
when Black's bishop is on QN4
instead of QR3.

| 20 Q–Q6 | |

White is not enamoured of the
position after 20 Q–B2 B–N4 21
N–QN3 B–Q6 22 Q–Q2 N–B5 23
Q–Q1, so has already made up his
mind to make a positional queen
sacrifice.

20 ...	B–N4
21 Q–K6+	K–R1
22 Q–K5+	R–B3
23 P–N3	

The point of Black's play is that
23 N–KB4 now fails to 23 ... R–K1!

| 23 ... | Q–R3 |
| 24 N–QB3! | |

Not 24 KR–K1? R–K1 25 Q–B7
R×P!

| 24 ... | R–K1 |

After 24 ... B×R 25 N×QP
N×N 26 Q×N R1–KB1 27 R×B
Black's KP falls.

| 25 N×B! | |

In exchange for his queen White
obtains rook and bishop and penetrates to the seventh rank with his
rook. Chances are at least even.

25 ...	R×Q
26 P×R	R–K3
27 R–B7	Q–R4?

An apparently logical move,

threatening both ... R–R3 and
... Q×KP followed by ... R–K2.
However, the move only loses time,
so 27 ... R×P was preferable when
Black can hold the game after 28
R1–B1 Q–KB3.

28 N–Q4!   **R–R3?**

Consequential but dubious. It was
essential to play 28 ... R×P 29
R1–B1 or 29 R×QRP with the
better game for White. After the
text-move White succeeds in doubling his rooks on the seventh.

29 R1–B1   **Q×KP**

Only now does Black realize that
after 29 ... Q×RP+ 30 K–B1 his
pieces are hopelessly out of play. If
then 30 ... N–B5 31 R–B8+ K–
N2 32 K–K2! N×N 33 N–B5+
K–N3 34 N×R K×N 35 R1–B6+
K–R4 36 R–B8! N–B6 37 R–KB5+
N–N4 38 P–K6 winning; or here
35 ... K–N4 36 R–KN8+ K–B4
37 R–KB8+ K×P 38 K×N wins.

30 R×QRP   **Q–N1**
31 R1–B7 (*132*)

White has achieved his aim and
obtained a won position. The next
moves followed at lightning speed and
it was not until move 42 that White
suddenly realized his superiority.

31 ...	**N–B1**
32 R.R7–N7	**Q–R1**
33 N2–N3	**N–Q3**
34 R–R7	**Q–KB1**

35 N–K2	**N–B5**
36 N3–Q4	**N–K4**
37 N–B4	**N–B6+**
38 N×N	**NP×N**
39 R–B7	**Q–QN1**
40 R.R7–N7	**Q–QB1**
41 R.B7–B7	**Q–KN1**
42 N×P	

This sealed move is sound enough,
but 42 P–QR4 is the most exact,
as 42 ... R–R3 fails to 43 P–R4
when there is no defence to 44 N–
R5. On the other hand the immediate 42 P–KR4 is bad because
of 42 ... P–Q5! 43 P×P P–K6 44
P×P Q×NP+ 45 K–B1 Q–N1.

42 ...	**R–Q3**
43 N–B3	**R–Q1**
44 P–KR4	**Q–K3**

Or 44 ... R–K1 45 K–R2 winning
easily, as R×P+ is threatened and
after 45 ... P–R3 (or R4) White's
knight can come into the attack.

45 K–R2	**P–R4**
46 R–K7	**Q–N5**
47 N×P	**Q–N3**
48 N–N5	**R–R1**
49 P–K4!	

An unobtrusive move containing a
trap aimed at Black's queen.

49 ...	**R–QB1?**
50 R–K6	**R–B8**

A last try, hoping for 51 R×Q??
R–KR8+! 52 K×R stalemate.
However ...

51 R–N8+	**1–0**

58 Nimzowitsch–Capablanca

New York 1927 Caro-Kann Defence

1 P–K4 P–QB3 2 P–Q4 P–Q4 3
P–K5 B–B4 4 B–Q3 B×B 5 Q×B
P–K3 6 N–QB3 Q–N3 7 KN–K2
P–QB4 8 P×P B×P 9 0–0 N–K2
10 N–R4 Q–B3 11 N×B Q×N
12 B–K3 Q–B2 13 P–KB4 N–B4
14 P–B3 N–B3 15 QR–Q1 P–KN3
16 P–KN4? This allows Black to

immobilize White's K-side pawns
and thus cut out all counter-play.
16 B–B2 was best **16 . . . N×B 17
Q×N P–KR4!** 18 P–N5 if 18 P–
KR3 P×P 19 P×P 0–0–0 threatening 20 . . . P–KN4 or 20 . . . R–R5
with a strong attack down the KR-
file **18 . . . 0–0 19 N–Q4 Q–N3 20
R–B2 KR–B1 21 P–QR3 R–B2 22
R–Q3 N–R4 23 R–K2 R–K1 24
K–N2 N–B3 25 R2–Q2** according
to Alekhine, White should play 25
N×N Q×N 26 R–Q4, but this only
shows that 22 . . . N–R4 is inexact
and that Capablanca only reverts
to the correct plan on move 26.

25 . . .	R1–QB1
26 R–K2	N–K2
27 R2–Q2	R–B5
28 Q–R3	K–N2
29 R–KB2	P–R4

Preparing for the logical breakthrough by . . . P–QN4–5 which
will open the QB-file. White's static
pawn structure condemns him to
passivity while Black manoeuvres at
will.

30 R–K2   N–B4!

At first sight it appears that Black
has achieved nothing by avoiding
exchange of knights on . . . QB3 and
now allowing it on . . . KB4. However, he obtains a vital strong-point
for his rook on . . . K5.

31 N×N+

After 31 R2–Q2 N×N 32 R×N
R×R 33 P×R R–B5 34 Q–K3 P–
QR5, or here 33 . . . Q–N4 Black's
command of the open file gives him
an advantage similar to the one in
the game.

31 . . .	NP×N
32 Q–B3	

Not 32 Q×RP R–KR1 33 Q–B3
R–R5 and Black regains the pawn
with advantage.

32 . . .	K–N3
33 R2–Q2	R–K5

34 R–Q4	R1–B5
35 Q–B2	Q–N4
36 K–N3	

Black obtains an advantageous
queen ending after 36 R×R.B4
Q×R 37 R–Q4 Q–N6 38 R×R
BP×R.

36 . . .	R.B5×R
37 P×R	

Not of course 37 R×R R–K7.
So Black has opened the QB-file
without having to advance his QNP
in the usual way, and this file will
be used exceptionally by the queen
rather than the rook!

37 . . .	Q–B5!
38 K–N2	P–N4
39 K–N1	P–N5
40 P×P	P×P
41 K–N2	Q–QB8!
	(133)

Capablanca's queen manoeuvre
has given him a position in which
neither the white rook nor the queen
can move without loss of material.
King moves allow Black to double
his pieces decisively on the eighth
rank. A rare case of zugzwang with
major pieces on the board!

42 K–N3	Q–KR8!
43 R–Q3	R–K8
44 R–KB3	R–Q8
45 P–N3	R–QB8

Again placing White in zugzwang,
as 46 K–R3 loses to 46 . . . R–B7!

46 R–K3	R–B8
0–1	

ACTIVE ROOKS IN FRONT OF THE PAWN CHAIN

In the previous sections we have dealt with the normal method of exploiting our major pieces by creating and utilizing open files. However, in certain positions the occupation of an open file is insufficient, or we cannot always open a file, even if our strategic plan points to the desirability of doing so. For example, when both sides have castled on the same wing, we cannot usually begin a pawn storm to open up a file against the enemy king, as this would often weaken the position of our own king. Therefore, in such cases it is preferable to post the rook in front of our pawn chain. Consider the old variation of the Queen's Gambit which runs **1 P–Q4 P–Q4 2 P–QB4 P–K3 3 N–QB3 N–KB3 4 B–N5 B–K2 5 P–K3 0–0 6 N–B3 QN–Q2 7 R–B1 P–QN3 8 P×P P×P 9 B–Q3 B–N2 10 0–0 P–B4.** Pillsbury now used to continue **11 N–K5** followed by P–B4, R–B3 and R–R3. We often meet similar manoeuvres whose object is to use the rook in the attack without having to open a file.

Many modern openings incorporate the use of a rook in front of the pawn chain, even when there is no question of an attack against the enemy king. The reason for this is that we must normally advance pawns to open a file, but Steinitz demonstrated that such an advance can lead to weaknesses in the endgame, and Réti remembered this principle when developing his own opening ideas. Positional players often strive to retain their pawns on the original square for as long as possible, which is why rooks are often utilized in front of their own pawn chain in modern chess. To describe this activity, Tartakower coined the term 'hypermodern rook'. Here are two games which illustrate such rooks in action.

59 Alekhine–Kmoch

San Remo 1930, Nimzo-Indian Defence

1 P–Q4 N–KB3 2 P–QB4 P–K3 3 N–QB3 B–N5 4 B–Q2 0–0 5 P–K3 P–Q4 6 N–B3 P–B4 7 P–QR3 B×N 8 B×B N–K5 9 R–B1 N×B 10 R×N BP×P 11 KP×P N–B3 12 B–K2 P×P 13 B×P Q–B3 14 0–0 R–Q1 15 R–Q3 B–Q2 16 R–K1

Although Black has now achieved full equality, Alekhine still decides to play for a win. For this reason he avoids the continuation 16 Q–Q2 and 17 P–Q5 eliminating his isolated QP, and prepares instead to attack on the K-side.

16 ...	B–K1
17 Q–Q2	N–K2
18 N–N5!	

The first attacking move which leads to the weakening ... P–KR3. White's main threat is 19 N×KP! P×N 20 R×P.

18 ...	N–Q4
19 R–KB3	Q–K2
20 R–KN3	

Threatening 21 Q–Q3 forcing a weakness on the black squares after 21 ... P–KN3.

20 ...	P–KR3
21 N–B3	Q–B3
22 R–K4!	

The second rook now joins in the attack and at the same time protects KB4.

| 22 ... | N–K2 |

In order to answer 23 R4–N4 by
23 ... N–B4.

23 N–K5	N–B4
24 R–Q3	QR–B1
25 P–R3!	

The back rank mate must be
avoided if White is to use his rooks
for the attack.

25 ...　　　　　**N–Q3?**

It is a mistake to exchange this
knight for White's bishop. Black's
defence is made more difficult,
whereas 25 ... B–B3 would have
given him equal chances.

| 26 R–B4 | N × B |
| 27 N × N | Q–N4 |

Or 27 ... Q–K2 28 N–K5 when
28 ... P–B3 is answered by 29
N–N4.

28 R–KN3	Q–Q4
29 N–K3	Q–B3
30 K–R2 (*134*)	

134
B

White's rooks are now strongly
placed and enable him to bring
about an energetic finish. Black can
occupy the eighth rank but this
leads him nowhere, as he has no
time to double his major pieces on
it and White's king is well protected
at the moment.

| 30 ... | Q–B8 |
| 31 Q–N4 | Q–B2 |

After 31 ... Q–QN8 White wins
by 32 Q–K7 R–B8 33 R × NP+
K × R 34 R–N4+ K–R2 35 Q–B6
R–R8+ 36 K–N3.

| 32 P–Q5! | P–QR4 |

Or 32 ... P × P 33 Q–Q4 with a
decisive attack.

33 Q–K4	R–Q3
34 Q–K5	P–KN3
35 Q–R5	R × P

Or 35 ... K–R2 36 N–N4!
P × Q 37 N–B6+ and mate next
move.

| 36 N × R | P × N |
| 37 Q × RP | 1–0 |

In the above game both rooks
were used to attack the king, but in
our next game they were deployed
successfully to exert pressure on the
Q-side.

60 Trifunovic–Pachman

Hilversum 1947, Four Knights Game

**1 P–K4 P–K4 2 N–KB3 N–QB3 3
N–B3 N–B3 4 B–N5 B–N5 5 0–0
0–0 6 P–Q3 B × N 7 P × B P–Q3
8 B–N5 Q–K2 9 B.QN5 × N P × B
10 Q–B1** 10 N–Q2 is better **10 ...
P–KR3 11 B × N　Q × B 12 Q–K3
P–B4! 13 KR–N1?** 13 QR–N1 is
better **13 ... B–Q2 14 P–Q4?** and
here White has better with 14 P–B4
QR–N1 15 R–N3 R–N3 with a
slight advantage to Black because of
... B–R5. Black also stands better
after 14 R–N7 KR–N1! 15 R1–N1
Q–Q1 **14 ... BP × P 15 P × P P × P
16　N × P　KR–K1!** in order to
answer 17 R–N7 with 17 ... B–B3!
and 18 ... B × P, and also threatening 17 ... P–Q4 **17 R–K1 QR–N1
18 N–N3**

White has been frustrated in his
attempt to seize the QN-file and has
to block the file himself in order to
stop Black's rook reaching the
seventh. This compels Black to find
another way of deploying his rooks.

18 ...　　　　　**R–N5**

19 P–KB3

Not of course 19 Q × QRP R5 × P

20 R × R R × R 21 Q × P? Q × R+!
22 N × Q R–K8 mate.

    19 ...   **R–R5**

And so one of the rooks has
already reached a most effective
square from which it both guards
its own QRP and attacks White's
QRP.

    20 P–B3   **R–K4!**

Now the other rook heads for the
Q-side. 21 P–KB4 fails to 21 ...
R4 × P 22 Q × R R × Q 23 R × R
Q × QBP e.g. 24 R–QB1 Q–Q6 25
R–K7 B–K3 26 R7 × QBP Q–K6+
with advantage to Black.

    21 R–K2   **B–K3** (*135*)

Black's Q-side pressure increases
with every move. Defensive play
would lose to the transfer of Black's
second rook over to the Q-side e.g.
22 N–Q4 R4–QR4 23 N × B Q × N
24 Q–Q2 Q–B5 followed by 25 ...

R–R6, or 22 R–QB1 R–QN4! 23
N–Q4 R4–QR4 24 N–B6 R–QB4
etc. After the text-move, White
blunders away a pawn and the
game is virtually over.

    22 R–Q1?   **R × RP!**

Now 23 R × R B × N wins. The
rest is a matter of technique.

    23 N–Q4   **R4–QR4**
    24 R × R   **R × R**
    25 R–N1   **Q–N3**
    26 P–N4   **Q–B3**

After forcing the weakening P–
N4, Black's queen threatens to go
to ... KR5 and this in turn compels
White to relinquish the QN-file.

    27 R–K1

He cannot play 27 N–K2 B–B5
and Black wins the QBP.

    27 ...   **P–B4**
    28 N × B   **Q × N**
    29 R–K2   **R–R6**
    30 K–N2   **Q–B5**
    31 R–QB2   **R–R8**
    32 R–B1

Or 32 Q–Q2 Q–B8+ 33 K–N3
R–Q8 34 Q–K2 Q–R8.

The game now ended: **32 ...
R–R7+ 33 K–N3 Q–N6 34 Q–N1
Q–N7 35 P–K5 P × P 36 R–N1
Q × BP 37 R–QB1 Q–Q7 38 R × P
Q–B5+ 39 K–R3 Q × BP+ 40
Q–N3 Q × Q+ 41 K × Q R–R6+
42 K–N2 P–B3 43 R–B7 K–R2 0–1.**

6 The Queen and Play with the Major Pieces

6 The Queen and Play with the Major Pieces

In our chapter 'The Value of the Pieces' we mentioned certain aspects of play with the queen, pointing to its great mobility due to its ability to change from a vertical or horizontal to a diagonal movement. These characteristics make it above all an excellent attacking piece, with the enemy king as its main objective. We see an example of this in a simple ending played in the 1907 Carlsbad tournament, Maroczy–Marshall (*136*)

136
W

1 Q–R4 K–N2 2 Q–KN4+ K–B2 3 Q–R5+ K–N2 4 Q–K8 Q–K7 5 Q–K7+ K–N3 6 Q–B8! P–K4 7 Q–KN8+ K–R3 8 P–KR4! Q–B7 9 Q–KB8+ K–N3 10 P–R5+! K×P 11 Q–N7! Q–Q7 12 Q×RP+ Q–R3 13 P–KN4+ K–N4 14 Q×P K–B5 15 Q×NP Q–R8 16 Q–N4+! K×BP 17 Q×P K×P 18 P–B4 P–K5 19 P–B5 P–B4 20 P–B6 Q–R1+ 21 P–B3 P–K6 22 Q–N6+ K–B5 23 P–B7 P–K7 24 Q–K6 K–B6 25 Q×BP+ K–N7 26 Q–N4+ K–B7 27 Q–KB4+ K–N7 28 Q–K3 K–B8 29 Q–B3+ K–K8

30 Q–B4 Q–QB1 31 Q–Q6 K–B7 32 Q–Q8 P–K8=Q 33 Q×Q Q–Q7+ 34 K–R3 Q–B8+ 35 K–R4 Q–B5+ 36 P–B4 1–0.

In the middle-game too the queen thrives on attacks against the king or against weaknesses in the enemy camp. Its mobility also allows it to switch fronts with great speed, a characteristic which is impressively demonstrated in our next two games.

61 Tarrasch–Chigorin

Match 1893, Ruy Lopez

1 P–K4 P–K4 2 N–KB3 N–QB3 3 B–N5 P–QR3 4 B–R4 N–B3 5 N–B3 B–N5 6 N–Q5 B–R4 7 0–0 P–Q3 8 P–Q3 B–KN5 9 P–B3 N–Q2 10 N–K3 B–R4 11 B×N P×B

  12 Q–R4

With this move White is the first to use his queen as an attacking piece, winning a pawn. However, Black has compensation in an attack against the enemy K-side which has been weakened by the white queen's sortie. The reader would be correct in assuming that White's manoeuvre, beginning 11 B×N, has little to recommend it.

12 ...	**B–QN3**
13 Q×BP	**0–0**

It is important to note that White cannot prevent the following weakening of his pawn by retreating his knight on KB3, as this allows 14 ... B–K7.

14 N–B5	**N–B4**
15 P–Q4	**N–K3**
16 P×P	**B×N**
17 P×B	**P×P**
18 K–R1? (*137*)	

18 Q–B4 is probably better, but Tarrasch himself admits that even then 18 ... Q–B3 followed by 19 ... P–N3 would give Black an excellent game.

137
B

After the text-move Black's queen enters the fray, winning the pawn back and weakening the enemy K-side even further.

18 ...	**Q–Q6!**
19 B–K3	**Q–K7!**
20 N–R4	

The natural defence 20 K–N2 fails to 20 ... B×B 21 N×B N–N4 etc.

20 ...	**B×B**
21 P×B	

After 21 QR–K1 Black could simply pick up White's QNP and

QRP, but even stronger is 21 ... Q×P.B7! 22 R×Q B×R 23 N–N2 B×R 24 N×B QR–N1 25 P–N4 R–N3 followed by 26 ... R–Q1 with a clear winning position.

21 ...	**Q×KP**
22 Q–B4	**KR–Q1**
23 N–B5	**Q–Q7**
24 R–KN1	**P–N3**

The threat was 25 R×P+! N×R 26 N–R6+ K–R1 27 N×P+ K–N1 28 N–R6+ K–R1 29 Q–N8+ leading to the well-known smothered mate.

25 R–N2	**Q–B5**
26 N–K7+	**K–N2**
27 N–Q5!	**Q–R3!**

But not 27 ... Q×KBP 28 R–KB1 when White obtains a strong attack down the KB-file. The text-move sets a pretty trap: 28 N×P N–B5! 29 N×R (if *29 R–B2 QR–B1 30 Q–B5 N–Q6*) 29 ... N×R 30 Q–B7! (if *30 R–KN1 N–B5 31 Q–B7 Q–R4 32 R–KB1 R–Q8 wins*) 30 ... Q–R4 (or *30 ... Q–Q7 31 Q×KP+ K–N1 32 R–KN1 N–B5* also wins, as given by Tarrasch) 31 Q×R Q×BP 32 Q–Q1! Q×KP 33 K–N1 N–B5 34 Q–Q2 (*34 Q–KB1! – Translator's note*) 34 ... N–R6+ 35 K–B1 Q–R8+ 36 K–K2 Q×R etc. wins (Chigorin).

28 R1–KN1	**R–Q2!**

Offering another pawn, this time on QR3, in order to seize control of the Q-file.

29 Q–B6	**R1–Q1**
30 Q×RP	**R–Q3**
31 Q–K2	**K–R1**

After the immediate 31 ... P–QB3 White has 32 N–K7 whereas now Black threatens to drive away the knight then play ... N–B5.

32 Q–K3	**P–N4**
33 Q–K1	**P–KB3**
34 R–KB2	**P–B3**
35 N–K3	**Q–R4**

36 N–N2

If 36 N–B5? R–Q6 37 R1–B1 N–B5 and 38 ... N–R6 wins.

36 ...   **R–Q6**

37 R1–B1 (*138*)

White's last few moves have consolidated his position to such an extent that Black has serious problems in finding a way of continuing the attack. However, Chigorin now discovers an excellent manoeuvre which exploits the active position of his major pieces. His mobile queen rapidly switches over to the Q-side where the open lines give it excellent attacking opportunities.

37 ...   **Q–B2!**

38 P–N4?

This weakening move only hastens White's defeat, but even waiting tactics would not save the game. Black can force White to play P–QN3 and P–QB4 which give him the ... Q5 square for his pieces. In addition Black can regroup his pieces by ... N–B4, ... R6–Q2 and ... N–Q6, a plan which the text-move aims to avoid.

38 ...   **Q–R2!**

39 Q–B1   **Q–R3!**

40 Q–B2?

Overlooking Black's pretty combination. He had to play 40 K–N1 Q–B5 41 R–B2 N–B5! 42 N×N KP×N when his pieces are tied

down and Black has the strong ... P–KN5 at his disposal.

40 ...   **Q–B5**

41 R–B1   **R×QBP!**

42 Q×R   **Q×Q**

0–1

After 43 R×Q R–Q8+ 44 N–K1 R×N+ White must give up his rook to prevent mate in three moves.

In this game Chigorin made maximum use of his queen's mobility. It is interesting that Chigorin was feared because of his splendid use of the major pieces. His games abound in examples of the queen's attacking powers and of the exploitation of open lines to penetrate into the enemy position.

62 Bogoljubow–Mieses

Baden-Baden 1925, Dutch Defence

1 P–Q4 P–KB4 2 P–KN3 N–KB3 3 B–N2 P–K3 4 N–KB3 P–Q4 5 0–0 B–Q3 5 ... B–K2! 6 P–B4 P–B3 7 N–B3 QN–Q2 8 Q–B2 N–K5 9 K–R1 Q–B3 10 B–B4! B×B 11 P×B Q–R3 12 P–K3 N2–B3 13 N–K5 N–Q2 14 R–KN1 N2×N 15 QP×N N N×N

16 P×N!

With this move White already intends to increase the scope of his major pieces. A good example of this is if Black accepts the pawn: 16 ... P×P? 17 QR–Q1 followed by 18 R–Q6. At the same time the QN-file is opened and a later threat will be P×P followed by P–B4.

16 ...   **B–Q2**

17 QR–Q1!   **P–QN4** (*139*)

Black attempts to forestall the above threat, probably only seeing the reply 18 P×NP? when he would have good counter-play down the QB-file.

In the further course of the game it is interesting to compare the

139
W

activity of both queens. The black queen's early sortie has placed it in a very disadvantageous position and it can do practically nothing for the rest of the game. On the other hand, White's queen now leaves its modest post and manages in a few moves to threaten the enemy position on both wings.

18 Q–N2!   0–0

Both 18 ... QP×P 19 R–Q6 and 18 ... NP×P 19 Q–N7 are good for White.

19 Q–R3!   KR–Q1

If 19 ... NP×P 20 Q–Q6 KR–Q1 21 R–N1 and 22 R–N7 wins.

20 P×NP   P×P
21 Q–R6!

Threatening 22 B×P P×B 23 Q×Q. Black should parry this threat with 21 ... Q–R5! when White continues 22 R–Q2 followed by 23 P–R4! P×P 24 P–B4.

21 ...   Q–R4?

As we shall see, this move only partially prevents the above threat. White can now bring off a splendid sacrifice which allows his queen to penetrate to the K-side and set up a mating net. What is so convincing about the coming combination is the logical way it is related to the open lines and to the preceding man-oeuvre Q–N2–R3–R6.

22 B×P!   P×B
23 R×NP+!   K×R

24 Q–KB6+   K–N1
25 R–KN1+   Q–N5
26 R×Q+   P×R

Black has obtained more than sufficient material for his queen, but he is lost against the advance of White's passed pawns supported by the queen.

27 P–B5   R.Q1–QB1
28 P–K6   B–B3
29 Q–B7+   K–R1
30 P–B6   R–KN1
31 Q–B7   QR–QB1
32 Q–K5   P–Q5+
33 K–N1   1–0

In modern chess we often meet extremely solid positions offering no pawn weaknesses and with the kings well protected from direct attacks. In such positions it is almost impossible to exploit the attacking power of the queen in the way we have seen in the above examples. In these circumstances the queen can usually show only part of its strength, either fighting for open files in conjunction with the rooks (see the chapter 'The Rooks'), or occupying vital diagonals and thus supporting or even replacing the bishop. The latter case often occurs in modern openings when the KB of White or Black has been fianchettoed. As the opponent often tries to exchange this bishop be-cause of its important defensive role, the queen can advantageously take over on the long diagonal. A simple illustration of this is found in the well-known line of the Queen's Indian Defence: 1 P–Q4 N–KB3 2 N–KB3 P–K3 3 P–KN3 P–QN3 4 B–N2 B–N2 5 0–0 P–B4 6 P–B4 P×P 7 N×P B×B 8 K×B when the usual continuation is 8 ... Q–B1 and 9 ... Q–N2+. The late Czecho-slovak grandmaster R. Réti was a specialist in this method of using the queen. His game against the World Champion of the time, Capablanca, made the rounds of the whole chess world.

63 Réti–Capablanca

New York 1924, English Opening

1 N–KB3 N–KB3 2 P–B4 P–KN3 3 P–QN4?! B–N2 better is 3 ... P–QR4! **4 P–N5 P–Q3 4 B–N2 0–0 5 P–N3 P–N3 6 B–N2 B–N2 7 0–0 P–Q3 8 P–Q3 QN–Q2 9 QN–Q2 P–K4 10 Q–B2 R–K1**

11 KR–Q1!

The first subtle move the idea of which is to post the queen on the long diagonal QR1–KR8. Black's previous move was apparently played to prepare 11 ... P–K5 but this would now allow 12 P×P N×P 13 B×B K×B 14 N–Q4 N2–B3 15 Q–N2! with the better game for White in view of his powerfully placed queen.

**11 ...   P–QR4
12 P–QR3   P–R3
13 N–B1   P–B4
14 P–N5!**

Admittedly, White could instead win a pawn by 14 P×RP R×P 15 N×P B×B 16 N×N B–B3 17 N×N+ B×N 18 B×B Q×B, but then Black's well co-ordinated pieces would give him attacking chances against White's weakened K-side.

**14 ...   N–B1
15 P–K3!**

Beginning a plan to open the Q-file and the long black diagonal.

**15 ...   Q–B2
16 P–Q4   B–K5
17 Q–B3 (?)**

A tactical slip which could have cost White a great part of his advantage. 17 Q–B1 was better, with a

subsequent transposition to the game line.

**17 ...   KP×P
18 P×P   N3–Q2?**

After this mistake everything is once again in order for White. Much stronger was 18 ... N–K3! 19 Q–B1 QR–B1 with complications.

19 Q–Q2!   P×P

It would have been better to maintain the tension in the centre with 19 ... QR–Q1. After the textmove Black wins the QBP in exchange for his QP, but he is left with serious weaknesses on QN3 and QB3, the latter square providing White with a vital strong-point (see his 26th move).

**20 B×P   Q×P
21 B×B   K×B
22 Q–N2+!   K–N1
23 R×P** (*140*)

It is clear that White's strategy has been successful. His queen controls the long diagonal, which means it is a potential danger to Black's king (see the note to Black's 27th move). Black now strives in vain to find points of attack for his queen which is already a source of trouble for him (24 N3–Q2 is threatened) and which will prove an object of tactical threats for the rest of the game.

23 ...	Q–B4
24 R1–Q1	R–R2
25 N–K3	Q–R4

A seemingly logical move by which Capablanca hopes to provoke the weakening 26 P–N4. However, 25 ... P–R4 is better, to prevent a subsequent N–N4.

26 N–Q4!

Capablanca was clearly expecting 26 R1–Q5!? B×R 27 P–N4 when 27 ... B×N! 28 P×Q B×P would give him good defensive chances.

| 26 ... | B×B |
| 27 K×B | Q–K4 |

He could not play 27 ... R×N 28 P×R Q×R, as 29 N–B5 (K6)! would suddenly reveal the latent danger of White's queen. However, he had a better defence in 27 ... N–K4 when White could maintain his advantage either with 28 Q–N3 or by transposing to an ending with 28 Q–K2, when Black's weak QNP will give him serious difficulties.

28 N–B4	Q–QB4
29 N–N6	R–B2
30 N–K3	N–K4
31 R1–Q5!	1–0

Black loses a rook after 31 ... N–B5 32 R×Q N×Q 33 R–B2 N–R5 34 N–Q5.

It is worth noting that White's queen, which occupied the long diagonal on move 22, remained on QN2 until the end of the game, yet proved the main factor in White's rapid victory. Black's queen on the other hand was always on the move, trying to create tactical threats, but its exposed position finally led to Black's downfall.

We often meet situations in which the queen exerts pressure along the other diagonal, bearing down onto the Q-side. Here is an example of this.

64 Alekhine–Rabar

Munich 1942, Catalan System

1 P–Q4	N–KB3	2 P–QB4	P–K3
3 P–KN3	P–Q4	4 B–N2	P×P
5 Q–R4+	B–Q2	6 Q×BP	B–B3
7 N–KB3	B–Q4	8 Q–Q3	P–B4
9 N–B3	B–B3	10 0–0	QN–Q2
11 R–Q1	P×P?	11 ...	Q–N3!
12 N×P	B×B	13 K×B	B–K2

14 Q–B3! (*141*)

White's queen is extraordinarily active on this square. If now 14 ... Q–B1, Alekhine would have continued 15 N–N3 followed by 16 B–B4 and 17 QR–B1, gradually building up winning pressure on the Q-side. We are denied the satisfaction of seeing such a positional exploitation of White's advantage, as Black commits errors which allow White to decide the game by a few tactical strokes. However, even here the white queen plays a vital part.

| 14 ... | Q–N3? |
| 15 B–K3! | 0–0 |

Black loses after both 15 ... Q×P 16 N3–N5 and 15 ... N–K4 16 N4–N5!

| 16 N–B5 | B–B4 |

Or 16 ... Q–Q1 17 N×B+ Q×N 18 Q×P KR–N1 19 Q–B7 R×P 20 B–Q4 with a winning position.

| 17 N–QR4 | Q–R4 |

18 N×B	**N×N**
19 N×P!	**K×N**
20 B-Q4!	

Not, however, 20 B-R6+? K-N3! etc. After the text-move 20 ... N4-Q2 fails to 21 B-B3 followed by 22 R×N.

20 ...	**N4-K5**
21 Q×N.4	**Q-KB4**
22 Q×Q	**P×Q**
23 QR-B1	**KR-K1**
24 R-B7!	**R×P**
25 R×NP	**K-N3**
26 B×N	**K×B**
27 R-Q6+	**1-0**

An interesting fact emerges from all these examples: compared with the other pieces, the queen's activity is predominantly of a tactical nature. Its many-sided powers enable it to assist in the execution of the most varied strategic plans. At one time it may be working with the rooks along open files and ranks, at another time it may be supporting or replacing the action of the bishops on the diagonals, and on many occasions its attacking powers help to create strong-points for the knights and to support pawn breakthroughs etc.

There is one time however, when the very pressure of this powerful piece exerts a decisive influence on the strategic nature of the position. This is when the major pieces alone are left on the board. Let us first examine the situation with rook and queen on either side. Such positions are unusual because they are poised between the middle-game and the end-game, the exchange of a single piece leading at once to a rook or a queen ending. At the same time, however, the rook and queen together present a formidable attacking force to be directed either at the enemy king or at his pawn weaknesses. The strategic principles that

apply to such positions are therefore a mixture of those that govern both middle-game and end-game. Let us now examine some typical examples.

65 Schlechter–Lasker

Match 1910, Ruy Lopez

1 P-K4 P-K4 2 N-KB3 N-QB3 3 B-N5 N-B3 4 0-0 P-Q3 5 P-Q4 B-Q2 6 N-B3 B-K2 7 B-N5 0-0 8 P×P N.QB3×P 9 B×B N3×B 10 B×B N×N+ 11 Q×N Q×B 12 N-Q5 Q-Q1 13 QR-Q1 R-K1 14 KR-K1 N-N3 15 Q-B3 N×N 16 R×N R-K3 17 R-Q3 Q-K2 18 R-N3 R-N3 19 R1-K3 R-K1 20 P-KR3 K-B1 21 R×R RP×R (*142*)

142
W

At first sight this position looks like a dead draw, and one might expect such an offer at any minute from one of the players. In reality, however, the next few moves tell us that Lasker is quite rightly playing for a win. His advantage lies in the fact that his king can reach the centre more easily than the white king if a rook ending should arise. Furthermore, White has an unpleasant weakness in his KP, and if he protects this by P-KB3 he gives Black the opportunity of playing ... P-KB4 or ... P-Q4 with advantage. This reasoning leads Lasker to the correct strategic plan: he will post his king in the centre, then improve as far as possible the placing of his pieces by offering the exchange of queens. At first Schlechter opts for the correct counterplay, using his queen to create weaknesses in Black's Q-side in order to have counter-chances once the black king advances.

22 Q–N4	P–QB3
23 Q–R3	P–R3
24 Q–N3	R–Q1
25 P–QB4	R–Q2
26 Q–Q1	Q–K4
27 Q–N4	K–K1
28 Q–K2	K–Q1
29 Q–Q2	K–B2
30 P–R3	R–K2
31 P–QN4? (*143*)	

143
B

White's previous move had already given the impression that he was about to make this tactical error. The correct move was 31 P–QR4! (or of course a move earlier), making it difficult for Black to undertake anything on the Q-side. He can then play P–QN4 later, threatening counterplay himself with P–N5. After the text-move Black can change the pawn structure to his advantage.

| 31 ... | P–QN4! |
| 32 P×P | |

After 32 Q–Q3 Romanovsky gives

32 ... Q–R8+ 33 K–R2 Q–R7! 34 P–B5 P×P 35 P×P R–Q2 36 Q–B3 Q–Q7 37 Q–K5+ K–N2 with a clear advantage to Black.

| 32 ... | RP×P |

The last two moves have favoured Black because an ending would now be won for him. Apart from the weakness of White's KP and QRP, there is the possibility of creating a passed pawn at a given moment by ... P–Q4 or ... P–QB4, White's king being too far away to stop it. For this reason the game is already strategically won for Lasker, and Schlechter can only look for tactical threats to make life as hard as possible for his opponent. The fact that this game is eventually lost by Lasker only goes to show how difficult such positions are to handle.

33 P–N3

Necessary to improve the position of his king, but now a new weakness appears on KR3.

33 ...	P–N4!
34 K–N2	R–K1
35 Q–Q1!	P–B3!

White's intended breakthrough with 36 P–QR4 will now be skilfully answered by 36 ... P×P 37 Q×RP K–N2 38 R–R3 Q×KP+ 39 K–N1 Q–Q5! 40 Q–R6+ K–B2 41 Q–R7+ Q×Q 42 R×Q+ K–N3 winning for Black, as White can only pick up one pawn on the K-side.

36 Q–N3	Q–K3
37 Q–Q1	R–KR1!
38 P–N4	Q–B5(?)

The first wrong step. After 38 ... R–R1 White would have had no counterplay whatsoever.

39 P–QR4!   **Q×NP**

It would have been more prudent to play 39 ... R–R1 40 P×P Q×NP.4 with a positional plus to Black. After the acceptance of White's pawn sacrifice, Black is driven back to defence because of the unfavourable position of his king. A new phase of the game now begins.

40 P×P	Q×NP
41 R–QN3	Q–R3
42 Q–Q4	

White now tries to seize the QR-file and is threatening both Q–N4 followed by R–R3, and R–N1 followed by R–QR1.

42 ...	R–K1
43 R–N1	R–K4
44 Q–N4	Q–N4

He cannot play 44 ... R–N4? 45 Q–B4.

45 Q–K1	Q–Q6
46 R–N4	

And now the strong threat is 47 Q–QR1. Black's safest defence lay in 46 ... R–R4! when Lasker gives: 'After 47 R–N3! Q×R 48 Q×R+ a queen ending arises in which my opponent could put up a tremendous resistance (e.g. 48 ... K–N2 49 Q–KB5 Q–B2 50 Q–R5)'. Nevertheless, this was the correct and logical plan. In the game Black wins a second pawn but this allows White to improve the attacking possibilities of his pieces.

46 ...	P–QB4(?)
47 R–R4	P–B5
48 Q–QR1!	Q×KP+
49 K–R2	R–N4
50 Q–R2!	Q–K4+
51 K–N1	Q–K8+
52 K–R2	P–Q4
53 R–R8!	Q–N5

Black could settle for perpetual check, but it is not easy to give up the idea of winning when you are two pawns up. As we shall see, there are no winning chances left.

| 54 K–N2! | Q–B4? |

Underestimating White's next move and losing with surprising speed. He had to play 54 ... R–N1

55 Q–R7+ R–N2 56 Q–R6! (if *56 Q–K3 Q–Q3* as given by Lasker) 56 ... Q–N3 57 Q–R3, or here 55 ... K–B1 56 Q–R6+ K–B2, with a draw in both cases.

| 55 Q–R6! | R–N1? |

Also insufficient is 55 ... R–N2 56 Q–K6 etc., but Lasker gives 55 ... P–B6! 56 R–QB8+ K–Q2 57 R×Q R×R still drawing.

56 R–R7+	K–Q1
57 R×P	Q–N3
58 Q–R3	K–B1
1–0	

If 58 ... Q–N5 59 Q–R7 wins. After the text-move Black resigned without waiting for the mate in three beginning 59 Q–B8+.

What conclusion can we draw from this very interesting if not faultless game? The first phase, moves 22 to 38, saw Black with a clear initiative in the struggle of the major pieces. It showed the strength of a centralized king and the disadvantage of having to avoid the exchange of queens. In the second phase, from move 39 onwards, White obtained a counter-attack by sacrificing two pawns. Black for his part refused the chance of transposing into a difficult but winning end-game and was finally mated after a few mistakes. We must point out that these mistakes by the World Champion of the time were no chance occurrence. In situations involving the major pieces serious mistakes occur with surprising frequency, even in master games. Indeed the play with major pieces contains so many strategic and tactical problems that it has proved to be one of the most difficult aspects of chess.

Our next position, played in the 1935 Moscow tournament, is an example of a successful transposition into an ending as a means of exploiting a slight positional plus. Romanovsky–Stahlberg (*144*).

144
W

White has the better pawn position, as Black's QBP and KP can easily be attacked. In contrast to the preceding example, there is much less danger to the kings. White's plan is to attack the black pawns after bringing his king to the centre. This will lead either to an ending or to the infiltration of White's heavy pieces down the Q-side.

36 Q–B3	R–B3
37 Q–B2	K–R1
38 K–B2	K–R2
39 R–QR4	K–N3

39 ... K–N1 is better, as the text-move only makes White's next move stronger.

| 40 P–K4! | P×P |
| 41 R×P | K–B2 |

The king cannot go to R2 because of 42 R×P!

| 42 Q–B3 | R–K3 |
| 43 P–R4 | K–B1 |

A better waiting move is 43 ... R–K2, in order to keep the king as long as possible in the centre.

| 44 Q–B4! | Q–Q3 |

The exchange of queens would give White an easily won ending: 44 ... Q×Q 45 R×Q R–QB3 46 K–K3 K–K2 47 K–K4 K–K3 48 P–R5 R–B1 49 R–R4 R–B2 (if *49*

... *R–B3 50 R–R7 P–B5 51 R×P P–B6 52 R–N6+*) 50 R–R6+ K–B2 51 K–Q5 etc. If instead 44 ... R–Q3 White can calmly play 45 K–K3 with a clear advantage.

| 45 Q–R2 | R–K2 |
| 46 R–R4! | R–N2! |

The only good continuation. After 46 ... Q×P 47 R–R8+ R–K1 48 R×R+ K×R 49 Q–N8+ K–Q2 50 Q×P+ K–B1 51 Q–R8+ K–Q2 52 Q×KP P–B5 53 Q–K3 Q–B7+ 54 K–K1 P–B6 55 Q–K2 White would have great winning prospects.

| 47 R–R8+ | R–N1? |

This shows that Black's previous good move was based on the faulty plan of transposing into a queen ending. He had an interesting way of drawing in 47 ... K–K2! e.g. 48 Q–N8 R–N7+ 49 K–K1 R–N8+ 50 K–Q2 R–Q8+! 51 K×R Q×P+ with perpetual check.

| 48 R×R+ | Q×R |

The queen ending is better for White in view of the more active placing of his king. It is not clear whether this advantage would be sufficient to win against the most exact defence, but this is irrelevant as regards the theme we are treating here. The game ended: **49 Q–Q5 Q–N7+ 50 K–K3 Q–B8+ 51 K–K2 Q–B7+ 52 K–K3 Q–B8+ 53 K–K4 Q–K8+ 54 K–B5 Q×P 55 Q×BP+ K–N1 56 Q–B4+ K–R1? 56 ... K–R2! 57 Q–KN4 Q–K8? 57 ... Q–B7! 58 K–N6 Q–QB8 59 Q–Q7 Q–KN8+ 60 K–B7 K–R2 61 Q–B5+ P–N3 62 Q–Q7 1–0.**

Our next game, in which both sides possess two rooks and a queen for a time, is a rather more complex example of our theme.

66 Alekhine–Bogoljubow

Match 1929, Queen's Gambit

1 P–Q4 N–KB3 2 P–QB4 P–B3
3 N–KB3 P–Q4 4 N–B3 P–K3
5 B–N5 QN–Q2 6 P–K4 P×KP
7 N×P B–K2 8 N–B3 0–0 9 Q–B2
P–QN3 10 0–0–0 B–N2 11 P–KR4
Q–B2 12 B–Q3 KR–K1 13 K–N1
N–B1 14 B×N B×B 15 N–K4 P–
B4 16 N×B+ P×N 17 Q–Q2 N–
N3 18 P–R5 N–B5 19 R–R4 B×N
20 P×B P–K4 21 P–Q5 Q–Q3 22
P–R6 K–R1 23 Q–B2 N×B 24
Q×N R–KN1 *(145)*

Black has managed to occupy the
only open file, but the position of
his king is most unattractive and the
mobility of his pieces is restricted by
White's protected passed pawn on
Q5. If White is to pose serious
threats to the black king, he needs
an open file, and as Black occupies
the KN-file it is imperative to open
another one. Alekhine achieves this
in a few moves with the help of a
pawn sacrifice.

25 P–B4!   R–N3
26 Q–B5   P–R3

As Black has no time to play . . .
P–N4, it would have been better to
play 26 . . . P×P at once.

27 R–K1!   P×P

If 27 . . . R–K1 28 R–R5! and if
then 28 . . . P–N4 29 P×KP BP×P

30 R×P R×R 31 Q×R.5+ Q×Q
32 R×Q R×P 33 P–N4! gives
White two connected passed pawns
which win for him.

28 R×P   R×P
29 R4–K4   R–KN1
30 R–K7   R–KB1
31 P–R4

Preventing 31 . . . P–N4 and at
the same time giving his king
another loop-hole.

31 . . .   R–R5
32 R–K8   R×R
33 R×R+   K–N2
34 Q–B8   K–R3
35 R–N8   Q–K2

White was threatening 36 Q–K8,
when the black pawn on KB2 could
not be defended.

36 K–R2   P–N4
37 R–N3!   P–B4

There is no better defence e.g.
37 . . . R–R4 38 P–B4! followed by
39 Q–KN8. Or 37 . . . K–R4 38
Q–KN8 P–R3 39 Q–R7 Q–Q2 40
R–N6! wins. After the text-move
White has an alternative win with
38 Q–KN8 e.g. 38 . . . P–B3 39
P–Q6, or 38 . . . Q–B3 39 P–Q6
R–Q5 40 P–Q7.

38 Q×KBP   P–B3

Not 38 . . . R×P 39 R–KR3+
R–R5 40 Q–B4+.

39 R–K3?

There was a quicker win by 39
Q–K6! Q×Q 40 P×Q R–K5 41
R–K3 etc.

39 . . .   Q–KB2
40 R–K6?

But this seemingly logical move
throws away the win. It was essential
to play 40 Q–K6! Q–B1 41 R–KB3
K–N2 42 R–KN3+ followed by 43
P–Q6 etc.

40 . . .   K–N2
41 R–Q6   Q–N3
42 R–Q7+

It was only now that Alekhine

realized that his original intention
of 42 Q–Q7+ K–R3 43 Q–K7
fails to the surprising 43 ... R×P!
44 R×BP R×P+ 45 K–N3 R–
QN5+ 46 K–B3 R–QB5+ 47
K–Q2 R–Q5+ 48 K–K3 R–K5+!
etc.

| 42 ... | K–R3 |
| 43 Q×Q+ | K×Q |

White now wins a pawn in the
rook ending but this should not be
sufficient to win. The game ended:
44 RP×P P×P 45 P×P R–R5+
46 K–N3 R–QN5+ 47 K–B3
R×P.4 48 R–QB7 P–R4 49 P–Q6
R–N1 50 R×P R–Q1 51 R–Q5
P–R5 52 K–B4 K–B2 53 K–B5
K–K3 54 R–Q4 R–QB1+ 55
K–N6 K–Q2 56 R×P R–B3+ 57
K–R5 R–B7 58 P–N4 K×P 59
P–B3 R–B6 60 P–B4 R–QR6+ 61
K–N6 K–K3 62 R–R5 R–KB6 63
P–B5+ K–K4 64 P–N5 K–B5 65
K–B6 K–N5 66 R–R1 R–B6+ 67
K–Q5 K×P 68 R–QN1 R–Q6+
69 K–B6 R–Q1 70 P–N6 K–N5??
The game is clearly drawn after 70
... K–K5! preventing the white
king's approach. 71 P–N7 P–B4 72
P–N8=Q R×Q 73 R×R P–B5 74
K–Q5 P–B6 75 K–K4 P–B7 76
R–KB8 K–N6 77 K–K3 1–0.

In play with the major pieces,
weak points in the enemy position
are of special importance. The
major pieces are poor in defence
but their long-range power is seen
at its best when they are attacking.
For this reason, it is often worth
more than an extra pawn if the
major pieces can switch the attack
from one weak point to another. As
we saw in the game Nimzowitsch–
Capablanca (p. 120), concentrated
pressure by the heavy pieces can
bring about a position in which the
mobility of enemy pieces is so restricted that they are finally left with-

out a reasonable move. Our next game
is an illustration of the same theme.

67 Rubinstein–Alekhine

Dresden 1926, Queen's Indian
Defence

1 P–Q4 N–KB3 2 N–KB3 P–K3
3 B–B4 P–QN3 4 P–KR3 B–N2
5 QN–Q2 B–Q3! strengthening his
central position and opening the
QB–file 6 B×B P×B 7 P–K3
0–0 8 B–K2 8 B–Q3 is better
8 ... P–Q4 9 0–0 N–B3 10 P–B3
N–K5 11 N×N(?) P×N 12
N–Q2 P–B4 13 P–KB4 P–KN4!
14 N–B4 P–Q4 15 N–K5 N×N
16 QP×N after 16 BP×N Black
could prepare a breakthrough with
... P–B5 16 ... K–R1.

17 P–QR4   R–KN1

Black now has a worse bishop
than his opponent, but his major
pieces have far more possibilities
of active play.

18 Q–Q2   P×P
19 R×P

Not 19 P×P? Q–R5 threatening
both 20 ... Q×RP and 20 ...
R×P+! and obtaining a winning
position after 20 Q–K3 R–N6.
However, after the text-move White
has a weak KP which the black
queen can attack at any time from
KN2, thus compelling the white
queen to be ready to go to Q4, which
in turn severely restricts its mobility.

19 ...   Q–N4
20 B–B1   Q–N6!

A very subtle manoeuvre. By
threatening 21 ... Q×RP Black
drives the white king into the
corner, thus gaining a tempo later
when White's rook will be un-
defended on KB2.

21 K–R1   Q–N2!

The weakness of White's KP is
already felt, as his queen must not

give up the defence of the KNP, allowing Black to exchange his 'bad' bishop.

22 Q–Q4	**B–R3!**
23 R–B2	**Q–N6!**

Black's four move manoeuvre has achieved two advantages; exchanging his bishop and driving the white rook from the KB-file. The point is that 24 K–N1 fails to 24 ... B×B 25 K×B (otherwise 25 ... Q×RP follows) 25 ... Q–R7! 26 R–Q1 QR–KB1 when Black carries out the breakthrough by ... P–B5.

24 R–B2	**B×B**
25 R×B	(*146*)

Although material is still equal, White's position can be viewed as hopeless. The weakness of his KP, the lack of co-ordination and passivity of his pieces, and Black's control of the KN-file all add up to a quick loss for White.

25 ...	**QR–QB1**

Threatening 26 ... R–B5.

26 P–N3	**R–B2**
27 R–K2	**R2–KN2**
28 R–B4	**R–QB2**

A well-known method of gaining a little time whilst preparing the final assault.

29 R–QB2	**R2–KN2**
30 R–K2	**R–N3!**
31 Q–N4	

An interesting position arises after

31 Q–Q1 R–R3! when none of White's pieces can move. Any rook move loses a pawn, 32 K–N1 allows 32 ... Q×RP, if the white queen leaves the back rank 32 ... R×P+! wins, and finally if 32 Q–K1 (or KB1) 32 ... Q–N2 wins the KP. However, if White plays 32 P–B4 then 32 ... P–Q5! 33 Q×P R×P+! wins.

31 ...	**R–R3**
32 P–R4	**Q–N2!**

This wins much more quickly than 32 ... R×P+ 33 R×R Q×R+ 34 K–N1. We have already pointed out that active major pieces are worth more than an extra pawn, and Alekhine demonstrates this fact once again by means of a few energetic moves.

33 P–B4	**R–N3**
34 Q–Q2	**R–N6!**

Threatening 35 ... R–R6+ and planning to answer 35 K–N1 with 35 ... P–Q5! 36 P×P P–K6! 37 Q–B2 R–KR6 followed by 38 ... Q–N6.

35 Q–K1	**R×NP**
0–1	

In the same way, an isolated pawn can become a fatal weakness with heavy pieces on the board, mainly because the defending pieces are driven into passive positions. Consider the following example: Vyzantiadis–Pachman (*147*).

At first sight this position seems tenable for White but in reality he loses very quickly. After **25 ... R–Q1** the threat of . . . P–K4 forces a further weakening of his pawn position. A conclusion to be drawn from this is that an isolated pawn should not be defended passively by the major pieces, but actively. In this case White would draw with his rook on QB4. The game continued: **26 P–B4 Q–K5 27 Q–KB2 P–N3 28 K–R2 R–Q4! 29 R–Q2 P–KR4 30 K–N1** after 30 P–KR4 the black king simply marches to ... KB4 **30 ... R–KB4 31 P–N3 P–R5! 32 R–K2 Q–Q6 33 Q–K3** or 33 P–KN4 R×P! **33 ... Q×Q+ 34 R×Q P×P 35 R–K4** 35 R–KB3 equally loses to 35 . . . K–B1 36 K–N2 K–K2 37 K×P K–Q3 etc. **35 ... K–B1 36 K–N2 K–K2 37 K×P R–Q4 38 R–K3** otherwise the black king penetrates on the Q-side **38 ... R×P 39 R–QB3 R–Q2 40 K–B3 K–B3 41 K–K3 K–B4 42 P–QR4 P–B3 43 P–R5 P×P 0–1.**

7 The King

7 The King

The king has a special place among the pieces. On the one hand it is the most important piece on the board, and on the other hand for the major part of the game it has the thankless task of defending itself from attacks by enemy pieces. For this reason, it is pointless trying to assess its value in relation to the other pieces. Nor can it be exchanged for enemy pieces, because the elimination of the enemy king (i.e. mate), even if it requires the greatest sacrifice of material, is the ultimate strategic aim of the game.

It is not until the end-game that we see a great change in this situation. As soon as direct mating threats are no longer an important factor, the king becomes active and begins to make its presence felt as a vital strategic element in the struggle. Experience teaches us that the king is a little more powerful than a minor piece, yet much less so than a rook. It is of course outside the scope of this book to deal with the strategic problems arising from the use of the king in the end-game (centralization, opposition etc.).

In the first section of this chapter we examine those exceptional cases when the king becomes active even during the middle-game. In the second section we look at the problems of where to post our king in the middle-game, and in the third section we consider cases which reveal the unfavourable posting of the king as a permanent strategic factor.

THE ACTIVE KING IN THE MIDDLE-GAME

The position in our next diagram (*148*) was reached in a game Pachman–Ujtelky played in the 1954 Championship of Czechoslovakia.

148
W

White's pieces have reached ideal positions and the sole question is to find the best way of exploiting this. White can hardly succeed in winning the QB pawn without losing his own QP which is threatened if he moves his knight on QB5. White's correct strategic plan is to create a break-through on the K-side by P–B4, P–KN4, P–B5. However, his KRP must be guarded first and this could be done by his knight on QN4 (N–Q3–B4–N2) or by his rook on QB1 (K–N2 and R–KR1). As this would displace valuable attacking pieces, White must consider using the one piece which is lying idle at the moment – his king. It can easily advance to KR3 and Black's pieces are too passively placed for him to undertake anything effective against White's exposed king.

35 K–R2	Q–N3
36 K–R3!	Q–R2
37 P–B4	P–N3
38 P–N4	N–Q2
39 B–Q3	N×N
40 P×N	Q–Q2

Black tries without success to profit from the position of the white king in order to make the pawn breakthrough difficult to carry out. All White has to do is move his king back a square before proceeding with the final attack.

| 41 P–B5! | KP×P |

| 42 P×P | P–N4 |

Not of course 42 ... P×P? 43 R–KN1+ K–R2 44 Q–B4 winning.

| 43 K–N2! | P–B3 |

At least preventing P–B6 when both black bishops would be shut out of play. Black also quickly loses after 43 ... Q–Q5 44 Q×Q R×Q 45 P–B6 B–Q1 46 P×P R–N5+ (if *46 ... P×P 47 R–KR1 R–R5 48 R×R P×R 49 K–B3* etc.) 47 K–B3 R×P 48 R–KR1! etc.

| 44 RP×P | RP×P |
| 45 P–K6 | Q–B2 |

The last try. 45 ... Q–Q5 also loses after 46 Q–R3 Q–R5 47 Q×Q P×Q 48 K–R3.

| 46 Q–R3 | R–Q5 |
| 47 R–KR1! | |

But not 47 Q–R5? R–R5 48 Q–N6+ K–R1 49 R–KR1 R–KN1!

| 47 ... | R–R5 |
| 48 Q–KB3 | R–KB5 |

Or 48 ... R×R 49 K×R when there is no defence to 50 R–R2.

| 49 Q–R5 | 1–0 |

In this case the king was used to support a pawn advance, but there are a few exceptional examples in chess literature when the king directly takes part in a middle-game mating attack. The following game is a case in point.

68 Teichmann–Players in consultation

Glasgow 1902, Two Knights Defence

1 P–K4 P–K4 2 N–KB3 N–QB3 3 B–B4 N–B3 4 0–0 N×P 5 P–Q4 P×P 6 R–K1 P–Q4 7 B×P Q×B 8 N–B3 Q–KR4 9 N×N B–K2 9 ... B–K3 is better 10 B–N5 B–K3 11 B×B N×B 12 N–N3 Q–R3 13 Q×P 0–0 14 QR–Q1 N–B3 15 Q–QR4 QR–Q1 16 N–Q4 N×N 17 R×N R×R 18 Q×R P–QN3 19 Q–K5 P–QB4? with 19 ...

Q–Q7 Black could achieve complete equality **20 P–KB4 B–B1 21 P–B5 B–N2 22 Q–K7 Q–QB3 23 R–K2 P–B3 24 N–K4 Q–Q4 25 N–Q6 B–B3 26 P–KR3 P–B5 27 P–B3 P–KR3?** (*149*)

149
W

Suddenly Black finds himself in a situation where none of his pieces has an effective move. His last move is an attempt to free his queen which was tied to the defence of the mating possibility after Q–K6+. However, this weakening move allows White to bring his king right up the board in an astonishing mating attack. It would have been better for Black to play waiting moves with his rook.

28 K–R2	**P–QN4**
29 K–N3	**P–QR4**
30 K–R4	**P–N3**

Black was probably relying on this defence, as now 31 P×P?? allows 31 . . . Q–N4 mate.

31 R–K3	**Q×NP**
32 R–N3!	**Q–KB7**

After 32 . . . P–N4+ White would not of course play 33 K–N4 B–B6 mate, but would brilliantly complete his original plan by 33 K–R5! Q×R 34 K–N6 followed by a quick mate.

33 P×P	**Q–B5+**
34 R–N4	**Q–B7+**
35 K–R5	**1–0**

It is much more common to see the king used in middle-game positions which are more simplified, especially those in which queens have been exchanged. The centralized king often develops great activity and is particularly well-placed for transpositions into the end-game. This is the main idea behind the Alekhine variation of the Orthodox Queen's Gambit which was first seen in the following game.

69 Alekhine–K. Treybal

Baden-Baden 1925, Queen's Gambit

1 P–QB4 P–K3 2 P–Q4 P–Q4 3 N–QB3 N–KB3 4 B–N5 QN–Q2 5 P–K3 B–K2 6 N–B3 0–0 7 R–B1 P–B3 8 B–Q3 P×P 9 B×BP N–Q4 10 B×B Q×B
    11 N–K4

With this move which is still regarded as one of the most promising lines, White deliberately allows the exchange of queens. During the course of the following middle-game without queens he obtains an advantage in the centre which is increased by the presence of his king actively supporting the advance of his pawns.

11 . . .   **N2–B3?**

Theory tells us that 11 . . . N4–B3! 12 N–N3 P–K4 is the continuation here, leaving the knight on Q2 to control the important strategic points on Black's QB4 and K4. White has more initiative after the immediate 11 . . . Q–N5+ 12 Q–Q2 Q×Q+ 13 K×Q, or after 11 . . . N4–B3 12 N–N3 Q–N5+, as shown in several games of the Alekhine–Capablanca match.

12 N–N3	**Q–N5+**
13 Q–Q2	**Q×Q+**
14 K×Q	**R–Q1**
15 KR–Q1	**B–Q2**
16 N–K5	**B–K1**
17 K–K2	**K–B1**
18 P–B4	**P–KN3**
	(*150*)

According to Alekhine, this is an unnecessary move which makes his task easier. Better is 18 ... QR–B1.

150
W

19 K–B3!

The difference between the two kings is now clear. Whilst the black king remains passive until the end of the game, the white king helps to prepare the pawn breakthrough, then eventually brings about the decision in the ending by penetrating into the enemy position (see move 48).

19 ...	QR–B1
20 B–N3	R–B2
21 N–K2	N–K2
22 P–N4	R1–B1

Black is clearly preparing the freeing move ... P–QB4, an intention which Alekhine nips in the bud in a subtle manner.

23 N–N3!   **N3–Q4**

After 23 ... P–B4 24 P–N5! White obtains a decisive advantage, as shown by Alekhine in the following variations:

a. 24 ... N3–Q4 25 P×P R×P 26 R×R R×R 27 N–K4 R–B2 28 N–Q6 N–QB3 29 N–N4!

b. 24 ... N–Q2 25 N×N+ B×N 26 R×P R×R 27 P×R K–K1 28 K–B2 winning a pawn.

24 N–K4	R–Q1
25 N–B5	P–N3
26 N–R6	R2–B1
27 P–K4	P–B3

Otherwise Black will be condemned to complete passivity, but he must now lose material.

28 P×N	P×N
29 P–Q6	R×P
30 BP×P	R–Q4

After 30 ... R3–Q1 31 B×P Black's game would be hopeless.

The game now ended: **31 B×R N×B 32 P–QR3 P–KN4 33 N–N4 N–K2 34 N–Q3 N–Q4 35 P–KR4! P×P 36 N–B4 N×N 37 K×N R–Q1 38 K–N5 K–N2 39 K×P R–Q4 40 K–N5 R–Q1 41 K–B4 R–Q2 42 K–K3 R–N2 43 P–N4 P–QR3 44 R–B1 R–R2 45 R–B6 R–K2 46 P–R4 K–N1 47 P–R5 P–N4 48 P–Q5! KP×P 49 P–K6 K–N2 50 P–N5 P–R4 51 K–Q4 R–QB2 52 K–B5 R–B1 53 K–N6 P–Q5 54 P–K7 1–0.**

As the above three examples have shown, it is only possible for the king to be a fighting piece in the middle-game when the enemy position is so constricted or the material so reduced that no immediate danger threatens. Other cases are extremely rare and really belong to the realms of chess tactics. For example, positions have occurred in chess literature in which an exposed king has won the game by marching straight into the enemy camp, but such combinations are outside the scope of this book.

THE CHOICE OF WHICH SIDE TO CASTLE, AND THE KING TREK.

In most games both kings castle in order to escape a central attack by the enemy pieces. At the same time castling is usually part of general development, being played during the first phase of the game, in the opening stage. However, the decision about which side to castle often determines the strategic plan of the entire middle-game. This is best illustrated by a few well-known examples from opening theory.

A After **1 P–Q4 P–Q4 2 P–QB4 P–K3 3 N–QB3 N–KB3 4 B–N5 B–K2 5 P–K3 0–0 6 N–B3 QN–Q2 7 Q–B2 P–B4** (*151*) White has two completely different plans at his disposal:

151
W

a. **8 BP×P N×P 9 B×B Q×B 10 N×N P×N 11 B–Q3 P–KN3 12 P×P N×P 13 0–0**, with the aim of concentrating on Black's weak QP.
b. **8 0–0–0 Q–R4 9 K–N1** setting up a very sharp position in which White intends to attack on the K-side by P–KR4 and P–KN4, whilst Black must try to counter-attack on the other wing.

Castling on opposite wings usually leads in fact to sharp struggles, as one can hurl pawns against the enemy king's position without the fear of denuding one's own king. For this reason the player who is behind in development (normally Black) does best to delay castling if possible, so that he can castle on the same wing as his opponent.

B **1 P–K4 P–K4 2 N–KB3 N–KB3 3 N×P P–Q3 4 N–KB3 N×P 5 N–B3 N×N 6 QP×N B–K2 7 B–Q3** (*152*)

152
B

White is a little better developed and could play for the attack after 7 ... 0–0? **8 B–K3 N–Q2 9 P–KR4!** so Black should first play the waiting move **7 ... N–B3!** to see which side White will castle. If White then castles on the K-side, Black can follow suit, and if White castles long, Black can prepare to do the same e.g. **8 B–K3 B–N5 9 B–K4 Q–Q2** etc.

Sometimes the whole character of the position is determined by whether or not a side castles at a given point. Take for example a well-known variation in the Gioco Pianissimo:

C After **1 P–K4 P–K4 2 N–KB3 N–QB3 3 B–B4 B–B4 4 P–Q3 P–Q3 5 N–B3 N–B3** White should not play **6 0–0? B–KN5!** with an unpleasant pin which White cannot shake off by **7 P–KR3** because of **7 ... P–KR4**. On the other hand, after the normal **6 B–K3** it is Black's turn to avoid **6 ... 0–0?** when White can afford to lose a tempo to play **7 B–KN5!** which is even better than **7 B×B**.

It often happens that in the opening stages one side may for various reasons reject normal castling and decide to secure his king by more involved methods. In these cases we talk of 'artificial castling'.

D After **1 P–Q4 P–Q4 2 P–QB4**

P–K3 3 N–QB3 N–KB3 4 B–N5
B–K2 5 P–K3 0–0 6 N–B3 P–KR3
7 B–R4 N–K5 8 B × B Q × B 9 P × P
N × N 10 P × N P × P 11 Q–N3
Q–Q3 12 P–B4 P × P 13 B × P
N–B3 14 B–K2 B–K3 15 Q–B3
Q–N5 White's strongest continuation is **16 K–Q2!** and if then 16 . . .
Q–Q3 (K2) 17 KR–QB1 followed by K–K1–B1 etc.

E After **1 P–Q4 N–KB3 2 N–
KB3 P–QN3 3 B–B4 B–N2 4
P–K3 P–K3 5 B–Q3 B–K2 6 QN–
Q2 N–R4 7 B–N3 N × B 8 RP × N,**
White has an attack down the KR-file if Black castles in the normal way, so the normal continuation is 8 . . . P–KN3 followed by . . . K–B1–N2.

Now let us examine a few more difficult problems connected with choosing which side to castle.

70 Szabo–Bisguier

Buenos Aires 1955, Queen's Gambit

**1 P–Q4 P–Q4 2 P–QB4 P–QB3
3 N–KB3 N–B3 4 N–B3 P–K3
5 P–K3 QN–Q2 6 B–Q3 B–Q3
7 P–K4 P × KP 8 N × P N × N
9 B × N N–B3 10 B–B2 B–N5+
11 B–Q2 B × B+ 12 Q × B 0–0**
(*153*)

In this position Trifunovic chose to play 13 0–0? against Bisguier

who quickly equalized after 13 . . .
Q–B2 14 Q–K3 P–QN3 15 Q–K5
Q–N1 16 N–N5 B–R3 17 P–QN3
P–B4 18 QR–Q1 P–KR3 19 N–K4
Q × Q 20 P × Q N × N 21 B × N
QR–Q1. However, the diagrammed position is advantageous to White who has a superior central position and a better bishop, whereas Black's bishop has difficulty coming into the game. Szabo finds the correct strategic plan:

**13 N–K5   Q–B2
14 0–0–0!**

This move enables White to advance his K-side pawns and creates serious problems for Black.

14 . . .   P–B4

A logical but stereotyped central counter. Black had bettter prospects with 14 . . . P–QN4! in order to create a strong base for his knight on . . . Q4. However, White still stands better after 15 P–B5 because the black bishop remains shut in for a long time.

15 Q–K3   P–QN3

15 . . . P × P 16 R × P would only help White's attack, but now he is denied the chance of an attack down the QB-file.

16 P × P!   P × P

After 16 . . . Q × P 17 Q × Q P × Q 18 P–B3, White has an end-game advantage because his king is nearer the centre and Black's QBP is weak.

**17 P–KN4!   R–N1
18 KR–N1   Q–N3**

18 . . . N–Q2 loses to 19 N × N B × N 20 Q–Q3.

**19 P–N3   R–N2
20 P–N5   N–K1**

Equally hopeless is 20 . . . N–Q2 21 N–N4 etc.

**21 B × P+!   K × B
22 Q–R3+   K–N1
23 R–N4   1–0**

Black cannot prevent mate down

the KR-file e.g. 23 ... P–B3 24
R–R4 P×N 25 P–N6 etc.

Just as in the A(b) example we
gave earlier, Q-side castling in the
above game was the basis of an
attack against the K-side. In some
cases, however, it is to our advantage
to castle on the wing where we are
preparing to attack. This is of course
only possible when our king is
protected from enemy attacks by our
command of space. The next game
shows the danger of exposing a king
in this way.

71 Pachman–Fichtl

Czechoslovak Ch 1954, Queen's
Gambit

1 P–QB4 P–K3 2 N–QB3 P–Q4
3 P–Q4 P–QB3 4 N–B3 N–B3
5 P–K3 P–QR3 6 P–B5 QN–Q2
7 P–QN4 P–QR4 8 P–N5 P–K4
9 Q–R4 Q–B2 10 B–K2 P–K5 (?)
11 N–Q2 P–KN3 12 N–N3 B–R3
13 B–Q2 0–0 (*154*)

154
W

14 0–0–0?

In this position it is clear that
White's main theatre of operations
will be the Q-side when Black's
QRP is a glaring weakness which
must fall sooner or later. At first
sight K-side castling seems the
most logical, but then after ...
N–K1 and ... P–B4 Black can set

up dangerous counter-play. White's
plan to castle long is correct, but
his tactical execution is inexact.
He should first play 14 P–N6!
Q–Q1 and only then 15 0–0–0!
when Black could not open a line on
the Q-side and would quickly lose
the QRP. Even though the position
is then semi-blocked, the extra
pawn should guarantee the win.
White thought that the text-move
was even stronger but overlooked
Black's next tactical counter which
poses serious threats to the white
king.

14 ...	P–N3!
15 NP×P	N–N1
16 P×P	Q×NP
17 Q–N5!	

The last few moves have dramatically changed the situation so much,
that White's original plan of capturing the QRP cannot be executed, as
Black answers 17 B–N5 with 17 ...
B–N5 followed by 18 ... R–B1.
Although the position of White's
king on the Q-side looks risky, he
nevertheless makes good use of it by
offering the exchange of queens.
The king will then be much nearer
than Black's king to the weak QRP
and QP. For this reason White aims
to simplify the position as much as
possible in order to exploit his end-
game advantage.

17 ...	Q×BP
18 Q×Q	N×Q
19 N–R4	B–N5
20 QR–K1!	

But not 20 B×B? N×B 21 QR–
B1 (or *21 B–K1*) 21 ... N–N5. After
the text-move White can quietly
answer 20 ... N–QN5 with 21
K–N1. Black now decides to play
passively and allow simplification,
but this only helps White to reach
his strategic goal.

| 20 ... | B×B? |

21 R×B	**N–Q2?**
22 K–N1	**KR–QB1**
23 R–QB1	**B–B1**
24 K–N2	**N–N5?**
25 R×R	**R×R**
26 B×N	**P×B**

Or 26 ... B×B 27 R–B2 R×R+ 28 K×R B–K8 29 P–B3 followed by 30 N–B3, or here 29 N–B3 B×P 30 N×QP with a won ending for White in both cases.

27 R–B2	**R×R+**

Or 27 ... R–R1 28 R–B7! N–B3 29 N–N6 R–N1 (if *29 ... R–R3 30 N–Q7*) 30 R–B6 etc. In the game continuation Black's QNP falls quickly, mainly because the black king is too far away to help. The final moves were: **28 K×R B–Q3 29 P–KR3 K–B1 30 N3–B5! K–K2 31 K–N3 B–R7 32 K×P B–N8 33 N–B3 N–B3 34 N–Q1 K–Q3 35 K–N5 K–B2 36 P–QR4 P–N4 37 P–R5 N–K1 38 N–R6+ K–N2 39 N–N4 N–B2+ 40 K–B5 P–B4 41 N×P 1–0.**

The following game by the ex-World Champion is a good example of the correct position of the king on the side where the breakthrough is planned, but this time there is no castling involved.

72 Tolush–Botvinnik

20th USSR Championship 1952, French Defence

1 P–Q4 P–K3 2 P–K4 P–Q4 3 N–Q2 N–KB3 4 P–K5 N3–Q2 5 B–Q3 P–QB4 6 P–QB3 P–QN3 7 N–K2 B–R3 8 B×B N×B 9 0–0 N–B2 10 N–KN3 B–K2

11 N–B3	**P–KR4!**

In this variation Black usually castles on the K-side, but his king is by no means secure there, as was seen in the game Kotov–Keres

(16 USSR Ch) which continued (from move 9) 9 ... B–K2 10 N–KN3 0–0 11 Q–N4 P–B4 12 KP× Pep R×P 13 N–R5 R–N3 14 Q–K2 N–B2 15 N–B3 with a clear advantage to White.

Botvinnik selects a completely different plan, aiming to block the K-side and play his king towards the Q-side where he intends to carry out a pawn advance. Black's space advantage on this wing is enough to ensure the safety of the king.

12 N–K1	**P–N3**
13 N–Q3	**Q–B1**
14 B–K3	**P–B5!**
15 N–B4	**P–QN4**
16 N–R3	**Q–Q1**
17 Q–Q2	**P–QR4**
18 P–QR3	**N–N1**
19 B–N5	

White exchanges bishops in the hope of exploiting the weakness of his opponent's black squares on the K-side, whilst Black prepares a pawn breakthrough on the other wing.

19 ...	**N–B3**
20 KR–K1	**B×B**
21 N×B	**N–K2**

Black must play his knight to KB4, even if this means weakening his pawns, or else his KBP cannot be guarded.

22 Q–B4	**N–B4**
23 N×N	**NP×N**
24 R–K3	**Q–K2**
25 R–N3	**K–Q2!** *(155)*

Black's plan is now clear. His king is safe and his rooks are ready to invade the Q-side.

26 N–B3	**R–KR2**

An unnecessary safety measure. He could play 26 ... QR–QN1 and if 27 R–N7 then 27 ... Q–B1 followed by 28 ... P–N5.

27 R–N5	**K–B3**

155
W

Even here 27 ... R–QN1 was preferable.

28 P–KR4	R–QN1
29 N–R2?	

White could have profited from his opponent's inaccuracies by playing 29 N–K1 and if 29 ... P–N5 30 RP×P P×P 31 N–B2 would be very strong.

29 ...	P–N5
30 RP×P	P×P
31 Q–B1	R2–R1
32 P–QN3?	

This understandable attempt at a counter-attack against the enemy king is dubious on this occasion. 32 N–B1 is better.

32 ...	NP×P
33 P×P	P×P
34 Q×P	Q–N5!

Black has obtained a definite positional advantage but one factor, which has nothing to do with chess strategy, prevents him from converting it into a win. This is an important factor in tournament games – time-trouble. Because of it, Botvinnik overlooked a threefold repetition of position, so only drew after 35 Q–B3+ N–Q4 36 N–B1 Q–B6 37 Q–Q1 Q–QN6 38 Q–K1 Q–QB6 39 Q–Q1 Q–QN6 40 Q–K1 Q–QB6? better 40 ... Q–N5 or 40 ... P–B6 ½–½.

In the three examples we have quoted, the active side posted his king on the Q-side. We selected examples of Q-side castling because to a certain extent they are exceptions to the rule. K-side castling is by far the most normal, requiring only four moves to be carried out, whereas Q-side castling needs at least five and usually six moves. Moreover, the position of a king on KN1 is much safer than on QB1, as the QR2 square remains unprotected and one must usually waste another move, K–N1, to guard it. Generally speaking, we can say that castling K-side is the norm and that one must have a definite strategic plan in mind before castling long.

In certain games the king's position after castling becomes so uncomfortable that the king must flee black to the centre or even across to the other wing. This of course is an emergency measure, as such a king trek costs a great deal of time, making it easier for the opponent to build up an attack. Our next game illustrates all the dangers involved in transferring the king to the opposite side of the board.

73 Capablanca–Ragozin

Moscow 1935, Nimzo-Indian Defence

1 P–Q4	N–KB3
2 P–QB4	P–K3
3 N–QB3	B–N5
4 P–QR3	B×N+
5 P×B	P–Q3
6 Q–B2	

More exact is 6 P–B3.

6 ...	0–0?

Dubious here. Black ought to continue 6 ... P–B4 7 P–K4 N–B3 followed by ... P–QN3, ... Q–Q2, ... B–R3 and ... 0–0–0, when his king would be much safer.

7 P–K4	P–K4
8 B–Q3	P–B4

Preferable is 8 . . . N–B3.

9 N–K2	N–B3
10 P–Q5	N–K2
11 P–B3	N–Q2?

From a strategic point of view this is already the decisive error. The correct move is 11 . . . N–K1 to prepare the freeing move . . . P–B4. If then 12 P–N4 Black can play 12 . . . N–N3 controlling the vital . . . KR5 square, and if instead 12 N–N3 White's attack is considerably slowed down.

12 P–KR4!	N–QN3
13 P–N4	P–B3?

Helping White to open lines. 13 . . . B–Q2 was essential, followed by . . . N–R5, . . . P–QR3 and . . . P–QN4.

14 N–N3	K–B2

Beginning a long trek with his king, as it would be fatal to remain on the K-side.

15 P–N5!	N–N1
16 P–B4	K–K1 (*156*)

An extremely interesting position. Black has momentarily succeeded in safe-guarding his king which will soon reach the Q-side. However, White will use this gain of time to strengthen his position in such a way that he can eventually break through on the Q-side, even though he has weak pawns on that wing. An important factor is that White's space advantage is so great that he does not need to castle himself.

17 P–B5	Q–K2
18 Q–KN2	K–Q1
19 N–R5	K–B2
20 P×P	P×P
21 N–N7	B–Q2
22 P–R5!	R–B1
23 P–R6	

White's knight is now very strongly posted, as Black must always be prepared for N–K6.

23 . . .	K–N1
24 R–KN1	R–KB2
25 R–N1	Q–B1
26 B–K2	K–R1
27 B–R5	R–K2
28 Q–QR2	Q–Q1
29 B–Q2	N–R5
30 Q–N3	N–N3

After 30 . . . R–N1 to prepare . . . P–N4, 31 N–K6 is immediately decisive e.g. 31 . . . B×N 32 QP×B N–N3 33 B–B7 wins, or 31 . . . Q–N3 32 Q×Q P×Q 33 N–B7+ K–R2 34 N–N5+ B×N 35 R×B followed by 36 B–Q1 winning the knight.

31 P–R4!

The culmination of White's Q-side attack leading to a total blockade of the black position. 31 . . . B×RP now fails to 32 Q–R2 B–Q2 33 N–K6 B×N 34 QP×B followed by 35 B–B7 winning.

31 . . .	R–N1
32 P–R5	N–B1

32 . . . N–R5 loses to 33 N–K6.

In the remainder of the game, Capablanca slowly but surely capitalizes on his positional superiority: **33 Q–R2 Q–B1 34 B–K3 P–N3 35 P–R6 Q–Q1 36 K–Q2 Q–B1 37 R–QN2 Q–Q1 38 Q–N1 P–N4** as White is threatening 39 Q–KB1 and 40 N–K6, Black tries a desperate

freeing move **39 P×P N–N3 40
Q–R2 P–B5 41 Q–R3 Q–B2 42 K–
B1 R–KB1 43 R2–N2** again threatening N–K6 **43 ... Q–N1 44 Q–N4
R–Q1 45 R–N3 R–KB1 46 N–K6!
B×N 47 QP×B R–QB2** to be able
to answer 48 B–B7 with 48 ...
R2–B1 **48 Q×QP N–K2** or 48 ...
R–Q1 49 Q×R.8 Q×Q 50 R×N
49 R–Q1 1–0.

Our next game is an instructive
example of a successful king trek
which arises logically out of the play.

74 R. Byrne–Kotov

USSR–USA match 1954, Nimzo-
Indian Defence

**1 P–Q4 N–KB3 2 P–QB4 P–K3
3 N–QB3 B–N5 4 P–K3 P–B4
5 B–Q3 0–0 6 P–QR3 B×N+
7 P×B N–B3 8 N–K2 P–QN3
9 P–K4 N–K1 10 B–K3 P–Q3
11 0–0 B–R3 12 N–N3 N–R4
13 Q–K2 R–B1 14 P–Q5 Q–Q2
15 P–QR4 P–K4 16 P–B4 P–B3
17 P–B5** (*157*)

Although the pawn structure is
similar to the one in the previous
game, Black has the superior position here. First of all White is a
long way behind with his K-side
pawn advance, and secondly the
black pieces are posted much more
actively, with an attack on ...

QB5. However, Black cannot afford
to waste time, as White will gradually begin his K-side pawn storm.
For this reason, Black's king must be
transferred to the other wing where
it will be safe.

17 ...   K–B2!

The tactical justification for this
move lies in 18 Q–R5+ K–K2
19 Q×P B×P with advantage.
After the text-move White blindly
sticks to his original plan of advancing his K-side pawns, a plan that is
now pointless. He could have
obtained near equality by 18 KR–
N1! followed by N–B1–Q2–N3,
exchanging off the knight and thus
freeing his queen from having to
guard the QBP. If then the black
king went to the Q-side, White could
prepare P–R5.

**18 R–B3?   K–K2
19 N–B1   K–Q1
20 R–R3   R–KR1!**

Weaker would be 20 ... P–R3
when White's knight could head for
KN6.

**21 P–N4   K–B2
22 N–N3   K–N1
23 K–B2   N–B2
24 Q–R2   R.B1–Q1
25 R–KN1   Q–K2
26 B–K2?**

White is suddenly content to make
planless waiting moves, thereby
completely handing the initiative
over to Black. It was essential to
play 26 N–B1 and 27 P–N5.

**26 ...   B–B1
27 N–B1   B–Q2
28 N–Q2**

This was White's last chance to
play 28 P–N5 with counter-play,
but 28 ... R.Q1–KB1 followed by
... P–N3, or an immediate 28 ...
P–N3 29 NP×P Q–B2! gives Black
active play against the exposed
white king.

28 ...   P–KN4!

By the following blockade of the K-side, Black obtains a free hand for operations on the other wing.

29 N–B1	**B–K1**
30 N–N3	**P–KR3**
31 N–R5	**B×N**
32 P×B	

After 32 R×B Black plays his knight to KN2, after which White has to reckon with the opening of the KR-file by ... P–KR4.

32 ...	**N–K1**
33 B–N4	**N–KN2**
34 K–K2	**K–B2**
35 K–Q3	**R–R1**
36 R–N1	**R.KR1–QN1**
37 R–N2	**P–R3**
38 K–B2	

The reader may ask why White's king has crossed over to the Q-side where it is more exposed to danger than on the K-side. The reason is that he requires the king here for the end-game! In fact, after ... P–N4 with subsequent line-opening, the major pieces could easily be exchanged and Black's king would be threatening to penetrate down the Q-side to attack the white pawn on QB3.

38 ...	**Q–Q2**
39 R–KN3	**Q–K1**
40 B–Q2	**R–R2?**

This last move before the time control throws away the win which could be obtained by 40 ... N× RP! 41 R–R3 N–B5 42 R×RP Q–K2 when his major pieces decisively penetrate down the KR-file.

41 R–R3	**P–N4**

Giving White the opportunity to save himself by a pretty tactical coup (see move 47). The position would be far better for Black, if his king could return to the K-side without risk. However, the blockade is not complete there, for White has P–R4 at his disposal.

42 RP×P	**P×P**
43 P×P	**R×P**
44 R×R	**Q×R**
45 P–B4!	**Q×P+**
46 Q×Q	**N×Q**
47 B×P!	

The point. Black would have nothing after 47 ... RP×B 48 P–R6 R–R1 49 P×N R–KN1 50 B–K2 and he even loses after 47 ... BP×B? when Romanovsky gives 48 P–B6 K–Q1 49 R–QB3 N–R4 50 R–B3 K–K1 51 P×N R×P 52 R–B6 N–B5 53 K–Q3 etc.

47 ...	**N×BP!**
48 P×N	**BP×B**
49 P–B6	**P–K5**
50 P–B7	**R–R1**
51 R–QB3	**N–K4**
52 R–QR3	**R–KB1**
53 B–K6	**K–N3**
54 R–QN3+	**K–B2**
55 R–QR3	**K–N3**
56 R–QN3+	**½–½**

THE EXPOSED KING'S POSITION AS A STRATEGIC FACTOR

The attack on the king is very often the object of the strategic plan. As, however, such a plan entails other positional factors, we have refrained from devoting a special chapter to this theme. The reader will in fact find the principles governing the attack on the king linked with each typical strategic element which is found in both attack and defence (see 'The Use of Open Lines in Attacking the King').

Basically we can term 'exposed' any king's position which can be successfully attacked by the enemy. Such weakened castled positions consist of pawn structures like KB2, KN2, KR3, which can lead to line opening if the opponent's KNP is advanced; or KB2, KN3, KR2 when the KB has been exchanged; or doubled pawns on KB2 and KB3 etc.

Our first example shows the attacking side basing his whole plan on compelling the enemy king to castle into an exposed position. We have deliberately chosen examples of attacks with greatly reduced material.

75 Alekhine–Winter

London 1932, Caro-Kann Defence

1 P–K4 P–QB3 2 P–Q4 P–Q4 3 P×P P×P 4 P–QB4 N–KB3 5 N–QB3 N–B3 6 N–B3 B–N5 7 P×P N.KB3×P 8 B–QN5 Q–R4 8 ... R–B1 is better **9 Q–N3! B×N 10 P×B N×N 11 P×N** not 11 B×N+? P×B 12 Q–N7 N–Q4+ 13 B–Q2 Q–N3! 14 Q×R+ K–Q2 with a won game for Black, as in Nimzowitsch–Alekhine, Bled 1931 **11 ... P–K3** (*158*)

Black has the superior pawn position and if he could only manage to complete his development and castle K-side, he would have very fine prospects. However, Alekhine's next two moves prevent this and drive the black king into an exposed position on the Q-side.

12 P–Q5! **P×P**
13 O–O **O–O–O**

As 13 ... B–K2 fails to 14 R–K1, there is no time for castling K-side, so that the black king has to make do with the insufficient pawn protection offered him on the Q-side.

14 B×N **P×B**
15 R–N1 **Q–B2**
16 Q–R4 **R–Q2**
17 B–Q2!

The obvious move 17 B–K3 would not threaten anything, whereas the subtle text-move allows Alekhine's bishop to reach QR5.

17 ... **B–B4**
18 P–QB4! **K–Q1**

The best defence. The threat was 19 Q–R6+ K–Q1 20 B–R5 B–N3 21 R×B! and if 18 ... B–N3 to prevent this, then 19 P–B5! wins.

19 B–R5 **B–N3**
20 B×B **P×B**
21 Q–R8+!

White's intention is not of course to win the insignificant black pawn on QN3, but to free his QR4 for the rook and at the same time (by his next move) prevent the black king escaping via K2.

21 ... **Q–B1**
22 Q–R3! **Q–N1**
23 P×P **P×P**

The alternative 23 ... R×P 24 KR–Q1 R–K1 25 R×R+ P×R 26 R–Q1 R–K4 27 P–B4 also gives White a sharp attack.

24 R–N4! **Q–Q3**
25 R–K1

It would clearly be pointless to play 25 Q–R8+ K–K2 26 Q×R Q×R.

25 ... **R–B2**

After 25 ... R–K2 White's best is 26 R–Q1! threatening 27 Q–N3.

26 Q–N3 **R–K1**
27 R–Q1 **R–K4**
28 R×NP **R–B3**

29 R×R	R–N4+

Not of course 29 ... Q×R 30 Q–N8+ winning.

30 K–R1	Q×R
31 R–K1!	Q–B3
32 Q–N8+	K–Q2
33 P–B4	R–N3
34 Q–K8+	K–B2
35 R–QB1+	K–N3
36 R–QN1+	K–B4
37 Q–N5+	1–0

Our second example shows a king's position fatally weakened by one of the pawns being advanced too far.

159
B

Matulovic–Pachman, Sarajevo 1961 (*159*) Black continued:

14 ...	P–KN3!

After this White has no means of preventing a file being opened on the K-side. If 15 P×P P×P, Black continues with ... N–B2–K3 and ... 0–0–0 followed eventually by ... P–KN4. White's next move is an interesting try, but he cannot consolidate his king's position.

15 P–KN4!?	R–KN1!

But not 15 ... BP×P 16 P–B5! and White really does have a strong attack.

16 K–R1	0–0–0
17 P–N5	N–B2!
18 B–K3	N–K3
19 NP×P	B–K2!

To allow the rooks to reach the KR-file without loss of time.

20 R–KN1	R–R1
21 P×P	R×P+
22 K–N2	P×P
23 R–R1	R1–R1
24 R×R	R×R
25 Q–Q2	Q–K1
26 R–R1	R×R

The black queen now takes over on the KR-file and soon White's position is without defence.

27 K×R	Q–R1+
28 K–N2	Q–R5
29 B–B2	

If 29 N–N3 P–KN4!

29 ...	Q–N5+
30 K–B1	

If 30 B–N3 B–R5 and 31 ... B×B.

30 ...	P–KN4!
31 P×P	P–B5
32 P–N6	P–B6
33 N–N1	Q–N7+
34 K–K1	B–R5!
35 N×P	Q×N
36 B×B	Q–R8+
37 K–K2	Q×B
0–1	

Our final example in this section could also be used as an illustration for 'The Active King in the Middle-Game'. Black's king remains in the centre, although this seems to place it at a serious disadvantage. However, such a centralized king can well be a decisive factor in the end-game. White does his best to exploit by logical means the exposed black king, but does not succeed against an interesting active defence. Spielmann–Tartakower (*160*).

21 ...	K–B3
22 Q×NP	

22 P–KN3 would give more equalizing chances.

22 ...	Q–B5+
23 K–N1	Q×P

160
B

24 Q-B6+   K-N4!
25 P-KR4+   K-N5!

But not 25 ... K-R3 26 Q-B6. By his surprising king march, Black not only eliminates all danger but even wins a pawn.

26 QR-KB1

White must keep both rooks on the board, if he is to pose any danger to the black king. If 26 Q-B6 Black can calmly play 26 ... R×R+ 27 R×R Q×KNP 28 Q-N5+ K-B6 29 Q-B1 (or R6) 29 ... P-K6 etc.

26 ...   Q-N3
27 Q-B4

Black's active king would guarantee him an easy win after the exchange of queens.

27 ...   R-Q7
28 P-N4   Q-K6?

After this error, however, White does get certain chances. 28 ... R1-Q1 was the correct move.

29 R-R3!   Q-N3
30 R3-B3

White has won a tempo which he now tries to use for a dangerous attack, but Black's king still manages to find a haven from the checks.

30 ...   R×NP!
31 R-B4+   K-N6!
32 Q-Q5

Threatening 33 Q-K5.

32 ...   R-K1
33 Q-Q7

After 33 R4-B3+ Black's simplest winning move is 33 ... K-R7! As Tartakower points out in his notes, the king's journey from K1 to KR7 creates an extraordinarily piquant effect.

33 ...   Q-R3
0-1

8 Exchange of Material

In the preceding chapters the reader has seen the connection between the strategic plan and the material on the board. The quality and quantity of the available pieces determine the character of the position, from which we can draw a logical conclusion: every important exchange of material affects in some way the nature of the position and this requires changes in our strategic plan and its tactical execution.

Not every exchange of a piece can be viewed as important in this respect, but we would single out the following as typical ones which have positional repercussions: bishop for knight, 'bad' bishop for 'good', all rooks coming off, and of course the exchange of queens. In the latter case we are usually witnessing a transition from middle-game to end-game. The reader has already become acquainted with a few problems that arise in such a situation. Sometimes this transition to the ending is the unavoidable result of tactical complications, but in general it is deliberately brought about by one of the players.

Usually the side with material advantage is the one who wishes to exchange queens and to introduce further simplification. This case is so clear-cut and occurs with such frequency, that no further explanation is required. The reader will know that an extra pawn can best be exploited in a pawn ending, or an ending with knights or like-coloured bishops, and that a greater advantage than this is usually easy to convert into a win. However, it is much more difficult to press home an advantage when there are major pieces on the board, or when we are dealing with bishops of opposite colour. Naturally, the side with the advantage should make every effort to transpose into the most favourable end-game, whereas the losing player, if he must go into the ending, should aim for the one which will make it impossible or at least extremely difficult for the opponent to exploit his superiority.

A transition to the end-game can be equally advantageous when the enemy pawn structure is weak. Exchange of queens then robs the opponent of any attacking chances he may have, as well as depriving him of a vital defensive piece, so that it becomes much easier to attack his weak points. Here are two examples of this.

Smyslov–Reshevsky (*161*) Black has a very weak QP and is behind in development. As his only developed piece, the queen, is guarding the pawn, it seems a good idea to exchange this important defensive piece. Play proceeded: **26 Q–R4! Q–Q2** if 26 ... Q×Q 27 P×Q followed by 28 R×P **27 Q–Q8+ Q×Q 28 B×Q N–Q2** if 28 ... N–B3 29 B–N6 etc. **29 B–B7 N–B4 30 R×P R–QB1 31 B–N6 N–R5 32 R×P N×NP 33 R×KP N–B5 34 R–K6 N×B 35 R×N R×P 36 R×NP** and White won on move 52.

Botvinnik–Sorokin (*162*) We have here a similar, although more complex, situation. White is better developed and controls the open

Q-file. Black is threatening ... B–N5 when he will be able to complete his development. However, his queen is 'over-loaded', having to guard the KP and at the same time to prevent P–R5 driving his knight back. Once again the exchange of queens is White's best method of exploiting his superiority: **20 Q–K3! Q×Q 21 P×Q B–N5 22 P–R5 N–B1** a little better is 22 ... N.N3–Q2 23 P–R3 B×N 24 P×B N–B4 25 P–N4 N–K3 26 B×N P×B 27 N–R4 with a good game for White **23 R–QB1 B×N 24 P×B N–K2 25 N–Q5! N–B3** or 25 ... N2×N 26 B×N N×B 27 R×N with a won rook ending **26 N×N+ P×N 27 R–Q7 QR–N1 28 K–B2 N×P 29 R1–B7** or 29 R–KN1+ winning the KBP **29 ... R.N1–B1 30 R×BP R.QB1×R 31 R×R.7+ K–R1 32 B–Q5 P–N4 33 P–N3 R–Q1 34 K–N3** and White won on move 55.

The next game is an excellent illustration of exchanges based on correct strategy, followed by a transition to the end-game.

76 Reshevsky–Waliston

New York 1940, French Defence

1 P–K4 P–K3 2 P–Q4 P–Q4 3 N–QB3 P×P 4 N×P N–Q2 5 N–KB3 KN–B3 6 N×N+ N×N 7 B–Q3 P–B4 8 P×P B×P 9 0–0 0–0 10 B–KN5 P–QN3 11 Q–K2 B–N2 12 QR–Q1 Q–B2 13 B×N P×B (*163*)
14 B–K4!

At first sight an illogical move, as Black's K-side is badly weakened, especially his KR2, and seems ripe

for storming. Yet here is White exchanging his attacking bishop! On what does he base this exchange? A more searching analysis reveals that Black's strong bishops prevent any real attack by White. He cannot sacrifice a piece by 14 B×P+? K×B 15 N-N5+! K-N3! winning for Black (but not here 15 ... P×N? 16 Q-R5+ K-N2 17 Q× NP+ K-R2 18 R-Q3 etc.). After 14 N-R4 Black plays 14 ... Q-B5 15 Q-R5 P-B4 16 P-KN3 Q-K4, and after other preparatory moves ... Q-B5 gives Black excellent counter-play. Reshevsky thus logically concludes that Black's weakened pawns cannot be exploited by a direct attack. However, the weakness of the doubled pawns would be clearly shown up in the end-game, as they are open to attack by White's pieces and make it difficult for Black to utilize his K-side pawn majority (more about this in the section on 'The Doubled Pawn'). Such a pawn structure also favours the knight rather than the bishop, so Reshevsky aims for this ending.

14 ...	QR-Q1
15 B×B	Q×B
16 N-Q2	B-K2
17 N-K4	R×R?

As we have already pointed out, exchanges help White, so Black should avoid them and play 17 ...

P-B4 followed by 18 ... B-B3. It is doubtful whether White's positional advantage would be enough for a win against accurate and active play by Black.

18 R×R	R-Q1
19 R×R+	B×R
20 Q-Q3	B-K2
21 P-KR3	Q-B2?

Once again 21 ... P-B4 and 22 ... B-B3 was the correct plan. By allowing the exchange of queens, Black gives White the very ending which offers him most prospects.

| 22 Q-KN3+! | Q×Q |
| 23 N×Q | K-B1 |

The remainder of the game is simply a question of the technical conversion of White's advantage into a win: **24 K-B1 K-K1 25 K-K2 K-Q2 26 K-Q3 K-B3 27 N-K2 B-B4 28 P-KB4 P-N4?** this helps White to create a passed pawn **29 P-KN4 P-QR3 30 K-K4 B-B1 31 N-Q4+ K-Q3 32 N-N3 B-K2 33 N-Q2 B-B1 34 P-B4 K-B4 35 P×P P×P 36 N-N3+ K-Q3 37 N-Q4 K-B4 38 P-B5 P-K4 39 N-B3** threatening 40 P-N5 **39 ... P-R3 40 P-KR4 B-K2 41 P-R5! B-Q3 42 P-R3 P-N5 43 P-R4 P-N6 44 N-Q2 K-N5 45 P-R5 K×P 46 N-B4+ 1-0.**

Occasionally positions arise in which simplification is sought by the side who has a positional or material disadvantage. This is because a transition to an end-game can sometimes reduce the opponent's advantage. For example, when a player is a piece down, he will try to eliminate all the pawns and exchange as many pieces as possible. End-game theory tells us that a minor piece on its own cannot win, and two minor pieces against one is almost always a draw (apart from a few positions with two bishops against knight). A rook can usually draw against rook and minor piece, albeit sometimes with great difficulty, whereas a rook and two minor pieces can in general win against rook and minor piece.

In the following game, the exchange of queens and minor pieces is the only way to avoid a serious positional disadvantage, even though this costs a pawn.

77 H. Steiner–Pachman

Venice 1950, Nimzo-Indian Defence

1 P–Q4 N–KB3 2 P–QB4 P–K3 3 N–QB3 B–N5 4 P–QR3 B×N+ 5 P×B 0–0 6 P–K3 P–Q3 7 B–Q3 P–K4 8 N–K2 P–K5 9 B–N1 P–QN3 10 N–N3 R–K1 11 P–B3 B–N2 12 0–0 QN–Q2

13 R–R2!

Black's game is based on control of his important K5 square, and the text-move poses a serious threat to this plan. White threatens to exert sufficient pressure down the KB-file to compel Black to play ... KP×BP which will strengthen the white centre.

13 ...   **P–B4**
14 R2–KB2 (*164*)

164
B

White now threatens to win the KBP after 15 BP×P and it is difficult for Black to counter this. As we have

already stated, 14 ... KP×P 15 NP×P is strategically hopeless, as White will dominate the centre after P–K4 and can easily prepare a K-side attack. And if 14 ... B–R3 15 N×P White's strong centre again gives him a clear positional plus.

14 ...   **P–Q4!**

Beginning a series of exchanges leading to a position whose assessment was the most difficult part of the whole exercise. Black sacrifices a pawn in order to eliminate the queens and minor pieces and to seek salvation in the rook ending.

15 QBP×P	B×P
16 BP×P	N×P
17 N×N	B×N
18 B×B	R×B
19 R×P	N–B3
20 Q–N3	Q–Q4!
21 Q×Q	N×Q
22 P×P	N×KP!

Better than 22 ... P×P 23 R7–B5 N×BP 24 R×P.

23 B×N	R×B
24 P×P	P×P (*165*)

165
W

After ten practically forced moves, the situation has drastically changed. The massive exchange of pieces has deprived White of any chances of deciding the game by a direct attack. Moreover, his extra pawn is insufficient for winning purposes, as his weak Q-side pawns can easily be attacked.

25 R–QB7	R–K3
26 P–QR4	P–R3
27 R–KB4	R1–K1
28 P–R3	R–N3
29 K–B2	R–K4!

Black must seek active counter-play by threatening to switch his attack to either wing. The game continued: **30 P–N4 R3–K3 31 P–R4 R–K7+ 32 K–N3 R7–K6+ 33 R–B3 R6–K5 34 P–KR5 R–K2 35 R–QB6 R2–K3 36 R×R R×R 37 K–B4 R–QB3 38 K–K5 R–B4+** 38 ... R–B5 allows 39 R–N3 R×RP 40 K–Q5 followed by 41 K–B6 **39 K–Q6 R–B5 40 R–N3 K–B2! 41 R–B3+ K–K1 42 R–N3 K–B2 43 P–R5!** 43 K–Q5 R–B4+ 44 K–Q4 R–KN4 draws **43 ... P×P 44 K–Q5 R–B5 45 P–B4 K–K1 46 K–B5 K–Q2 47 K–N5 K–B2 48 P–B5 R–B8! 49 P–N5 R–QN8+ 50 K×P K–B3 51 P×P P×P 52 R–N6+ K×P 53 K–R6 R–KR8 54 R×P K–Q4 55 R–R8 K–K3 ½–½.**

In all the examples we have seen, one side was striving to obtain the advantage by exchanging queens. However, the resulting positions can be so difficult to evaluate correctly, that we sometimes have the bizarre situation of both sides aiming for the queen exchange, with only one player justified in doing so! Our next two games are interesting illustrations of this.

78 Lasker–Tarrasch

Mährisch Ostrau 1923, Alekhine's Defence

1 P–K4 N–KB3	2 P–K5 N–Q4
3 P–QB4 N–N3	4 P–Q4 P–Q3
5 P–B4 P×P	6 BP×P N–B3
7 B–K3 B–B4	8 N–QB3 P–K3
9 N–B3 B–QN5 10 B–Q3?	10 B–K2!
10 ... B–N5 11 B–K2 B.KN5×N
12 P×B Q–R5+	13 B–B2 Q–B5

14 R–KN1 0–0–0	14 ... P–KR4!
15 R×P 0–0–0 15 R–N4	Q×RP
16 R–R4 Q–N7 17 B–B1	Q–N4
18 Q–B2 P–KR4 19 R–Q1	Q–R3
20 P–R3 B–K2 21 R–R3	B–N4
22 Q–K4 P–B3 23 P×P	Q×P
24 B–K2! (*166*)	

After an opening mistake by White, Black has won a pawn, but Lasker's last few moves have consolidated his central position and his two bishops give him definite counter-chances. He now sets up a 'psychological' attack against his opponent by allowing him to 'force' the exchange of queens which will apparently help him to exploit his material superiority.

24 ...	Q–B4?

A serious strategic error which hands the advantage over to White. The exchange of queens does not produce an ending, but rather a typical middle-game without queens. At the same time Black's K-side advantage is reduced, and the white centre pawns become a force to be reckoned with.

25 Q×Q	P×Q
26 B–Q3	P–N3
27 N–K2	P–R5

Better is 27 ... N–K2, as Black's pieces are now tied to the defence of the KRP.

28 P–B4	B–B3

29 P–N4	K–N1
30 P–Q5	N–K2
31 K–B1	N3–B1?

Intending . . . P–B3 which cannot be played at once (31 . . . P–B3 32 P–Q6! and 33 P–B5), but this 'freeing' move only hastens Black's defeat. 31 . . . N–R5 would have worried his opponent more.

32 P–N5!	P–B3?

Consequential but bad! Tarrasch should have tried 32 . . . N–Q3 followed by . . . N–K5 sacrificing a pawn but easing his defence somewhat.

33 NP×P	P×P
34 R–N1+	K–R1
35 N–Q4!	B×N

After 35 . . . P×P 36 P×P, both 36 . . . N×P 37 N–B6 and 36 . . . R×P 37 N–K6 R–Q2 38 B–K2 (threatening 39 B–B3+) lose for Black.

36 B×B	R–R2
37 B–K5	N–Q3
38 P–B5	N–N2
39 P–Q6	N–Q4
40 R–B1	R–KB1
41 B–R6	N–B3
42 B5×N!	R×B
43 R–K3	R–B1
44 R1–K1	R2–R1
45 P–Q7	K–N1
46 R–K8+	K–B2
47 B×N	1–0

79 Capablanca–Bogoljubow

London 1922, Ruy Lopez

1 P–K4 P–K4 2 N–KB3 N–QB3 3 B–N5 P–QR3 4 B–R4 N–B3 5 0–0 B–K2 6 R–K1 P–QN4 7 B–N3 P–Q3 8 P–B3 0–0 9 P–Q4 P×P 10 P×P B–N5 11 B–K3 N–QR4 12 B–B2 N–B5 13 B–B1 P–B4 14 P–QN3 N–QR4 15 B–N2 N–B3 16 P–Q5 N–QN5 17 QN–Q2 N×B 18 Q×N R–K1 19 Q–Q3 P–R3 20 N–B1 N–Q2 21 P–KR3 B–R4?

21 . . . B×N! 22 Q×B B–B3 22 N3–Q2! B–B3 23 B×B Q×B 24 P–QR4 P–B5 25 NP×P N–B4 26 Q–K3 P×RP 27 P–B4! Q–K2 28 P–N4 B–N3 29 P–B5 B–R2 30 N–KN3 Q–K4 31 K–N2 QR–N1 32 QR–N1 P–B3 32 . . . R–N7! 33 N–B3 R–N7+ 34 R×R Q×R+ 35 R–K2 Q–N6 (*167*)

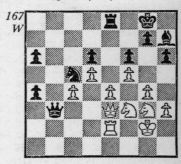

167
W

Black's last few moves indicate that he is happy to exchange queens. His reasoning: a passed pawn and strongly posted knight on the Q-side! However, White's next move shows that he too does not mind exchange of queens. His reasoning: Black's bishop is completely shut out of play on KR2! The game continuation reveals which player's judgement is correct.

36 N–Q4! Q×Q

Not 36 . . . Q×P? 37 N–K6! (*37 R–QB2? Q×QP 38 N–K6 R×N!*) 37 . . . R–N1! 38 N×N P×N 39 R–Q2 R–N6 40 Q–B2! with a winning game in view of his strong QP.

37 R×Q	R–N1
38 R–B3	K–B2
39 K–B3	R–N7
40 N3–K2	B–N1
41 N–K6	N–N6

He cannot play 41 . . . N×P 42 K×N R×N+ 43 K–Q4! winning easily.

42 P–B5!	P×P
43 N×BP	N–Q7+
44 K–B2	K–K2

Preferable was 44 . . . N–N8!

45 K–K1	N–N8
46 R–Q3	P–R6?

Black had a last chance to draw with 46 . . . K–Q3. White now wins quickly.

47 P–Q6+	K–Q1
48 N–Q4!	R–N3
49 N4–K6+	B×N
50 P×B	R–N1
51 P–K7+	K–K1
52 N×P	1–0

The rook has no good move, as 52 . . . R–R1 or 52 . . . R–N2 allow 53 N–B7+, and 52 . . . P–R7 fails to the simple 53 N×R.

It is not only the exchange of queens which produces interesting strategic problems. The exchange of minor pieces, which sometimes has a purely tactical aim such as the removal of an important defensive or attacking piece, can often prove a vital strategic factor. We have already seen examples of this in our chapter on 'The Minor Pieces', where it was shown that we must try to exchange well-placed enemy pieces for our own ineffective ones e.g. a 'bad' bishop for a 'good' one. To allow the opposite to happen can almost always be considered a serious positional error and often occurs when a player is in too much of a hurry to draw by exchanging pieces. Consider the next diagram; Esposito–Pachman (*168*).

This position occurred in a game played in the 1950 Buenos Aires tournament. White could have obtained a completely equal game with 19 Q–Q2, but wrongly decided to exchange his actively placed bishop, after which Black obtained a decisive advantage as follows: **19**

B–K4? B×B 20 R×B KR–K1 21 R1–K1 R×R 22 R×R R–Q1 23 K–N2(?) P–QN4! 24 P–N3 P×P 25 P×P Q–N2! 26 K–B2 Q–R3 27 Q–K2 P–B4 28 P–KR4 P×P 29 B–N4 Q–R5 30 Q–Q2 P–Q6 31 K–N1 Q–B3 32 R–B4 B–K4 33 R–B5 Q–K5 34 R–B1 Q×BP 0–1.

In the following game, the loser misses the opportunity of reducing his opponent's advantage by exchanges (move 12), and the winner greatly increases his advantage by exchanging knights (move 19).

80 Botvinnik–Zagoriansky

Sverdlovsk 1943, Réti System

1 N–KB3 P–Q4 2 P–B4 P–K3 3 P–QN3 N–KB3 4 B–N2 B–K2 5 P–K3 0–0 6 N–B3 P–B4 7 P×P N×P 8 N×N P×N 9 P–Q4 P×P? 10 Q×P B–B3 11 Q–Q2 N–B3 12 B–K2 (*169*)

12 . . .	B–K3?

A grave positional error. We shall explain at another time the basic principles that apply to positions containing an isolated pawn, but we can say now that from White's point of view the control of his Q4 square is of supreme importance. As the white knight is required for this task, Black should play 12 . . . B–N5! 13 0–0 B×B 14 Q×B B×N

169
B

15 B×B Q-R4 16 KR-Q1 KR-Q1
with equality.

13 0-0	B×B
14 Q×B	Q-R4
15 KR-Q1	KR-Q1
16 R-Q2	R-Q2
17 R1-Q1	R1-Q1
18 P-KR3	P-KR3
19 N-K5!	

By eliminating both knights in this way, White obtains a positional superiority on the dark squares in the centre. The Q4 square is especially important in this respect and the exchanges have only helped him.

19 ...	N×N
20 Q×N	Q-B4
21 B-B3	P-QN3
22 Q-N2	R-QB1
23 Q-K5	

White tacks about a little before embarking on his final plan, but Black can do nothing in the meantime.

23 ...	R1-Q1
24 R-Q4	P-QR4

As White cannot put any more pressure on the QP, it is at first sight unclear how he can win. However, Botvinnik's next move reveals his winning plan: Black's passive set-up will be exploited by a K-side attack. It is worth noting that Black's 18th move has helped White, for otherwise he would have been forced to

manoeuvre with his major pieces to bring about the required weakness of Black's K-side. In contrast, White's 18 P-KR3 effectively improves his position. It is in differentiating between such apparently equal and insignificant moves that real chess understanding lies.

25 P-KN4!	Q-B3
26 P-N5	P×P
27 Q×P.N5	P-B3
28 Q-N6!	B-B2
29 Q-N3	P-B4?

In order to bring his queen over to defend his KNP against the threat of K-R2 followed by R-KN1. However, this further weakening of the black squares makes White's task easier.

30 Q-N5	Q-K3
31 K-R1	Q-K4
32 R-KN1	R-KB1
33 Q-R6	R-N1
34 R-KR4	K-B1
35 Q-R8+	B-N1
36 R-KB4	R1-N2
37 R-N5	R-KB2
38 Q-R5	Q-R8+

Black's KBP is without defence and the game is over.

39 K-R2	P-N3
40 Q×P	B-R2
41 Q-Q6+	R.N2-K2
42 Q-Q8+	1-0

In the next game White succeeds in obtaining a strategically very advantageous position by exchanging three minor pieces.

81 Lasker-Tartakower

Mährisch Ostrau 1923, Caro-Kann Defence

1 P-K4 P-QB3 2 P-Q4 P-Q4
3 P×P P×P 4 B-Q3 N-QB3
5 P-QB3 N-B3 6 B-KB4 P-KN3
7 P-KR3 B-N2 8 N-B3 N-K5

8 ... N–KR4! **9 QN–Q2 P–B4**
10 0–0 0–0 (*170*)

In this position most chess-players, even the best, would play 11 R–K1 to apply pressure down the K-file onto the backward KP. However, the black knight would sooner or later need to be driven from its strong post on K5 by a manoeuvre such as N–R2 and P–B3, when White's pieces would become a little disorganized. For this reason, Lasker chooses a completely different plan. With his next move he prepares to exchange three minor pieces, leaving Black with a passive QB. At the same time the pawn structure will be altered, creating a strong-point for White on Q4.

11 N–K5!   **N3×N**

After 11 ... B–Q2 12 N2–B3 White would control his K5, but this line would be better than the game continuation which clearly favours White.

12 B4×N   **B×B**
13 P×B   **N×N**

An unpleasant move to have to play, but otherwise White's knight reaches the beautiful square Q4, then the black knight is driven away e.g. 13 ... Q–B2 14 N–B3 P–K3 15 Q–K2 B–Q2 16 N–Q4! followed by 17 P–B3.

14 Q×N   **P–B5?!**

A sharp attempt at a counter-attack, as 14 ... P–K3 15 KR–Q1 Q–B2 16 P–KB4 followed by QR–B1 and P–B4 gives White an undoubted advantage, albeit difficult to convert into a win.

15 QR–Q1!   **Q–B2**

But not 15 ... P–B6? 16 B–K4 P×P 17 Q×P+ etc. According to Tartakower, 15 ... B–K3 and 16 ... Q–Q2 was best.

16 KR–K1   **P–K3?**

He had to try 16 ... P–B6, when, admittedly, after 17 B–B2 (or 17 B–B1) 17 ... P–K3 18 P–KN3 Black's KBP looks weak, but he would at least have some counter-chances.

17 R–QB1   **Q–Q1**
18 B–K2   **Q–R4**
19 P–QN4   **Q–B2**
20 P–B4!   **Q×KP**
21 P×P   **Q–Q3**

After 21 ... Q×P White can either play for a strong attack by 22 Q–N2 or reach a clearly won end-game by 22 Q×Q P×Q 23 B–B3.

22 B–B3   **R–Q1**
23 Q–Q4!   **B–Q2**

He cannot play 23 ... P×P 24 B×P+! Q×B 25 R–K8+! etc.

24 Q–B5!

The simplest winning method! After the exchange of queens White immediately wins a pawn.

The game ended: **24 ... Q×Q 25 P×Q! QR–B1 26 P–B6 NP×P 27 P×BP B–K1 28 P–B7 R–Q2 29 R×P B–B2 30 R6–QB6 B–Q4 31 B–N4 was threatened 31 B×B+ R×B 32 R–R6 K–B2 33 R×RP K–K2 34 R–R4 P–N4 35 R4–B4 K–Q2 36 R–B5 R×R 37 R×R R×P 38 R×R+ K×R 39 K–B1 K–Q3 40 K–K2 K–Q4 41 P–QR4 K–Q5 42 K–B3 1–0.**

Finally, exchanges are often the

correct defence in positions where the opponent has a space advantage. Consider an example from opening theory: **1 P–K4 P–K4 2 N–KB3 N–QB3 3 B–N5 N–B3 4 0–0 P–Q3 5 P–Q4 B–Q2 6 N–B3 B–K2 7 R–K1 P×P 8 N×P 0–0** (*171*)

This is a well-known position in the Steinitz Defence to the Ruy Lopez, in which theory recommends **9 B×N**, when the central pawn structure gives White a certain space advantage. After the natural developing move 9 B–N5 or 9 P–QN3 Black exchanges two minor pieces by ... N×N and ... B×B, obtaining a good game, as practical play has shown. In other words the exchange of one piece (9 B×N) prevents the exchange of two and so reduces Black's chances of equalizing the game.

To sum up this chapter, we can say that exchanges are advantageous in the following circumstances:

1. When a badly placed or inactive piece is exchanged for a more favourably posted enemy piece.
2. When the exchange will prevent the opponent defending weak points effectively.
3. When the exchange makes it easier for us to exploit our material or positional superiority, or makes it harder for our opponent to do the same.
4. When the exchange eases a cramped defence and reduces the effectiveness of an enemy space advantage.

On many occasions exchanges are made in the hope of cutting out complications and reaching a quick safe draw by means of simplification. With the present advanced state of opening theory and the highly developed playing technique, such a strategem is often successful. However, many examples also show that simplification does not always bring equality in its train. On the contrary, in some case exchanges can seriously alter the equilibrium of the position. Exchanges should therefore never be undertaken lightly, as purely mechanical exchanges bring little reward.

Index of Games

Index of Openings

Index of Positions

Index of Openings